REFINEMENT OF MANNER

Manners, Etiquette & Elegance for the Twenty-First Century Woman

~

The 21st Century Woman's Guide to a Refined Manner & Elegant Lifestyle

Melanie Jarrell

ISBN: 978-0-9975884-0-8

Refinement of Manner

With special thanks for edits by Joy Waldron, Kay Jarrell, Carolyn French, Lisa Clemenceau, and Tammy Bernard

Original illustration designs by Melanie Jarrell; final drawings by *Tatiana*. Cover design by: Madeline Taylor

Published 2016 by Blue Ox Publishing

Printed and bound in the U.S.A.

ISBN: 978-0-9975884-1-5

Blue Ox Publishing, LLC

Post Office Box 82566

Lafayette, LA 70598

CONTENTS

CHAPTER 1 – REFINEMENT FOR TODAY

"There is no outward sign of courtesy that does not rest on a deep moral foundation…The way you see people is the way you treat them, and the way you treat them is what they become." Goethe

The ideas and questions posed to you in this book will challenge you to see yourself differently – as more confident, desirable, attractive and smart. The concepts offered here are simple, yet for many, they have remained hidden.

Reading through this book may give you a better idea of the world and how you fit into it, and introduce new ways you can use to achieve your desires, hopes, and dreams by just being you . . . but with a new awareness that will serve you well in life.

Ten results you can achieve from reading my book:

1. Understand quality versus quantity
2. Improve your looks and image
3. Feel great about your choices and lifestyle
4. Train your eye on beauty and how to identify something of the highest quality
5. Be confident in crowds and in every social situation
6. Build your best wardrobe while investing less financially
7. Know how to relate to people in every kind of circumstance
8. Learn to notice details
9. Work smarter, accomplish more, achieve your goals, and realize how wealthy you really are
10. Add a bit of mystery and intrigue to your life
11. The possibilities are endless!

Don't you love being a woman? We are complex creatures. We can be wise and intuitive, mysterious to the opposite sex, attractive, poised, graceful, charming and delightfully creative. When given a challenge, we sense we should rise to the occasion and reach our goal. In those cases, we actually see what we can really accomplish. When assigned a task, we can feel compelled to execute it fully and correctly. We tend to be detail-oriented. We are truly fit for purpose. We can be exceptional and distinct. Our femininity sets us apart: it is part of our manner, and it is how we do what we do.

Refinement is beyond elegance and demeanor. It is ingrained in your nature and personality.

The question remains: Is one more etiquette book (one specifically about pointing you in a direction to become who you would like to be) outdated, old fashioned, and unbeneficial to the twenty-first century woman of today? What about becoming a more "refined" you? Is timeless elegance still to be sought after? What are the benefits of such a life, such a change and refined approach to living?

The refined manner, whether it is acquired early or later in life, must be cultivated and nurtured through a discerning eye and discerning taste. A refined woman possesses a certain calmness and confidence. She retains that quiet inner demeanor when facing anything that comes her way. She has discriminating taste that sets her apart and states her allegiance to a stricter "code."

Refinement is *beyond* elegance and demeanor. It is ingrained in your nature and personality. It is not achieved through outer means only, but consists of a development of a certain set of qualities in a person. It is not about status or social standing, yet those things can develop out of refinement.

Whether you are just beginning to understand manners and refinement or you have always been a student of etiquette – or even *well-bred* – it is helpful to have a historical overview of the ideas and concepts around courtesy, manners and etiquette in order to realize the importance of proper etiquette. It reinforces the impact this behavior has on you and society as a whole.

Politeness

Politeness, historically, has been the "socially acceptable standard" of how to treat others. Even as early as the 1700s, gentlemen had a code of honor on how to behave among society. Later that century, a trend emerged among the upper class and their understanding of certain "polite norms," thus separating themselves from the common folk. Middle-class *bourgeoisie* followed this trend and attempted to identify themselves with the elite by following a precise set of rules of etiquette and behavior, hoping their actions would become acceptable in the courts and perhaps lead to invitations of the higher class. These rules became the standard of expectations by the courtiers of all others who were in their presence, and became the criteria of socially accepted behavior for all who attended any function of social stature.

The rules of etiquette evolved into a set of standards that were exacting on the individual to the point of defining when to show emotion, how to dress for any occasion, what was acceptable or *not* acceptable conversation. Letters from fathers to sons included such instruction as when to smile and not to laugh out loud for that was considered vulgar in public. The Mr. Darcys of *Pride and Prejudice* were instilling in their sons the proper and appropriate behavior to continue the gentlemen's class to the next generation. Acting "courteously" was a preoccupation, particularly with the women of the day, and much was written during this time about how to behave. One writer in the early 18th century, in writing instructions to his son, defined politeness as "the art of being pleasing in company." It is easy to see that not much has changed since then. He (Lord Shaftesbury) went on to write:

'Politeness' may be defined a dexterity of the management of our words and actions, whereby we make other people have better opinion of us and themselves.

The writings attempted to balance morality with wit – enlivening morality and tempering wit – even to the extent of offering "talking points." *(Is this a full circle of today's rhetoric at social gatherings?!)*

Some went on to say: the notion of "civility" referred to a desired social interaction which valued sober and reasoned debate on matters of interest." During this time the "polite class" arose. They set the rules and procedures for proper behavior, acceptable etiquette, and do's and don'ts even for gentlemen's clubs and English coffeehouses. The purpose of the polite class was to reform English manner and morals in private and public gathering places.

As mentioned, men were known to write letters of instruction to their sons in hopes of making them aware of the "do's and don'ts" of modern civility; by the time of the Victorian Era, etiquette had developed into a very complicated system of rules for gentlemen and ladies, even to the extent of how to treat different classes and genders. Etiquette had evolved into a sort of systematic approach to interacting together.

Over the centuries of history, as nomads gathered and formed colonies and towns, and later cities, there was a need to regard others – their feelings, their rights. It was the formation of "society" – of getting along and behaving toward others in a way that allowed commerce and neighborhoods to flourish under minimal law and order. Proper etiquette was the philosophy among the well-bred of previous generations and has been handed down through family tradition and upbringing ever since.

Etiquette is more than a list of social rules and requirements. It is not merely a surface observance of customs, but rather stems from the essence of a person.

For further refinement in manner, we can actually change the way we think. We are capable of behaving and reacting to society by becoming acquainted with the ideals of the manner of the socially adept on correctness.

Now more than ever, proper etiquette plays out in our daily interaction with others, as the human sharing in an organized civilization. Society has become highly developed in a fast-paced and very intellectual, sophisticated and growing worldwide social order.

Etiquette is much more than a list of social rules and requirements. It is not merely a surface observance of customs, but rather stems from the essence of a person. It is in the broadest of senses about the blossoming of that inner *instinct* for peace and harmony and good fellowship among those we are around. Our actions and demeanor affect those we socialize with day in and day out. Etiquette is not just something we put on once a year for a special occasion, but must be inherently born in us – something that we own and is ours to flourish or diminish based on our actions.

We might say the test of one's breeding is how one interacts under social pressure. How one behaves when they think no one is looking. It is the test of one's grit and gumption, of how one acts and interacts with others in our deepest humanity. It is the basis of treating everyone the same and being simple in our requirements of others. Our etiquette never projects our own requirements, responsibilities and demands on anyone else.

MANNERS & POLITENESS

When thinking of an etiquette makeover, manners are of secondary importance to the real issue: your natural MANNER toward yourself and others. *"Manner"* is the spirit of your will; *"manners"* are an expression of the spirit. Some common definitions of *manners* (from Merriam Webster):

- *A characteristic or customary mode of acting: the custom; a distinguished or stylish air –manner;*
- *A mode of procedure or way of acting – fashion; a method of artistic execution or mode of presentation: style.*

Manners could also be understood as social conduct or rules of conduct as shown in the prevalent customs such as, Victorian manners; or, with characteristic or distinctive bearing, air, or deportment; such as: his poised gracious manner. Manner is also considered by most to be a habitual conduct or deportment – such as "mind your manners." Or "good manners."

When you study the full meaning of a word, you begin to understand its application more accurately. The word *manners* has come to mean that knack of protocol that one "uses" to behave properly. Most people believe it has nothing to do with the demeanor of a person. Manners are the requirements of social life, the external actions we adopt when with others, the little allowances we make to the idiosyncrasies, habits and customs of those around us.

Manners are really an expression of one's inherent desire to adjust herself to her surroundings and conform to the established customs of her neighbors. Manners have been thought of as rules: *do not do this*, and *always do that*. Manners are *the tools of social life*. But what are the timeless manners that will benefit you and me, learned from previous generations? How can the past hand off the baton of etiquette smoothly and effectively to the future?

A Reason for Manners

There is always a reason for manners. Proper manners sets you apart from the crowd and shows you are managing your life elegantly, with determined refinement. Your manners exemplify the taste and simple elegant way about you. No one can make you act one way or another without some sort of control over you, which is not the purpose of this book. This book is a selective systematic handbook to help you initiate new concepts and ideas into your lifestyle and enjoy your life so much more. This book attempts to help you understand and grasp for yourself how elegance and refinement can add to the quality of how you live.

Refinement is intended to cause you to begin to think about your life in a more elegant way. Although plenty of books exist on manners and etiquette, this book goes much farther: *Refinement* is a gentle reminder of the way you can enjoy your lifestyle by making subtle changes to your attitude and manner, and by making simple changes to your ideas and concepts of how you treat others – and yourself.

These changes give you the opportunity to enjoy more in your life by being a gentle person who enjoys little pleasures from a refined way of thinking and a more pleasurable lifestyle.

In becoming a genuine and unpretentious person you attain a sort of *manner* that is your own.

By educating and training and forming new habits, your *manner* evolves into a more genteel person, and it comes from the inside out.

My desire is to be a person who considers others as well as myself, a person who treats everyone the same, a soft-spoken person who automatically takes all into consideration before forming a judgment or even hearing a word of gossip. I want to be that sort of person. So I read and study and practice the art of good manners, from the little things like handling a napkin at table, to the weightier matters of being the proper guest at a dinner party. All those things matter to me in how I handle myself. I also want to be confident enough to walk into a room and understand my place and be a person who enriches others and improves myself through their company. This metamorphosis has to start somewhere. It does not just happen.

Life is a journey and the people you meet and the things you do make you who you are. It is your actions that exemplify you. My hope is that after you have read this book you will enjoy the journey even more each day.

Homework: Jot down your top ten "manners rules". As you read through the book look to add more favorites to your list. This will keep you focused on your goals for change and refinement.

Defining Refinement

There is no better way to believe and trust in yourself than to know how to behave and know what to do in every situation. This book defines the attitude behind the eloquent ways to behave not only every day but also on special occasions. Your worth is tied to how you look at yourself. Your value lies in who you are inside and how it is portrayed outside. You may feel very feminine and demure inside but your outer image may not show it effectively. This book includes proven ways to enhance your own unique beauty through the ease of understanding certain principles of action. This is a book that can offer you the lasting changes to your life that you have been desiring.

Refinement is a small change that improves something. It is the act or process of improving something.

I love, love, love the idea of being refined, so I am constantly adding to the arsenal of ideas to enhance one's self-image. Here you will find a lot of things you already know about manners and etiquette and you might discover a few new ideas you can relate to. As you take them in, these concepts will become your own, and will be seasoned with your own personality.

Refinement, by definition, is:

1. Removing unwanted substances from something; the act or process of making something pure.
2. The *act or process of improving* something.
3. A *small change that improves* something.

Refinement of Your Manner

It is easy to use buzzwords to relate to something you understand but cannot quite convey to someone else. I realize that this book is titled *Refinement* but it could equally be called "Enrichment" or "Finer Life." The title does not always reflect the entire content. Your challenge is to read the book and then decide how it relates to what you want out of life, how you want to live your life and enrich it. Adjectives describing refinement results might include:

Advanced	Betterment	Improvement
Perfection	Excellence	Highest Quality
Flawless	Impeccable	Developed
Cultivated	Finished	Cultured

REFINEMENT *of* MANNER
Becoming an Elegant, Distinguished, Twenty-First Century Woman

You may want to consider reading *Refinement* as your *etiquette makeover*. When you get a makeover, you usually go in looking one way and come out looking another. In this tone, we could say you have been thinking one way about yourself and your life, but after reading this book, you might begin to think another way, to think in a broader, more enriched way about yourself, to reconsider what you want to be, how you want to behave and how you want to speak.

Refinement may offer you options you had not considered before. It might suggest other options for investing your time, energy and resources. Or the book might reinforce what you already know. It can provide a great opportunity to reintroduce yourself to a refined manner in public and private.

The number one rule of etiquette is to make people comfortable around you. Your manners should be so flawless that everyone around you is totally comfortable. If something happens, you are kind and civil. You never panic or create a scene. You avoid drama when you are behaving correctly. You are exemplifying a genteel and refined *manner*.

REFINEMENT IS QUALITY

The art of refinement might be considered *"the quality of a person who has the good education and polite manners that are expected in people who belong to a high social class."*

What is usually expected of persons of a high social class? Most people would say it is education, manners, proper etiquette, social leadership, and common courtesy.

One of the major differences between people who are successful at accomplishing their objectives and those who are not is whether they are able to defer immediate gratification, develop their long-term thinking, and keep track of their goals. If becoming refined were simple and quick, most girls and women would be eager to become refined. However, excellence in behavior and thinking is really a lifelong pursuit . . . and yet it begins with who you are today.

 Have you ever noticed that people who have a good work ethic and are habitual "doers" with lists? They prioritize their actions to make sure the important ones get done and are not skipped over.

This ability to focus is how successful people pull out in front of the pack. They defer the instant gratification of doing the easy things and go after those difficult not-so-pleasant things on their list that will actually move them along in the long run. These people make themselves do what needs to be done, on a regular, routine basis. It is a habit to them and they get ahead in life because of it. They are considered "disciplined" in this undisciplined society and world we live in. This discipline and reliability builds character and trustworthiness.

Eating the elephant. Becoming a disciplined and task-accomplishing woman creates personal responsibility. *I must do it, because no one else is going to do it for me. I must do this mundane task to get farther in life. I must take up the baton and move forward and exercise myself to get things accomplished, to complete my goals – no matter how hard it is or how long it takes.* You may know the saying; *how do you eat an elephant?* The answer is: *One bite at a time.* Building character and trustworthiness and self-confidence happen in small but constant increments. The task might be an elephant, but it will get done – one bite at a time.

Success in any endeavor comes from raising your mindset over a long period of time.

it is not just a "good idea" for a week or two, or even a summer or a year. It is building and developing your character into someone who is self-disciplined sufficiently to finish what you begin. You become someone who sees her goals as challenging *but achievable* and who desires to accomplish them.

Refinement begins with character. Ultimately you will never build character unless you take personal responsibility. You can get what you want out of life if you want it badly enough. It might take humility, but you must be willing to take that chance and make something of yourself, even if you start at the *bottom*. Take a no-excuse approach to achieving goals, and rely on those who are strong in areas where you are weak (think teamwork and humility). Lose your ego, and admit you do not know it all, nor do you need to! Open-mindedness, determination and courage are the characteristics of a person who will discipline herself to achieve great things in her lifetime.

A Type of Excellence

Excellence can be your goal in living an enriched life of quality. No matter your age and situation, you can always make the choice to develop that special value of excelling, of possessing good qualities to a high degree. In order to achieve this, you must choose those changes to make *now*. Take the person you are now and begin to refine your lifestyle wherever it makes sense in your own personal life and personal goals.

One goal you might decide to make is *a list of changes* you desire in your life this year. Make that list based on the ideas, endeavors and dreams you always wanted to do or become. Every January, I write down one hundred things I would love to do during the upcoming year. It is a list of things (small and great) that I want to accomplish. My annual lists have included things like:

Have lunch with my financial adviser every month
Learn about the National Monuments
Use eye cream *consistently*
Write more interesting thank-you notes
Stop saying *uh*

Although these might seem unimportant to anyone else, many of the items on my lists from the last three years have become a part of me. It's been fun to see how many things on my lists I actually incorporate into my life.

This is a book on refinement of taste, ideas, and general outlook on life. It is often said that moderation in all things is a good idea. This book brings forth the ideas of so many areas of life that we sometimes barely touch on during our brief time here. That is, we often get caught up on so many unrelated time-consumers that we don't understand what happened to our life.

Refinement is a key to the mystery of lasting beauty. A tactless woman may appear beautiful in her twenties or even her thirties, but there has to be more to her. If that certain polish to her personality, appearance, speech, and actions is missing, she will not continue to appeal to others as a beautiful person.

Here is a chance to look at a way of life that is fuller and richer than the average – and how to create the opportunity to enjoy it.

You may be that woman who has achieved many things in her life and feels accomplished, and confident, but you might now at this moment be on a "plateau" and need encouragement to reach the next level of your career, social or personal life.

Desire for Refinement

One of the ways to learn about something new or deepen our understanding of a subject begins with *research*. In that vein, let us take a look at refinement and etiquette – etiquette and elegance begins with what we know and how we apply ourselves to understand more about the subject and incorporate that information into our daily lives.

There are several wonderful times to take stock and invest in a *makeover*. One obvious time is the transitional summer between high school and college, a great time to look at how you lived your life in high school. What has been the structure of parental guidance, teachers, peers and guys? And how do you plan to move forward into college? For most high school graduates, the next step is often a junior college near home, or a university within her state or region of the country. Even this small stepping stone into the future brings anxiety and trepidation that cannot be easily appeased by parents and those ahead of the young woman experiencing this important life change.

High School to College

Is that limbo time between high school and college a woman's most traumatic time? Even with the finest parental preparation, most girls don't know how to plan ahead for this rite of passage and often find themselves losing a semester or even a year in a sort of high school/freshman limbo trying to grasp the new world they have been thrown into. Is this the defining moment in life, where she reaches out to see who she really is? What happens when she experiments in her new nest, being away from home for the first time in her life? How will she deal with leaving behind the life of structure, where most of it was planned for her, to begin her own designed life and experiences? She knows and understands a general outline for living *within the parameters defined mostly by parents and a home.*

After she leaves that home, she must decide for herself what comprises her life, how she will handle her own choices, how she must develop integrity in all she does and craft her own ideals. The challenges ahead will call for decisions and awareness from the girl to understand the world she is entering. This book can assist that *girl* in learning the ways of a woman. Elegance and etiquette are intended to prepare her for the more sophisticated world she will soon embrace – *or not.*

In any case, her own manner and demeanor will eventually come forth. She has either taken steps to become well-suited for society or she has not. This conscious approach to refinement is an opportunity to learn from years of experience, study and research in the lives of women who have done it well.

The girl knows there is much preparation ahead during the weeks and months before going away to college, but sometimes does not realize the preparation is not all outward. Much of it must be inward to be successful. Those days and evenings are full of developing and executing the greatest plans for her own happiness and readiness to cross this passage successfully, with grace and ease. Emotions run high and can often spark some painful times of anxiety and fear of the unknown.

Through *Refinement*, the young woman will learn the importance of preparation for the scenarios she will face in the very near future.

Under the tutelage of her parents and teachers, a basic understanding of general etiquette terms and behavior have been established in her life and heart and she must then choose how to broaden her experiences and knowledge to become the woman she wants to be. She might begin to travel abroad and need the essential information that manners and etiquette could afford her as she meets foreigners and finds herself in strange accommodations, eating strange food, and attempting to communicate in strange languages.

This can be the time to take a good hard look at who she is and who she wants to become.

But we all need the tools to succeed in any new venture. These chapters offer the ingénue the tools and ideas to guarantee a greater element of success in determining how she desires to look, feel, act and become in the upcoming years.

College to Career

Another life transition is between college and career. This step is probably the greatest life change a woman goes through. An etiquette makeover might be critical to establishing oneself as a forerunner and polished person for the many years she will be enlarging her influence on the job market. As stressful as this time is, she can circumvent much of the disastrous stress of the unknown by taking time to assess her strengths in pursuing the challenges that lay ahead of her.

Perfecting a good first impression is the key to the next step in job interviews, meeting company officials, being wined and dined by corporate headhunters or corporate executives. They say that the decision to hire is made by executives over coffee *once they have seen your etiquette when dining.* In fact, the how-to's of fine dining are critical, whether at home or at a restaurant. Your makeover should include the tips you need to make the difference in any interview process, including those all-important coffees, lunches or dinners.

Career and Homemaker

Another enduring change in a woman's life is when stepping into the role of wife or mother. Maybe you've learned already how to handle a job and a boyfriend. Now, learning to elegantly handle a husband, his career demands, your career demands, children and home is much more challenging, and it is never simple or easy.

As homemaker, entrepreneur, or company officer, wife and mother, you desire life to flow more graciously, but there can be so many anxieties during this period that it's easy to lose sight of which end is up. Meeting realistic expectations in these roles might be the greatest challenge of all, *but it is not the time to lose all of your cool, etiquette, elegance, and social savvy.* Instead, it's the time to step up your game. An etiquette makeover at this period in your life would be beneficial to your very soul.

Empty Nester

The next big makeover might be the time you find you are an "empty nester." This time is a great opportunity to reinvent your life with your spouse and find the time to do the things you may have put off. Rediscovering the art of cooking rather than just feeding the "meals on wheels" crowd, or visiting faraway or not so faraway places are some ways to reinvent your lifestyle. An etiquette makeover is perfect for you right now because you will want to have the best quality of life available to you in your new way of life.

Whatever the reason, here is an opportunity to look at yourself in a fresh new way and add some character, class, style and protocol to your life for the proper etiquette makeover – becoming refined.

PERSONAL CHOICE: TIMELESS OR CLICHÉ
"Insist on yourself. Never imitate." Ralph Waldo Emerson

This could be the beginning of a life-long journey – a quest – to make yourself the polished person you desire to be. It always begins with "desire." If you want to change, you can, if not, you will never create a lasting ideological change in your life just by reading a book, or taking a class. But changes do take place. It is said that habits take an average of sixty-five days to really take over. You can change some old bad habits with good new ones in a few months, so here is the challenge. By the time you get through this book you will have the opportunity to add new lifestyle tips to your daily routine. It is that simple.

This could be the beginning of a life-long quest to make yourself the polished person you desire to be. It takes a passion and desire to change and enjoy the process.

How do we explain the timeless etiquette to a generation as unique and special as ours? How do we expound on the information that has separated the crass from the well-bred through the previous generations and what is still fitting for our next generation?

It begins with a book of ideas and concepts –the *strategy* behind being mannerly and refined, not a list of "do's" and "don'ts." It includes suggestions to make your life more valuable in society. It is intended to influence you to be more beneficial and enjoy a fuller life while being on the cutting edge of *this* generation's society.

Like it or not, people judge us by appearances. They make an initial assessment according to the things we do and say, and how we look – our appearance and our behavior.

It is the little things that add up to an overall impression:

- Our coordinated outfit.
- An introduction graciously acknowledged.
- Neat, shiny hair.
- The right word at the right time.
- Gracious posture.
- Courtesy on the crowded subway or boarding lines at the airport.

In short, our *appearance* amounts to the hundreds of little things we are called upon to do and say daily in association with our neighbor, our friends, casual acquaintances, even the random stranger on the train or at the airport. It is truly the little things (on the outside, and from the inside) that make life finer. They win us friendships, and they bring us pleasure and happiness.

But how can your *manner* be right *if you are not sure of your manners?* How can you be poised, calm, and at ease if you don't know what to do, what to say? How can you radiate confidence when you are puzzled by doubt, embarrassed by mistakes? Whatever your personality may be, your confidence and overall disposition can be made more attractive by the added touch of complete self-possession – by knowing how to act (manners), and by learning how to adjust to the established customs. You must find out what is "correct" in the situation, and make it a practice to do that correct thing always, in private and in public. Practice so it becomes natural and instinctive for you to do it – so it becomes as simple as saying "good morning" – and *that* will give you poise and confidence, and will make you sure of yourself. Once you are familiar with appropriate *manners,* you'll be able to forget about the details of conduct and devote yourself to your *manner* (your overall demeanor) – and move along the path to the enrichment of your personality.

The Ideals of Good Manners

"The essence of politeness consists of so conducting ourselves in word and manner . . . that others may be pleased both with us and with themselves. Your manners are the printed page on which people read of what you are inside." Unknown

The ideals that come with good manners include:

- Do not estimate people for what they possess, but for who they are.
- There is "new" money and there is "old" money, but any indication of the glorification of money and the display of wealth are essentially vulgar.
- The truly well-bred man or woman has simple tastes and fine discrimination, judging people not by their tangible wealth or their ancestors, but by their own worth.
- A sense of values will teach you to have a good-humored tolerance of others, to be in sympathy with whatever society you are mingling, and to look for beauty everywhere.
- There is a charm in candor, yet, if the thing you have to say is in some way painful or disagreeable to those who are present, you should ask yourself: "Is there a real necessity for saying it?"

A refined woman's manner is never aggressive. She is truthful but not blunt. She is sincere but not rude or hurtful. She makes allowances for the differences of character and temperament in people. She never acts on dislike for someone, but always judges in fairness.

There is nothing that costs less and at the same time is of more value to you than good manners.

Pretense for the purpose of impressing others is always futile. No refined person pretends that she is more than she really is – whether it is her material wealth, education, social standing, or professional success. This gives all the more reason to be truly and sincerely ourselves, fearing nothing except injuring others, affecting nothing except a whole-souled interest in our fellow beings, living the simple, elegant, generous philosophy that is the polished woman's allegiance.

In the truest sense, etiquette and manners are concerned with those rules of the "game of life" that make it easier and simpler for us to socialize with one another. The primary and fundamental rule is a regard for the rights and the feelings of others. Sane, sensible rules of conduct improve confidence, make social contact smoother, and prevent misunderstanding. The final test of being courteous in character and manner is not whether you can host a formal dinner party or make a correct introduction, but whether you can mingle comfortably and pleasantly in any social circle.

Homework: Be on the lookout for persons with refined, good manners – what is the common thread among these people? Notice their ease, insouciance, upbeat, but reserved approach. Think about how to emulate these traits you see in other refined persons.

THE VALUE OF GOOD MANNERS

In social and business life we seek the people with whom we can feel at ease. We gravitate toward the people whose manners do not offend us. There is nothing that costs less and at the same time is of more value to you than good manners.

"Manners" means many things to various people. It may mean using a knife and fork properly. It could mean acknowledging an introduction in a pleasing, gracious way. To others, manners means overlooking some mishap in your midst and quietly discounting it so as not to embarrass the person causing it. The more manners you have and practice, the more it permeates all you do and say. For some people, manners mean the strict adherence to rules and Victorian principles. To you, manners should simply become the normal way of life.

When you hear someone say "she has impeccable, or flawless manners," this means she knows what to do in every situation and responds graciously, as one who is well-bred. She enjoys the finer way of doing things and handling herself.

You will be surprised at the dividends your good manners will pay. You yourself will be infinitely happier. You will make friends wherever you go. You will be conscious of a new sense of power and assurance in your contact with people. Once you begin to integrate refinement in your life, you will find you instinctively know how to behave based on the good manners you have been practicing.

You will realize that your desire to behave appropriately will guide you without any "do's and don'ts" from a book or any need to "look up" the proper way to behave since you have instilled within yourself an understanding of what is appropriate.

Refinement is meant to motivate you to study good manners and etiquette for your own personal lifestyle, to give you an overall approach to enhancing your manner, which is your behavior and your image. Ultimately your goal is to refine your taste, speech and actions to a level that pleases and satisfies you.

As kindness must be genuine, it is important to practice kindness to the postal deliverer as well as to the person you most admire.

A good disposition/manner:

- Is truly interested in people – looks for the joy and the sunshine in life, rather than the gloom and the shadows.
- Is cheerful, kind and courteous.
- Does nothing to hurt anyone's feelings, says nothing that will cause anyone pain.

- Is courteous and considerate no matter the circumstances.

FINDING THE COURTEOUS WAY

In the present-day, American, non-gracious attitude, courtesy ranks low. The new simplicity and informality that characterizes American life seems to allow rudeness and invite discourtesy in our contact with one another. This is not the only country that has forgotten their rich heritage. Europe and Asia have not winced at the lower standards of the new generation. The real foundation of good manners is to have an honest desire to please. Courtesy is the balanced expression of this desire to please. If you are courteous, you will elicit courtesy in response.

You will always find it worthwhile to cultivate the habit of courtesy. Choosing to be courteous at all times, even under the most difficult conditions, is the true test of having a courteous manner. Think *courtesy* no matter where you are or who is with you. Make every effort to avoid the little discourtesies we slip into so easily.

Meg Ryan, in a scene in the movie "You've Got Mail," realizes that she does not want to belittle someone just because they are unkind to her. She decides she will be civil and courteous toward all persons alike, no matter how they treat her. This is her ideal – and yet her goal is not always automatically accomplished; even though her upbringing taught her good manners, when she is "confronted with a horrible person," she responds back with a retort – and then quickly feels terrible for succumbing to someone else's bad habits. When manners are ingrained in you, even if you do not follow them in all your actions, you realize you would be more comfortable and be yourself by doing the *right thing*, the thing you *know* to do.

For the sake of your own social happiness, it is important for you to cultivate a sense of the true value in people. This empathy will put you at ease in being kind to all, and after all, being kind and putting people at ease is one of the first duties of a mannerly person.

CHAPTER 2 - THE BASICS

"It is very hard to be a woman. It is not enough to be supposedly intelligent, you have to be glamorous and elegant, too. And if you're not, men are very disappointed. If I only had to put on a tie and run a rag over my shoes, that would be just wonderful." Joanne King Herring

We each have as much time as the next person during a day, a week, a month, and a year. What we do with our time, particularly time not already allotted to career, family, and other commitments, says more about us than any other thing. If you are not the best at time management, you must approach time management as a "boot camp."

If you are a born procrastinator, you must motivate yourself to get up, get moving, and be organized and disciplined about it. Make lists, set goals and make sure you can meet them; then, reward yourself. Put a white board in your closet and schedule your hours.

Your challenge today is to determine what motivates YOU to change.

I coached a young woman with her first sales job. She could not get motivated to call on doctors and nurses, so we created a "points" scorecard whereby if she called on a certain number of potential customers, she received points. She could tally double points if she called on someone "cold." The points system worked for her because the rewards were gift cards to exclusive boutiques, specialty coffee shops, and restaurants. Her motivation was to be rewarded with presents. Increasing her confidence that her products, presentation, and follow-up were getting results (sales) turned out to be a great motivational tool for her, and the positive feedback inspired her to follow through. She developed good sales habits that brought her great results and eventually did not need a points card to motivate her to get sales. You can determine right now what motivates *you* to utilize your time wisely. Finding your own best motivator (or reward system) is a daring approach to managing time and making changes in your life. Determine what motivates you and use that tool to accomplish your goals.

So, really, when looking at the basics, it comes down to: Who are you? What's important to you? Are you confident in who you are? Do you wish to expand your horizons and capabilities? Answering these questions is a good starting point. The dialog you have with yourself will initiate a healthy curiosity about etiquette and manners and how you might become a more refined individual.

COMMIT TO A NEW START

Today is the best time to set a new direction. Become a "self-starter" and set a new course. I encourage you to highlight or write in the margins of this book those ideas that resonate with you. If this is an E-book, keep a "personal growth" notebook handy to write down page numbers or ideas to review and incorporate into your life.

What motivates you to change? It could be a certain person's admiration, or a goal reached, or boredom and discontent with your present lifestyle. You might be motivated by the satisfaction you have when you complete something or make a positive change in your life, or receive compliments. Whatever your motivation, once you identify it, you will move forward and accomplish more than you may have thought you could.

The best place to start with any new idea or endeavor is with your "why?" Why would I do this, and what am I aiming for? It's similar to a Mission Statement, such as the ones companies use to inspire their employees and keep them focused on the company's message and goals. Have you ever written a mission statement? A personal mission statement provides clarity and gives you a sense of purpose. It can be an important tool to help determine your calling or purpose in this next stage of your life. Once you are clear about your purpose, you will bring more enrichment into whatever you do.

Seeking your purpose – your calling – should be a personal priority. In a personal mission statement, you outline and define who you are and how you will live. The statement establishes what is important to you. If you desire to be a more elegant woman, then it should be in your personal mission statement. If you desire to become more cultivated, or want to give to others, or desire to become a mentor, that should be included. It is not about the roles you play in your everyday life; it is about your overall nature.

Writing a mission statement is important to identify your life and how to enrich it. Demands run high every day for our energy and attention, yet there are ways to handle any priority in your life. You could stay up a few minutes later each night, or get up a few minutes earlier each morning.

You may need to say "no" to less important time-consumers, such as television shows or movies or social media sites. If change is truly a priority for you, then you will make time to attend to it. You will see immediate and lasting results from applying principles in this book to your life. You will be happier and more confident as a woman. This confidence and sense of self-worth will, in turn, assist you in all your other priorities.

Choose Refinement. This is your time to become more refined as a woman, a professional, and in all the other roles you fulfill in your life. A woman who is certain about what she wants will not make excuses about an inability to find the time – she will *make* time to attend to what matters. You need to consider your philosophy and your goals. Why do you want to change at all? What is the driving desire within you that makes you want to be a better version of yourself? This awareness can be the start of a more interesting life for you and you need to understand your "mission statement" for getting started. Compelling reasons for an Etiquette Makeover might include the following:

- You are tired of the life you live and want to elevate yourself in a positive manner and become more interesting to yourself and others.
- You'd like to know what to do in every situation, giving you the self-confidence and assurance that you are always acting appropriately and handling yourself with poise and grace.
- You want to be "relevant" – and to reinvent, redesign or "refine" your own personal brand or style from time to time to

ensure you are age-appropriate and perfect for every occasion that you encounter.

- You desire to "upgrade" your taste and usual regimen with concepts that will improve your life as a feminine and "to-be-taken seriously" woman.
- You have a few months to invest in this venture and a real desire to see some personal growth. (*Think: over the summer, or a long winter vacation*).

Commit to doing something great for YOU this year. It is up to you to make the finer changes to your life and then enjoy the benefits every day.

Now is a good time to list some of the objectives you have for reading this book. Commit to doing something great for YOU. No one else will drive you to do this, or encourage you to change. It is totally up to you and your desire to improve yourself, reinvent yourself and be happier with yourself – with all your beautiful, unique qualities. It has often been said of famous women that it was not their looks that made them beautiful or desired, but deeper, more authentic qualities: kindness balanced with strength, grit mellowed by composure, and charm in their distinctive manner. Beauty on the outside, but steel inside.

Homework: Draft a Personal Goals and Mission Statement today. This is the chapter to get it down on paper or on your electronic device. You can even speak it to your notes app. DO IT. This will keep you on course to complete the book and make those little changes that will enhance your inner beauty and outward style and grace.

Take the time while reading this book to identify the longing within you for change. Know that, with a little discipline and understanding, you could really embrace formal and socially-correct behavior at all times, no matter the circumstance, no matter who is watching or not watching. This will be your life – no one else's. The advantages of learning general etiquette are that you will certainly know what to do and say in nearly all circumstances: You will better relate to each situation with the right responses, the right words and the right behavior. Here are a couple of rules for better conduct.

Rule 1 – Be Focused and Attentive

One of the first things you may notice about a refined woman is that she is focused and attentive. She is truly present with the person in front of her. She is not distracted, or absentminded. She is disciplined. She engages in conversation and shows an interest in that individual with a genuine and deliberate concentration. She exhibits a real interest in others and seeks to be interesting to others.

Allowing distractions during social interactions is unattractive and shows a sign of vulgarity and rudeness. It is like the date who continues to scour the room for every interesting-looking woman except the one in front of him. That kind of vulgar and self-centered behavior portrays someone undeserving of an elegant woman as a date, companion, friend or wife. Rude behavior and total lack of manners toward the person who should be the center of his attention should leave her wondering why she is even there.

Rule 2 – You Are How You Look

You are how you look. People form a first impression and judge you in the first five seconds they see you. Fair or not fair, that is the way it happens. So what can you do about it? Who you are is displayed all day, every day, by how you <u>look</u> (first), and <u>speak</u> <u>(second)</u>. You can only pretend with people for so long, and then when you begin to speak, you are known for who you are. How you <u>conduct yourself</u> can overpower the first impression. Beware: your actions can sometimes contradict your words!

If you are interested in developing the "whole package," integrating the principles of elegance and etiquette will make it possible for you to move forward and to advance in life as a refined woman, no matter your age, background, financial situation or social status. You become a well-mannered woman from the inside out. Your manner is established within you before it ever shows outside.

Although it begins inside, at the same time you are being judged by your "outward appearance" which reflects the way you think about yourself. This popular comment may sound crass, but it's true: "You can put lipstick on a pig, but at the end of the day, it is still a pig."

You can wear designer clothes and purchase expensive accessories but they will always wear *you*, unless you confidently make them a part of your very own signature style and appearance that reflects who you are.

It is important, to establish a signature item for your overall appearance. Each of us is remembered in all we do and say, but also in how we looked.

Elegant women are not opposed to shopping in thrift shops, boutiques, or even lower retail chain and discount stores. The idea here is that they know what to look for in a garment, such as fit, fabric, color, and fine attention to detail in how it is manufactured. They procure items for their wardrobe in many diverse locations. I received many compliments over the years for my 1990 banana republic suit. The suit fit well, and was made of great fabric in a beautiful color. Elegance is very much within your reach financially.

It is important, (and fun), to establish a signature touch for your overall look, such as always wearing the same perfume, or the same lip color, or incorporating the same accessories in all that is worn, or the same hairstyle. If you find an elegant classic cut or style, it keeps you from aging (think: Lady Diana, and Princess Grace of Monaco). In later chapters we will explore the types of hairstyles that will make you look your best. With very small changes over the years, you can have this timeless approach to your coiffure.

What is your signature touch? My dear cousin wore the same type of silver brooch every day of her working life. The brooches she owned all had one thing in common, which was a small vase for one tiny flower. She wore a flower every day and elevated her normal beauty to elegance beyond words. You just knew something was "right and beautiful" about Edith. At her funeral a few of us who were impressed by her style wore a similar silver vase pin with a single flower in it.

She left an impression of elegance and we remembered her that way. Each of us is remembered in all we do and say and, conversely, in all we do *not* do or say.

So, what are the guidelines for how to dress? Do you have a few particular rules you always follow when you dress? Do you wear only strapless underwear under black, or always tie your hair back when wearing turtlenecks? Perhaps you wear certain colors in combination as a rule, such as navy pants with grey blouses, or ruffled silk blouses with suits. Other example "rules" might include: *Flats with shorts, no sandals after September 1st, flip flops only at the beach or pool, and exercise clothing only in a class or the gym. Perhaps you always wear dresses when shopping.*

Here are some things you might always do. Keep a pair of flats inside your purse when you wear high heels on a long day. Carry a small clutch after five o'clock, wear drop earrings only in the evening.

- Identify what you LOVE and what you HATE. Clean out and organize your closet with this in mind.
- Be emotional and feel elegant as you put on your new clothes. Touch the gorgeous handbag that you purchased with three months' budget.

- Experiment with the way you want to look. Pay more attention to what makes you look grand, and what makes you look plain. Perhaps orange is not your color, if it doesn't flatter your complexion! Or maybe you believe that cut offs (shorts) are not elegant at any age, or mid-length skirts don't work for you unless paired with great heeled boots. *Never, never. Always, always.*
- What rules dictate your day to day choices? Consider rules that bring out your best features and play down your worst. Sometimes a good friend can give objective advice.
- Your life should have luxurious moments. You are feminine, womanly, and alive. Experience the sensuality of your wardrobe and your life as you discover how you want to look, feel, behave.
- Resist buying numerous items cheaply. Instead, acquire great pieces, which may take longer, but they will be ones that you absolutely LOVE to wear and feel good wearing. This approach to dressing will give you a timeless yet fresh appeal.
- Develop what you wear into a "code" or formula for looking more elegant and well put together. This is when you begin to style your personal "Look Book[1]" based on that tried and true best wardrobe in your closet.

Always purchase items made of the best fabrics and quality you can afford. Choose quality over quantity and you will have far less regrets.

Once you have some absolutes, you can then move to all of the possibilities: Sometimes this, or possibly that. You can be caught

---

[1] A **Look Book** is a compilation of photos and notes on your best ideas and colors for reference when shopping, or preparing for every occasion. Personal shoppers usually prepare one for their clients, but we will discuss how to create one as a useful fashion tool.

up in endless choices if you do not have some rules and boundaries for your personal style, which can evolve to always be fresh.

More On Your Appearance

"You have got to have style. It helps you get up in the morning." Diana Vreeland (former editor in chief, Vogue magazine).

As we look at arriving at dressing with style and elegance, here are some helpful ideas worth considering. Your style should reflect your individual personality. If you are more serious, then your wardrobe will reflect that intellectual, quiet and sophisticated look. It may contain all neutrals but you can still integrate fresh ideas into a neutral palette. Many neutral colors become exciting when combined, such as matching grey wool trousers with a crisp white blouse and a tobacco bomber jacket.

If you are gregarious and fun-loving, you will gravitate toward the best colors and fit that you feel confident in. You will take risks with combining some of your best colors and looks to create a more "edgy" style. Elegance is in the fit, color combination, and fabric choices.

If you are easygoing and relaxed, your personality should be reflected in what you wear and how you wear it. This does not mean "casual Fridays" every day. Even casual Friday clothing choices should be crisp, elegant, sophisticated and uncomplicated, not comfortable "jammy wear" such as stretch pants and long T-shirts. (Here is where the elegant woman has the *"never, never"* approach).

What you wear is only as elegant and fitting as HOW you wear it (Think: Lauren Bacall, Kate Moss, Mary Crowley of Downton Abbey, and Queen Elizabeth). How you walk and talk in your outfit makes it appear appropriate or inappropriate.

Elegant women in the 20th century – Grace Kelly, Iman, Aerin Lauder Zinterhofer, Princess Mary of Denmark, Jackie Kennedy

Onassis, and Queen Rania of Jordan, (you should discover your own favorites) – may or may not have had professional assistance in choosing their apparel, yet they rarely made mistakes when it came to their overall appearance. These women seemed to understand what worked best for their lifestyle and presence. They utilized their "signature colors" and wore them with style and substance. Who will stand out in the 21st century as elegant examples of refinement?

These are just a few examples of prominent women, and are not necessarily the finest-ever examples of elegance. Each one of these women made her mark in society with how she presented herself, found her own style and wardrobe, and acted before the public. These women were considered popular enough in social circles to have much written about them. You can research these women and find interesting information to glean for your own "road map" to becoming more elegant.

When determining how much effort you are going to put into becoming more refined, everyone (including men) finds certain attributes attractive. It is important to find those attributes that will make you more refined and attractive. Here are a few features of the attractive, confident and stylish woman:

- She generates an air of happiness
- Her facial expression is pleasant
- She has a natural fresh look (in makeup)
- Her approach to life is always feminine and confident
- She understands the importance of good body form and posture
- She always has a neat appearance
- She wears clothing that is appropriate for each activity

What do you highly esteem in women who are considered attractive? Is it the way they walk, or talk, or seem to be at ease with everyone? Determine what it is that makes others attractive, then list the qualities that you find make you attractive. There are many globally acceptable "attractiveness factors" that you might want to study and reflect upon, and then learn how to incorporate them into your own life.

REFINING YOUR LOOK

There is a way to find your unique and elegant style. It might take some work and a bit of trial and error, but there is that special *something* that makes each of us uniquely beautiful and elegant as we attain that self-confidence in what works for us in terms of style. Find out what inspires you. Determine at least two style icons that typify what you like to wear and what makes you feel chic. Consider your selected style icons: Ask yourself if they would wear *this,* try this on, or even consider it? *If she (the Icon) were shopping with me, would she want me to purchase and wear this?* Even if your body type is not like hers, she would advise you to look your best. It is her attitude and flair that has made her your icon; having the same body type and hair color as your chosen icon would be even better. Either way, ask yourself: "Would she look elegant in it, or even be seen in public in it?"

Asking these questions regarding items already in your closet is where it becomes bittersweet. As our taste becomes more refined, we have to lay aside some of the garments that we dearly thought were great. Perhaps they never were and never will be. There are items in our closet we have difficulty parting with for sentimental reasons, not for reasons of style. There is something in all of us that has a difficult time letting go of something we purchased for an occasion that once might have "worked," but just doesn't now! Or we've kept an outfit for emotional reasons, and now have to reconsider as we go back to look in our closet.

Face it. That garment, that item, that accessory – no matter how much affection you have for it – is never going to be stylish on you. This is tough love. Find a wonderful replacement that will elevate your wardrobe, and say goodbye to your old item (RIP). Closet cleaning is probably the most difficult part of the process. Perhaps trade that wonderful item with a friend for one of her newer iconic pieces.

When considering new pieces, ask a few questions about this purchase, such as:

1. Is this going to be my "go-to" or "anchor" outfit?
2. What would I trade in my closet for this outfit?
3. Does this color accentuate my best features?
4. Is it in line with my other newest garments to move toward more elegant outfits?

If your answer is no to any of your initial questions, ask yourself why you want to purchase the item or outfit.

When you have fallen in love with an outfit, scrutinize it again for details:

1. Does your eye focus on the overall look of the outfit or is there something that seems out of place?
2. Are the buttons too large?
3. Is the zipper exposed?
4. Does the item slip on and off comfortably?
5. Does the hem hit you at the wrong place?
6. Are the darts aligned with your bust line?
7. Does the pattern line up or is it skewed?
8. Do the shoulders fit just right? (It is difficult to alter shoulders).
9. Is this piece well-made and will it take you through years of happy use?

This is where you have to honestly and objectively analyze your potential purchase. This technique takes more effort when shopping, but fewer mistakes are made when you begin to purchase "smart."

There are other questions you may want to ask yourself:

a. Would you wear this instead of something else already in your closet for the same occasion?
b. Do you say "wow" when you see it on you? Do you look and feel fabulous in it? Or, are you just settling for it, since you did not find exactly what you really wanted? *Closets are cluttered with such items.*

c. What is it that keeps the outfit from being perfectly elegant and stylish?
d. Where would you wear this?
e. Is it the finest item you can afford?
f. Will you want to continue to wear it for the next ten years?
g. Does it upgrade your look, your style?

You have to determine what style changes and upgrades are right for you. You will find it gets easier as you consider these things.

Are you changing from a high school senior to a college coed? Are you going through a style make-over? Did your stylist/personal shopper recommend the item based on *her* taste, or based on *your* needs? Did you end up with several frumpy dresses one season and cannot see past them to the next fresh iconic pieces this season?

Shopping for iconic pieces can be daunting but as you develop in refinement, you will be able to manage your wardrobe choices more fluently. You become discriminating, so shopping gets easier because you can cull out many items that are definitely not suited for you. It will take less time and effort to locate those items you: 1) need; 2) will love wearing; and 3) are suited to your particular lifestyle and taste.

The refined woman must be committed to her decision to be elegant at all times. She must understand her place in society and her way of life and which outfits are necessary, and which are not in her type of lifestyle at this time. No slouching ever again in public. Private is no longer very private. You are on display most of your life. Time at home is spent on important ventures, so you dress smart, even at home, as you do these things. There are now a few very fine designers who create looks for home wear and offer us ensembles of pants, jackets or sweaters and blouses that look well-put-together in a moderate way. Some are versatile for the woman who is on the go to luncheons, meetings, and fund raisers. If you have found a designer or label that really suits you, it may be wise to purchase a few items together to mix and match, and then add to that collection over the years to update it.

Suits are making a comeback and with those suits come the color and design of the elegant woman who is advancing herself. Make an effort and allow enough time each day to look your best. Then it will become something you automatically do with less thought and it will begin to make an impression on others, even when you "dress down". With sufficient practice it will become second nature.

Determine why certain things, when paired together, are not elegant. Consider why they do not work or ask a trusted friend. You will get differing answers, but sift through their "pro's and con's" to arrive at a look that works best for you, and stand your ground about it.

It is sometimes best to start with a fresh color palette. Even with a closet full of clothes, you may need to just invest in a few basics to work with first. Use solid colored sheaths or dresses or monochromatic looks, and then add the statement accessories to get that "look." Put old things next to the new items and see if they come alive or just fade. Remember, it is your taste that is changing, and you are moving toward refinement, which is a good thing. This could create a dilemma for you, however, if you are adamant about wearing those old, tired items in your closet that have no elegance factor to them. Some tailors have a knack for revitalizing a tired outfit. Find one.

Once you are comfortable with some items to work with and create outfits, find a balance in your "sum total" appearance. Tousled hair and dark, lean denim. Sleek bob and little black dress. Think combos that are classic and fresh. Then add your own personality and continue to add your own character to make it your look.

Find fashion ideas in magazines or catalogs and retain them in your Look Book for inspiration before you plan to shop for specific items or clothing. Bring your Look Book with you or capture photos on your phone of the outfit you are shopping for. Think about what works best for your height, weight, and the occasion you are shopping for. Determine a few do's and don't's. It is about training your tasteful eye, your desire to look the best you possibly can, with pulled together looks that are timeless but fresh, looks that whisper, "This is the real me." Remember, this is like going to the gym and exercising, using more weights than before and getting a better result in your overall physical condition. It takes some exercise and practice to get your look all together.

ELEGANT IN APPEARANCE

"The only real elegance is in the mind; if you've got that, the rest really comes from it." Diane Vreeland

We have discussed how your refinement will be a lifelong endeavor, but you will begin to reap rewards almost immediately as you train your elegant eye. Even though there is a learning curve and you will not always get it exactly right, there are ways to be successful in "upping" your style next time you go shopping. Do not be discouraged if you make a few mistakes.

It is important that you develop an elegant refinement in taste and lifestyle for your own reasons. When you are well put together, you can actually forget about yourself, and you appear more relaxed and self-confident.

Grace Kelly, a style icon for many women, even missed the mark a few times in her lifetime. When invited to the White House for lunch with President and Mrs. Kennedy, she chose a beautiful green Givenchy dress with matching bolero, but finished the look with a fitted headpiece that social columns and the media in general scoffed at, saying it was more like a swim cap than a hat. Imagine the humiliation she had to bear before the entire world. But what did she do? She went back out there and wore the most elegant eveningwear imaginable. She WORE it! It did not wear her. She refused to feel beaten just because of one fashion flaw. We know that fashion icons take risks in order to look different from everyone else. If you research Sara Jessica Parker, you will see a certain quirkiness to her fashion choices. She was criticized greatly for taking risks, but she continued to find her own unique look. Why? Because she, and others are the *trendsetters,* not followers. Grace Kelly was known for her ladylike demure look, and even with the "swim cap," she was enchantingly beautiful and graceful; Anyone could critize the choice of hats, but not how she wore it. Photographers even captured President Kennedy being flirtatious with her. While it is good to work on refinement, it is not the end of the world when your look does not work as planned. Don't give in to it and feel poorly, and do not give up. Try again with a revision to include the one thing that did work in that outfit, and give it another try. Try a lot of looks. You will eventually settle into a particular style that is definitely you.

Elegance and style is about how you live. Being selective characterizes you as making very careful choices.

Bubble bath, champagne or sparkling water, old 1940s black-and-white movies with Humphrey Bogart, Lauren Bacall, Barbara Stanwyck . . . what do they have in common? All are elegant, refined, enchanting. Icons from the 1940s and '50s are timeless examples of what you can have if you aspire to it. You have become more self-confident, have a fond affection for others, and sincerely enjoy being among them. You are content with who you are and what you are, so you desire to reach out more, and not be needy and insecure. You begin to grow to love yourself, and enjoy being that person who adapts to an occasion.

It is important that you develop an elegant refinement for your own reasons. Eventually, you will be able to focus less on yourself – and when you are well put together, you can actually forget about yourself. You prefer to focus on other people, putting them at ease, making them feel good when they are around you, and you will have the confidence to give them your presence, your time, your energy.

Elegance and style is about how you live. HOW you live. Being selective characterizes you as making very careful choices. It is about the HOW, not the what. Whether you have a million dollars in the bank or not, you have become selective in your purchases, how you spend time, and your commitments. And you are giving people your full focus and putting them at ease while you are at ease.

While it is important to work smart and accumulate wealth, refinement is not about how much you spend, but who you are inside, which eventually begins to reflect positively on the outside.

Refinement Within

You have learned here that refinement takes effort and diligent research, along with some soul-searching for who you want to become and what you want to be known for. I have always loved elegance and etiquette since I was very young. I loved going to shops and choosing my own dresses as a little girl, which tested my dear mother's patience, but it was important to me to develop my own taste, which was definitely not mom's taste for me at the time. We had "discussions" and sometimes I won, but mostly she won. That did not deter me from finding my own style, look and attitude.

I was headstrong and wanted to know more about fashion, shoes, handbags, perfume and makeup, and how to put it all together for a "look." I tried to express my own personality at private school when all of us wore the same uniform and nearly all decisions on looks were determined by the strict faculty. But when it came to weekends and evenings, I was determined to find my own style: I learned to sew and create new outfits from time to time or alter what I owned to suit my taste. This often ended up a great big mess, but I learned from each experience and would seek out what I thought was elegant, based on my small-world perspective.

You must have this sort of determination to find your style and become elegant and refined. Super models are pawns by the great design houses, but when left to themselves, they have discovered their own look for everyday living. Jackie Onassis, a WASP [2] by upbringing, changed her look several times over her public lifetime. After leaving the White House and moving to Greece, her lifestyle and activities changed dramatically. She became a fashion icon in a new way with her panache for wearing headscarves and her famous dark glasses. Her casual look of white jeans and black shirt was so chic. Even though it was easy to find those items, it was more difficult for others to carry it off like she did. It was her style, her swoosh, her nonchalance, her attitude in those garments that made them work. Later, she again reinvented herself as a New York book editor. She changed her look, but never lost her style.

In fashion, it is not only the "what" you wear, but the "how" you wear it.

What makes your fashion wardrobe work for you? Is it just a matter of being yourself through the clothes you wear, do you think, and not having the outfit the center of attention?

Think about it…for fashion icons – and for you – it is not only the what, but the *how*. Carefully selecting your wardrobe through mindful shopping habits and considerate dressing is *always* the *how*.

Fashion and Style Icons

Who are your favorite icons of fashion? If not specific persons, what designers best define your taste in clothing, style and color? Once you determine what appeals to you, you can start to narrow down your standard looks and make better choices. Everything out there is made to sell, sell, sell. The way it is presented is to sell it to you, the consumer. You must be selective in order to focus on developing your own distinct style. The result of not doing

---

[2] WASP ("White Anglo-Saxon Protestant") became a style of dressing considered "preppy" to non-WASPs.

so is that you will have an array of items in your closet with no plan or focus or overall "look" that is decidedly you.

Find icons you really want to follow for fashion ideas, icons who have retained their own style over the years. Then, review your own closet with a style in mind. What do you see? Can you define the style or styles you have been wearing? Are there sufficient clues to tell you what you really love to wear?

Make your "A" list of famous style icons and what you like about their style. It might just be "ballet flats." Keep your list handy so that you begin to create your own look based on the elegant items worn and adorned by those you emulate. A list might include:

Sophia Loren -Her scoop necked tops framing her Italian full figured look.	**Katherine Hepburn** – the way she wore trousers – leaning back a bit and gliding across the room.	**Brigitte Bardot** - Her hair. How she wore simple dresses – how French she always looked.
Tory Burch - Even with her line of goods, she is a classy lady and exemplifies classic sporty chic: fresh, but simple and always demure.	**Ingrid Bergman** - Those cinched forties suits that made her look so unapproachable and mysterious. Her collar always seemed to lead you to her piercing eyes.	**Lauren Bacall** – Her evening wear was structured and chic. She wore stunning gowns and loungewear that idealized elegance.

When I look in my closet, I find I am always lured by the sheath created of a fine fabric, sometimes in a solid color or sometimes an interesting graphic print or herringbone. All of my clothes seem to have a structured look with a few nice details to make them elegant. Less décor is more for my petite frame. Everything I reach for seems classic yet with a splash of French messy. Not too boringly neat, but elegant with a good mix of old and new. A cross between Grace Kelly and Karly Kloss. I am not six feet tall, however, so some of the looks that work for Ms. Kloss will not work for me. I need to elongate my torso and look longer. The monochromatic effect adds height to my small stature and I am remembered as being taller than I am when in that sort of look.

Your personal style must be developed by your attitude and interests of life. Being well put together means everything is in harmony.

Although I have fashion icons that I look to for style sense, I also realize that the clothes and accessories they wear do not always translate to a demure, petite woman like me.

Your Personal Style

The purpose of personal style is to express your taste and preferences, to be individualized and clearly defined enough to show your selectiveness and originality. There are more clothing designers per capita than ever before, so you have plenty of opportunities to mix and match items from various designers. Think of various designer clothing at Target, Saks, Ann Taylor, Anthropology, Macy's, Nordstroms, Talbots, Amazon, EBay, Bonanza, ModCloth, local boutiques and specialty shops. How you approach living is how you approach your dress code. What do you want to do tomorrow? Do you have the wardrobe to pull it off? Are there sufficient basics in your wardrobe to make your own style achievable? It takes some basics to undergird any look that will last. You must exert sufficient thought to create a look for day and one for night based on the clothing in your closet and the accessories you choose for your unique style.

 Begin to work on your Look Book and create an elegant personal style that is fashion-forward with timeless hints of the greatest eras of glamour. Do not be afraid to try vintage pieces from your great aunts' closets, or little shops on the left bank in Paris. Elements from a previous era are recycled every season on designer runways with a twenty-first century twist to make it work for the style-conscious woman of today.

The first step in transforming your style is to develop a desire to change and be willing to invest the time and resources to make the changes that resonate with you while reading this book. Be a bit daring. Take a risk. Realize that your style encompasses all that is <u>you</u> – your clothing, your hair and makeup, your walk and talk. Remember that transforming your style is *a way of life,* not just a list of do and don'ts.

Thinking once more of the refined monochromatic look, I was first impressed with this look during a visit to my cousin's new home. She began taking her guests through her lovely place with windows open to river views, and spacious rooms with fine furnishings. It was at that moment that I realized how elegant she looked. Not particularly because of the designer labels of the outfit or anything blatant. It was very subtle. She was dressed in winter white from head to toe, her hair was a caramel honey color and coifed perfectly around her face. The look was stunning on her. Here we were, as casual as a Saturday afternoon can be, and her demeanor, as well as the décor surrounding her in her home, seemed to accentuate her monochromatic color palette with an air of elegance. Her hair and makeup was fresh and delicate. She looked as if she had stepped out of a magazine. She flowed through her home, which was perfectly appointed. It was also very neat and clean, with no clutter, no odd pieces out of order or screaming at you. It whispered *refinement.* It all flowed as if it were a master painting before me. Her accent pieces in each room did not distract but supported the architecture and rich colors of her wall fabrics, rugs, and furniture. Small details on tables, and other areas seemed to blend in just like her outfit. They worked simultaneously to give an air of sophistication and elegance.

Similar striking appearances have impressed me from women I know and fashion icons I have followed over time. For example, Marie Antoinette was aware of the value of her appearance in court and in the country, where she loved to spend time. Her choice of style and clothing and accessories were varied yet with an underlying consistency. She had a signature color: blue. Our styles can be just as consistent, with varying styles of dress depending on the occasion, the consistent connection being the signature colors we wear, or the accessories we always choose, or the hair and makeup combination for which we have become "famous."

Being "well put together" means everything is in harmony, a feature of the refined woman. Harmony is not just about the beauty of your face or the charm of your walk, but your entire look – that is what style does for a woman. It is a finished and uncomplicated "look" from head to toe. This is the elegance of simplicity, based on fine fabric, attention to detail and fit, well-made fashion that has good lines for your body type, colors that enhance your best qualities and features, and do not compete or distract from the look you is attempting to achieve.

If you are looking to reorganize and upgrade your closet and its contents, you may want to consult with a professional.

This overall look will bring out your better traits, your own personality, and *not* make you an unknowing model to advertise the latest fashion designer. A good test of style is to look back at photos taken of you last year, two years, or even five years ago. If you feel you look "dated" in that apparel, you were. If you look "timeless," you have discovered a look that you can continue to count on with variations depending upon the occasion.

Look at photos of various style icons over time. Their "look" may have changed, but most of these icons stayed with one personal designer who tastefully designed outfits for that woman over the years to keep her looking her age, yet timeless.

By studying other women over a period of a few years, one can train one's eye to look for similarities that withstand the test of time. Research one of your favorite style icons and study her look at different ages.

Adjusting Your Wardrobe

If you are re-inventing yourself based on a transformation in your life or some momentous decision, here are some ideas for making some things work well. If you are looking to reorganize and upgrade your closet and its contents, you may want to consult with a professional. I have friends who include this personalized service in their personal budget twice a year to help them come up with fresh new ways to combine items, to choose the right things to keep, give away or have altered.

When making a commitment to purchase new items for your wardrobe, sometimes it is worth spending more money on the consultant than the clothes. These professionals will also help you determine which quality pieces you are missing in your overall look and can save you money by directing you away from things that are not a good investment.

If you choose a consultant, be sure to research and interview at least two or three (and you will learn something from each of them during the interview process) before you make your choice. Many times consultants are specialists in specific age groups or styles; some could have other limitations that may not have your best interest in mind.

If your budget is tight, try using a stylist or personal shopper for one important iconic item and get her to take you through the entire range of outfits – day, evening, gala, and weekend looks. Make sure you are serious about discovering your best looks because these personal shoppers are professionals. When they see you really want to learn, they will share ideas with you.

You may want to schedule your stylist appointment on a Tuesday morning. Most clothing and department stores are least crowded early in the week. Be on time with ideas about the item or items you are specifically looking for or the look you want to achieve. Explain what you are attempting to accomplish during this session so that your consultant understands that you are developing a look, and also developing a trust with her.

The "personal shopper" is a great connector to you and your closet.

Tell her up front that you hope to work with her long term, but only want to be shown things within your budget and look. Expectations will be met or exceeded in this manner of shopping. The more developed the ideas and plan you present to her, the better the result. By planning ahead, you show the stylist that you are serious and value her time.

Make sure anything you purchase is returnable, and consider a separate visit for any necessary alterations. The most important aspect of working with a stylist is FIT. Ask for alterations to pin the garment to see the actual fit, but insist on coming back for final alterations. If you purchase the item, take it home with you, mix it up with your current wardrobe, and make the final decision.

The personal shopper is a great connector to you and your closet, and the way to get the most out of your time with her is to be honest about your preferences, budget and lifestyle. Expect to spend about ninety minutes with the stylist on the first appointment. The stylist will ask you about your lifestyle, hobbies, work environment, and expectations. Once you develop a rapport with her, she can notify you when items suitable to your look arrive or go on sale. Communicating what you really want to accomplish with her will get the best results. You can utilize these services to update your wardrobe with new items, but you may want to find a closet organizer to help you with your current clothing, first. She can assist you in photo-documenting your current wardrobe into your Look Book. As you upgrade items, you can delete and add various outfits and accessories into your Look Book to keep it current. This will give you a better understanding of how to work with your stylist.

The overall goal of the first meeting with a stylist is to develop a relationship with her so that you have someone you can rely on to discuss seasonal changes to your wardrobe and changes to your lifestyle. Expect that the stylist will be helpful with various suggestions until she understands you and your likes and dislikes. It is up to you to ask a lot of specific questions. She should not be intimidated by your questions but willing to explain her reasons for the items she finds for you.

Here are a few questions to relay to your stylist:

1. What are the maintenance requirements of this garment? Will it possibly shrink over time?
2. Which brands are keyed to my figure *(the fit is key)* and lifestyle? This allows you to research those brands online and discuss them with your stylist prior to purchase.
3. Are the clothes well made, with French seams, secure buttons, and details done to your expectations? You may choose to purchase such an item or decide to pass on one that has good qualities but was poorly made. You will not regret refusing items of lesser quality than what you are accustomed to, no matter how much pressure you receive from your stylist. You must feel comfortable saying no to items that will just hang in your closet.
4. If your budget is minimal, does the item translate into work and play? Can this item be versatile enough to wear on weekends and holidays as well as to the office? For example, a great jacket over a day dress will take you everywhere.
5. Has your stylist given you at least five ways to wear this item?

6. And finally, if you ask friends and relatives what they think of your potential purchases, be ready to stand your ground if this is something that is flattering but not what they are used to seeing you wear. Think about how you feel when you put it on. How do you appear to others?

Aside from hiring a professional, finding a "clothing mentor" is a good way to upgrade your wardrobe.

If you know someone (personally, or by internet and magazine fame) in your age group or perhaps someone a few years older, by watching her fashion choices you may find the motivation to change or upgrade your own style. If she is someone in your town or city who is amenable to meeting with you and discussing your fashion preferences, she can help you develop your new wardrobe from things in your closet or help you make a fashion shift that would get you into the next phase of your life, at least. If it is in person, make sure you choose someone willing to do this, someone with taste and style, and then find a way to compensate that person in an equitable way.

At any point during your lifetime, it is best to try to mix classics (purchases that will be worn for the next ten years) with new, trendy items. A good black, navy, or dark grey wool pencil skirt is a staple classic in any elegant woman's wardrobe. Pair this with trendy boots (in a neutral, or make it the "pop" color) and you will add a fresh look to the routine skirt, giving it a new life every year. At least 50 percent of your wardrobe should be timeless and can be worn for the next 7-10 years, if necessary.

Determining how much you can spend will determine your classic clothes purchases versus fad and trendy clothes.

A good rule is 75 percent classic / 25 percent trendy until you have all the necessary staples in your closet. At that point you can move to 50/50 and have more fun with seasonal, trendy looks, if that is how you want to dress. Remember that shoes will take a certain percent of your budget as they will wear out sooner than most of your clothing items.

> Having fewer, well-fitted items in your closet will take you farther than having volumes of "off the rack" clothing that says nothing about you.

Accessories are another important part of any wardrobe budget. Watch for great accessorizing ideas in magazines, on Instagram, blogs, and in store windows. You can always make a great scarf with a yard of beautiful fabric. Fray the ends and – *voila!* – you now have a $7.00 scarf with a $100.00 designer look. But if you really want a wow piece, try finding a vintage Hermes scarf and determine to wear it out! Sometimes the main reason why women do not accessorize properly is because they do not know how. Look for various ways to wear and tie a scarf. Once you learn a few ways, you will find you are more confident wearing it, rather than leaving that beautiful accessory in a drawer.

If you are creative, you can stretch your wardrobe even further by mix and match techniques that will make you look so totally diverse even your friends will think you have an endless wardrobe of great items. Scarves and belts are a great way to wear the same classic suit every week. The idea is to create "looks" based on a few basics and accessories to change the impression.

Sometimes it seems that even if we attempt to put ourselves together with a basic ensemble, we have not made the very best impression by not becoming a "stand-apart" individual. I was always told to wear one memorable thing (a statement piece of jewelry, or a hairband, or scarf, or great blouse, or skirt, or handbag) and I can get away with all my other wardrobe items from last year. Why? Because the "pop" in your outfit is what people will remember, whether it is a scarf, a blouse, fantastic shoes, or a great handbag. The rest of your outfit should blend with the one memorable thing and not compete with it. A confident smile will finish that gorgeous look every time. You will appear relaxed, confident and happy, which is an appealing look for anyone.

Another few words on fit and shape: Whether you buy all of your clothes from a low-end department store or a fine store carrying a couture line, the same rule applies: Good fit and form make the outfit grand and appropriately classy. Clothes, no matter the origin, are made for the masses. Often the best fit requires your willingness to have the garment fitted by a professional tailor. If your outfit has sleeves that hang below your fingertips, or a skirt that needs a hem, no matter how much you love the color or style, the wrong fit will make you look less than fabulous. If the buttons hang outside the buttonholes, find a way to reinforce those buttons immediately. Work with a good seamstress or tailor and bring all of your wonderful outfits to be fitted to your figure, particularly if you have lost or gained weight. Remember, your goal is to always look your best and always look well-put-together.

The Cost of a Garment

Have you ever considered the price of a garment you are about to purchase? Have you thought about what you are getting in exchange for x number of hours on the job, or $x sales commission, or $x bonus check, or $x clothing allowance? The full cost of a garment can include some or all of the following (and perhaps things not mentioned here):

- The price tag plus tax, plus the income tax you paid on the income you worked for to purchase this item. If you are a working woman, and in a state that pays income tax (or just federal tax) add the income bracket (10-30 percent) more to the price tag. This is what you will actually pay for the item.
- The actual expense of a garment can also be calculated by the "price-per-wear" cost. If you can reasonably estimate wearing this

garment ten times a season, and cleaning it five times during the season, factor that into the equation and perhaps this is an item that will be a staple or "go-to" that you do not want to pass up.

- Consider your time taken away from friends and family to find an item. A personal shopper can help you reduce shopping time by pre-shopping for you. (I usually call ahead and have my favorite shops place a few things in the dressing room before I arrive.) Once there, I discuss specific items I am looking for, if those items were not a good match). This allows you more freedom to be with others rather than in a dressing room. Here is another cost justification for a personal shopper. Other justifications include avoiding costly mistakes of impulse purchases, or settling for something because you did not have time to search for what you really wanted.

Other Things to Consider Before You Buy

1. Is the garment in perfect condition? If it is not (button missing, small tear, or something else, hem, darts, zipper hard to zip), then you might want to discuss a discount with the manager – say 10 percent (that will cover the tax). Then find a good tailor and get the garment fixed correctly before you wear it.

2. Is this a sale item and would you normally even try this garment on if it were NOT on sale? Before you try on anything on sale ask the question: "Is it one of my best colors or acceptable colors?" Stick to your taste and style. Sales typically include the last few pieces of a designer's collection for that season, or items passed up at retail because they were too odd, ornate or extravagant to include in a woman's typical wardrobe. You can, however, chance upon a great item that you can incorporate into your wardrobe as either a "wow" piece or something for a special occasion. Only then is the sale price a true bargain. Your stylist can always be on the lookout for sale items you liked earlier in the season.

3. Keep your clothing list of "must haves" in your wallet so that you can decide whether to purchase that sale item or spend a

little more on one of your great MUST HAVEs. Sometimes it's a tough choice.

4. Gather color swatches of your best colors and keep them in a Ziploc bag for shopping excursions. Or keep a small mini-Look Book in your purse or on your phone. This will help you steer away from sale items that are definitely not your color, or don't match your lifestyle.

5. Is the garment something that is wearable for your lifestyle? Or will it just sit in the back of your crammed closet? If it is a heavy wool coat and you live in Florida, will you wear it much, or at all? How many times a year will you wear it? Wouldn't it be better to find a coat on sale at the end of the season to justify buying a coat?

6. Purchases should always reflect and complement your look and style, not deflate it. Fad fashion and cheap bargains may make you feel better for a few minutes – but always consider the question: Is it better than what I already have in my closet? Will it replace one of my "go to" outfits? Would I wear this to a party instead of my wonderful Armani or vintage Oscar de la Renta? Will I wear this for the next ten years? If you can say "Yes" to all of those questions, *then* you should consider the purchase.

7. Also ask yourself: How do I feel emotionally today? Am I buying this for the right reasons, or is it an impulse buy to feel better about myself, to soothe a hurt or be someone I am not?

Ten Purchases You Will Not Regret

1. Day and evening handbags: A great black designer purse, medium size, of excellent quality leather. Too much hardware is not elegant and will date your purchase. You might want a silver or single color beaded *minaudiere,* the small ornamental case for a woman's cosmetics, jewelry, or personal items that is often carried as a handbag. You can find good ones at second-hand shops, because some women buy new ones every season – and the recycled ones rarely look used!

2. Spandex undergarments. There are now several brands of this type of underwear and they all serve a great purpose, they smooth out the bodylines for those in-between days when you are not an eight but not a ten either.

3. Good-quality pumps. You will need to try on several brands to find the one that is made for your foot, but once you do, make the purchase. Take good care of that investment. It can work for you for several seasons depending on the amount of wear and maintenance. Be careful not to wear soft-soled leather shoes in water or on rainy days. Keep a pair of inexpensive flats and heels in your trunk or in your desk for unexpected weather. Try to wear your best shoes only on smooth pavement or carpet. Treat your good shoes like you would treat your feet – only wear them on tender flooring. Cedar shoehorns are a sound investment in maintaining your shoes longer. Taking care of your shoes will make them look new for a longer period of time.

4. Beautiful lingerie. Do not skimp on a proper fit. This is what makes you actually feel good underneath whatever you are wearing. If your bra or panties are not good quality and fit, they will make you most miserable all day and will affect your outward appearance faster than anything else. Make sure the straps of your brassiere do not cut into your shoulders. There is nothing worse. Make sure your bra straps do not show. You can have small bra strap carriers inserted into your dresses to secure bra straps on sleeveless items.

5. A good quality cashmere sweater set. It is amazing what you can do with two pieces in a great color that accentuate your features, hair and coloring. If the sweater set has a fine ribbing, it will actually fit and last longer than a smooth nap. Find the right weight cashmere, and get the color that goes with

everything. You will be surprised how often you reach for it before anything else.

6.   A white blouse. Always in fashion and always looks chic. (Think: Meg Ryan and how many ways she wore that white blouse in "French Kiss.")

7.   An Hermes, YSL or great designer scarf. This "go to" for any occasion will dress up jeans and a top or keep your black dress from being drab. Learn to tie it several ways to mix it up. Hang your scarves in your closet rather than folding them in drawers, to air them out and remind you to wear them often.

8.   Good fitting dark navy denim jeans. The mid-rise straight-leg style is the most flattering to most figures. The tight-ankle cigarette style really makes most women look like a stuffed sausage, no matter how thin they might be. The most elegant and flattering jeans are the ones that are all one dark color, with no variations in the stitching color, buttons, or zipper. Make sure the zipper is a very good flat fitted type so that there is no bulge. *Pockets should be sewn closed in front to keep the front lying flat, and should be flat in the back with no detail, if possible.* Dark jeans can take you from day to evening with the right shoes, accessories, and a great clutch.

9.   A good fitting single-breasted button-front black or navy wool blazer. Choose the length that is right for your body type. This staple will serve you well in many different scenarios, paired with jeans, leggings, dresses, slacks, skirts, even walking shorts.

10. A simple black or navy dress at or above the knee; one made of silk, satin or crepe cut on the bias and intended to show off your shoulders will be suitable for office parties, teas, and socials, even cocktail parties. Cap sleeves can look very chic and adds a bit of elegance to your look. This dress can be worn

every season, depending upon the wrap or accessories you wear. A dress cut on the bias, made of a mid-weight fabric, will fit you like a glove, no matter how tall or short, and no matter if you are one size too small or large – it is very forgiving (don't forget your spandex undergarments). This staple will take you out on the town at night for dinner dates and, if you add some sparkle, it will carry you through formal events. You need this garment in your closet for last-minute invitations.

BONUS: A single strand of pearls that rests along the throat. Pearls go beautifully with a white shirt, or sweater and jeans. Simple chic always prevails.

CHAPTER 3 - A REFINED BEAUTY

"I am intrigued by glamourous women. A vain woman is continually taking out a compact to repair her makeup. A glamorous woman knows she doesn't need to." Clark Gable

This book *Refinement* is the result of research spanning the past twelve years, research on the changing attitudes of becoming an elegant woman in our society in the twenty-first century. What was considered "gauche behavior" in the twentieth century is now accepted, and what was once considered "proper" is now often viewed as outdated, stale and boring. Sadly, what was once unacceptable has now become acceptable. The well-mannered woman, however, has not "evolved," nor does she follow the current norm. She has a nobler path she chooses to take. Let the rest of society grab and begrudge and scratch their way among each other: she delights in her refined and more socially discreet approach to life.

Beauty is not rooted in the ordinary. It is a unique visual effect that causes a joy to spring up – a delight in the beholder's eye. It brings a sense of wonder, and sometimes awe. When understanding how to train your eye for beauty, consider "Hogarth's curve," which is a serpentine curve (S-shaped) found within certain objects of attractiveness. The line itself is never the end, it is a part of the whole. It appears within an object, as the boundary line of an object, or as a virtual boundary line formed by the composition of several objects. Even men use the Hogarth curve when describing a voluptuous woman –they outline a serpentine curve with each hand, opening their hands then bringing them closer as they outline the tiny waist (a delight to all men), then outward again as they form the shape of the hips.

The perception of lasting beauty is not just skin deep. It includes contentment within.

"Line of beauty" is a term and a theory in art or aesthetics used to describe an S-shaped curved line. Sometimes considered "serpentine" in shape, this line usually appears within an object or as the boundary of the object and signifies liveliness and activity – it is intended to excite and elevate the experience of looking at the object, as opposed to neutral parallel and straight lines. This theory was first described by Hogarth in his *Analysis of Beauty* (1753). Baroque and Rococo art used this serpentine curve in many of the creations during those periods. The sense was beautiful, ornate, moving figures, objects and ideas. Modernists such as Picasso used lines to create tension and emotion. His lines were straight or jagged but always dramatic. In the Rococo and Baroque periods the Hogarth curve assisted in moving the observer's eye from one area of the piece to another in a pleasing way.

THE REFINED YOU

By reading this book, you are embarking on a journey from your current level of sophistication and culture to a more refined point of view. You must be open to new ideas and concepts that will allow you to think on a larger scale. The journey will take you through some concepts that perhaps you already know about, or may want to study more and incorporate into your life. With the electronic age we live in, all you have to do is push a button or type a few keystrokes and find what you are looking for, but if you are looking for a new IMAGE, that comes with careful study, self-examination and some work. If you apply yourself, you can learn what it is to become a more refined woman in this fast and often vulgar world. Vulgarity has many forms and is often rooted in ignorance.

Refinement studies the forms of etiquette leading you to a more polished persona, no matter what your background or pedigree. Class and style always come with a price. It is not necessarily the price tag of expensive draping on an unrefined body, but an investment in working on your inner attitude to discover a more sophisticated way of life for yourself.

The Price of Being Beautiful

Jacqueline Bouvier Kennedy and Grace Kelly were considered beautiful women. What made them beautiful might be the totally different perspectives on how they chose to live their lives, yet, they were icons. Many beautiful women exist in the world (and we use the term beautiful to mean beyond the looks a person has at age twenty-one), yet we are not made aware of their beauty unless they are on display by the media.

Observing and learning from historical examples of beauty helps to train the eye to discern true exquisiteness. What makes a woman unforgettable and what makes her uniquely attractive? Is it the clothes, the way she speaks or acts or carries herself? Or is it simply the exquisite beauty of her face and features?

It seems that our perception of lasting beauty is not just skin deep. There is a certain "something" that continues in some women over time to make them even more beautiful as they age (Think: Catherine Deneuve). What is this necessary quality for lasting beauty in your own life? What makes a woman appear her very best at all times?

Refinement is one of the keys to the mystery of lasting beauty. An unrefined woman may appear beautiful in her twenties, or even her thirties, but there has to be more to her – a certain polish to her personality, appearance, speech, actions – to continue to appeal to others as a beautiful person.

Jackie Kennedy Onassis may not have had the most beautiful features, yet her speech, her overall appearance or "demeanor," her tone of voice and manner were so stately and regal she appeared beautiful and elegant.

Other beautiful women have chosen to be the "woman behind the man". Their influence is greater by acknowledging how powerful and influential their husbands' roles in society are, while they quietly forge their own way. This is perceived as a strong, beautiful woman who is so confident in herself that she gets things done, influencing opinions and decisions just by her subtle effect over others in power. Her sway is so solid that she can change the course of many decisions by her discreet counsel. There is a certain beauty and charm to this woman as her wisdom exhibits itself over time. These women do not need the limelight or have the desire to be known for what they accomplish. Candice Bergen was such a woman in the late 1960s and early 1970s. Because of her beauty, she was chosen for film roles, but her passion was actually to be behind a camera, making enduring statements with her photographs.

Remember that lasting beauty includes contentment within yourself, which comes when you take on the mindset that you are sufficient for anything that may come your way. Those of us who have real peace within ourselves can honestly say we are content with our state of being, which removes self-pity, pride, and competitiveness from our thinking. As we move from one life stage and setting to another (high school to university life, to young career, to middle age, to widow or divorcee' or Grand Dame) we go through transitions.

Refinement can help you determine how to move from one stage of your lifelong journey to the next. It considers how to grow into a more refined person with more influence, charm, self-respect and admiration of others. The price of ongoing beauty is to develop your image, taste, sense of worth and value to others, exemplify a humble mind and empathy toward the less fortunate and, finally, be able to adapt to change.

Becoming Attractive – Personal Grooming

Teeth, hair, nails and complexion: first appearances are telling. They tell everyone what you think of yourself, how you treat your health and overall looks, and how well-groomed you are, even if you are dressed very casually. The essentials are straight, clean white teeth; shiny, well-groomed hair and nails; and finally, a healthy complexion free of acne, red spots, and dry skin.

The challenge here is to think more about personal grooming as a part of developing your refined style.

- How much time do you devote to caring for yourself?
- Do you know the basics of personal grooming?
- Are you aware of the many ways you can care for your skin? Do you have a skincare regimen?
- Do you attend to grooming your hair as you would the rest of your body?
- Do you have a budget to spend on your grooming?
- Your hair has a way of telling your age and showing neglect when it does not appear clean with a healthy shine.
- Do you have your hair cut regularly?

Even these basic questions will remind you of the care that is necessary for you to be elegant all the time, not just for parties or in the midst of a crowded room or office.

I am a creature of habit and have established good habits for caring for my teeth and gums (good toothbrush and floss), my hair (deep conditioners once a week, at least, and a trim once every six weeks), and my skin (exercise, loofah, and moisturizer). Because this sometimes seems daunting, I combine some of these rituals together to save time, and I make sure I do them regularly.

Personal grooming is the proper way to look and feel attractive all the time. Try to incorporate more personal grooming techniques into time slots during your day or late evening, such as: apply a conditioning mask on your hair while you brush, floss and whiten your teeth; rinse hair, groom eyebrows and clean skin while your hair air dries to a shiny luster. Apply Vaseline to your nail cuticles and brush your dry hair 100 strokes with a good boar-hair bristle brush. Wash and moisturize your hands for the evening. (Total time: 20 minutes) Try to combine some easy 1, 2, 3 steps and you will find yourself always looking and feeling appropriately elegant at all times. Keep a basket or box with all the essentials handy and get some "me time" in a quiet bathroom.

Personal grooming is not an option to the elegant woman. It is the start of a great look and feel for her day.

It is easy to forget about these routines when you have a busy schedule. The purpose of reminding you of proper personal grooming is to encourage you to enhance your beauty while being a student, mother, wife, career woman, philanthropist, caregiver – whatever your chosen path. Self-neglect is a way you compromise your self-worth. You should care for yourself, because no one else will.

 Your personal routine sets a good example for your daughters, nieces, staff, and others, elevating you as a polished woman who takes her self-image seriously.

There are so many wonderful articles and books on personal grooming. Let it suffice to say that personal grooming is not an option. Every elegant woman has a refined approach to her own beauty routine that keeps her skin, nails, teeth and hair healthy, youthful, fresh and lovely – develop these timeless skills and be rewarded by an ageless beautiful appearance.

 *Honework: In your notes, list the beauty skills and routines you have learned over the years and desire to reincorporate into your daily routine. Jot down the three most important beauty routines you will commit to do each evening before retiring for the night.*

It takes work, time and effort to effectively perform any kind of personal makeover. Books, programs and videos abound on this subject, so discover ideas from them. You must make the decision to look and feel your best all the time, which means organizing and continually evaluating what you do with your time. Remember, since we are discussing an etiquette makeover, some rules in beauty still apply to your overall etiquette learning process.

Tim Gunn of the reality show *Project Runway* continued to tell contestants to "make it work" in reference to their half-started outfits. He challenged them to not give up on something they started; after all, finishing what they started built confidence and self-esteem – and a lively show! So *make it work*. Decide to delve into some of the ideas in this book. Do it for YOU. This is the time to learn about information on body type, best colors, and beauty maintenance routines that get results, *and apply it to your own life.*

Enhancing Your Body Type

There are three basic body types:

- Linear (boy shape)
- Curvilinear (larger bust and hips with a medium waist)
- Curved (larger bust and hips with accentuated small waistline)

Each body type has specific "best" looks. It is important to know your body type, and the best looks for it. Examples include: for a curved body type, the waistline should be accentuated when possible for a very feminine look. Sheaths work well for the curvilinear body type as they show the full contour of the body shape. A linear body needs some fullness such as ruffled blouses and cinched full skirts to appear more feminine.

At first, it may not seem very important, but there are clothing styles for each body type intended to create a great silhouette. (Now, I *know* you may want to continue to wear those baby-doll tops that cut you across the midriff at barely five feet tall! But please bear with me.) There are ideas on tall and petite versions of each body type that will either make you look taller, if you wish, or less tall, depending on your need. Various television programs and many style books identify body types and best-suited styles of clothing for each type. Knowing your own type can prevent you from making costly mistakes as you build a lasting wardrobe.

You may already know what does and does not look good on your body type, but by researching this topic, or getting a resource book, you can review before shopping and save time at the store when you know which dresses will look best on you. It is a good idea to put this information in the front of a binder of your "Look Book" of your best looks, garments you own, other garments that need pairing with something new, your measurements, a list of items you are budgeting for, and other information you may want to discuss with your stylist, personal shopper, or clothes mentor.

Here are some ideas to help you think of items in your wardrobe that may not be as elegant as you wish. This list should help you brainstorm about your outfits that you think are not as lovely on you as others. Here are some issues to consider:

- Exposed large zippers. When zippers become a part of the outfit (and fashion houses have placed zippers as part of the design to be seen across the back), it is rarely considered elegant. The more elegant choice is a hidden zipper on the side or back.
- Fabric that is too stiff or too clingy or too lightweight. No matter the weather, thin clingy fabric is never elegant on any woman's body type.
- Patterns that are too loud or large for the item or the person. When patterns or designs are too loud, they take away from the elegance of the fit, shape, and cut of the clothing. Usually the smaller the pattern, the more formal the item (this rule applies to men's shirts and ties as well).
- Bows, ties and sashes are difficult to keep in place and may create a distraction to your overall elegant look. Be cautious when purchasing items with these additional frills.

 Homework: When adding to your Look Book, start a list of ***"items I want to avoid when shopping."*** *These might include items you own and love, items that never look good on you, colors to avoid, designer labels that do not fit your body type. Bring this list when you shop.*

Quality Fit

Some hints on quality and fit when trying on clothing:
- No pulling or puckering at seams.
- Closures do not pull open between buttons (or add small snaps between buttonholes).
- Pleats should lie flat. On longer straight styles, look for a slit or kick pleat for walking and sitting (particularly in vehicles).
- Make sure the hemline rests smoothly on the legs and is parallel to floor and not curved, unless it is exaggerated for the

look/style of the item, *which usually does not look very elegant.*

- Matching patterns at seams – this seems to be an "elegance rule" even designers don't always follow.
- Jackets not too tight or too loose, not baggy or looking stretched (no bulges, pulling, or wrinkles across back). Most jackets usually require slight alterations before they really fit correctly.
- On sleeveless items, armholes should give sufficient room for movement, but not show any bagginess across the bust line
- Pants and trousers should create a smooth line from waist to tip of shoe when observed from the side and should not be tight in front or back; that creates pulling or stretching. If the hip and derriere portion of the pant fits, that is the correct size. You can take in the hem and waist accordingly.
- Normal length for trousers is to the front tip of the shoe; this usually requires alterations (or a tailor) to hem the pant leg at the exact length.

Fabric & Texture

Natural fabrics are sometimes the most elegant but they also require more maintenance and care. Polyester and other synthetics are now being used by all fashion houses and, depending upon the cut and fit of the garment, can sometimes give a more elegant look than natural cotton, linen or silk. Remember to read labels before purchasing items to make sure you are willing to care for your garment as prescribed.

Cotton – This fabric lends itself to more casual clothing, although I have purchased 100 percent cotton dresses made so well they look and feel like silk, but breathe better.

Linen – This looks better the more it is worn, washed and pressed. It gets softer and drapes better after a few wears and feels better on the skin.

Wool – This is a year-round fabric. There are lightweight wool fabrics for suits and dresses that can be worn year-round. In various climates, light-weight wool will vary, but wool is the best choice for retaining its shape.

It is a good idea to always throw your spandex undergarments in your purse when you know you will be shopping.

The heavier the texture, the more weight it adds to your look. Beware of those wonderful textured bouclé fabrics. Once you try a piece on and look in the mirror, you may choose a lighter, streamlined-looking fabric to ensure you are always looking as sleek as you really are.

Shiny textures also make you look larger. They reflect light and have a sense of largeness to them. They usually do not drape easily and will be unforgiving as you try to cinch your waist or wrap the fabric around your shoulders. If you go for a shiny silver top or skirt, create a monochromatic palette for the rest of the outfit with a color such as grey or blue.

Stiff fabrics are best for outerwear like jackets and coats. There is no reason to purchase a garment that does not have a little stretch in it to make it more comfortable for the hours you may wear it. Your outfit should give and take with the activity you wear it for, and most stiff, heavyweight fabrics are just too bulky to look elegant on a busy, focused woman.

Soft, pliable fabrics such as lightweight polyester and unlined silks may cling to the body, depending on the cut and style of the item. Without the support of the proper undergarment these fabrics have the tendency to show every curve in a most unflattering way. It is a good idea to always throw your spandex items in your purse when you know you will be garment shopping.

Face Shapes – Contour or Geometric

Here are the basic face shapes – in two categories: angled and curved.

Geometric/Angled Face Shapes	Contoured Face Shapes
Diamond	Heart
V-triangle	Pear
A-triangle	Oblong
Rectangle	Oval
Square	Round

Angled face shapes are best paired with angled patterns and prints in clothing, with angled jewelry framing the face, or scarves with angled prints on them. Think geometric prints, not curly rounded shapes. As you play with edgy shapes, you will find that your overall look is sharp, attention-grabbing, and yet classy. Your angled shape can handle this.

Contoured face shapes are best paired with rounded patterns and prints in clothing, jackets, scarves, and round jewelry shapes framing the face. Even collars should be rounded for this face shape. Remember that Hogarth curve? Having it in various areas of your style will enhance your overall look.

If you find an opportunity to have your face and body shape evaluated, do it! This is a marvelous way to determine the types of accessories that look best on you.

By knowing your face contour, you can determine your best choice of shapes for hats, collars, jewelry, and even haircut options. By knowing your body shape, you can determine your best jacket, dress, and pant styles, where sweaters should land on your hips or waist, and your most flattering skirt shapes and hemlines.

The late Jackie Kennedy Onassis did a great job of putting this together: her face was square, and she coordinated her accessories to balance that shape. She also knew her body shape and seemed to flow with ease in Pierre Cardin sheaths at White House formal events. Her bateau necklines and famous pillbox hats exemplified her knowledge of personal style and she always seemed to be comfortable in her choices. Her large squared sunglasses were coordinated to balance her squared jawline and soften her face shape to make it more appealing. Her haircut (a little flip at the bottom but never longer than her jawline) was selected to frame her face in such a way that it made her appear more feminine and graceful.

It is your unique look, sense of attractiveness, and femininity that sets you apart as someone memorable.

There are some things you cannot change about yourself. Even if you are not the beauty of the ball (remember, there is only one at every ball), you can be the most memorable. Learn the best ways to make the most of your facial features, shape and figure. This maximizing of your personal assets will make you appear more confident in who you are and how you approach life, and you will be attractive and interesting.

Grace Kelly was a stylish and beautiful actress in her day. She learned how to pose for the camera and show off her best features. Her eyes and mouth were beautiful and well-proportioned. Not all women are as beautiful outwardly, but Grace Kelly did not just have outward beauty – she was known for her intelligent wit and spirited laugh. She made men melt and women feel at ease in her presence. Her attraction was not just skin deep.

Princess Diana had a demure and shy look. She would tilt her head down and look up with her large brown eyes, a fetching look that was appealing to photographers and subjects alike. The media saturated the magazines and papers with that "look" from Diana. With a Roman nose and simple, pale lips, her eyes were the captivating feature. Her adoring fans fell in love with her total look; it was mesmerizing and it drew you into her mood, which was always a bit sulky-shy.

It is most appealing to everyone to display your most feminine side. While not a fashion statement in itself, it enhances any wardrobe a woman can possibly wear. Her look and her sense of attractiveness and femininity set her apart as someone memorable. If you have a sporty figure, sometimes lace will work against you – try a more sophisticated look that enhances your features, and softens your overall look; keep in mind, it is not necessarily "pink" or "lace" that will give you the most feminine look. And, of course, it is not just beauty that causes people to take a second look, it is that wonderful air about us that tells everyone you are a "force to be reckoned with."

Portrait artists have identified a significant elemental characteristic of faces we deem beautiful. They have incorporated the component of creating analogous lines, such as having a hairstyle that parallels the jawline, or creates a royal pose.

As you try on various looks, think about whether your face shape is angled or contoured. Take a look at your face with your hair pulled back: do you see a square (with a wide jaw) or an oval, or perhaps a round face, or triangle (wide forehead, pointed chin). If your face is round or oval, you have a curved face. If it is square or triangle or even diamond (wide cheekbones but small forehead and pointed chin), then you have a geometric face. This determines whether rounded or boat-neck collars are better than V-neck collars for you.

Your face shape can even affect which shapes in jewelry are best for you. Your face shape may favor round earrings versus geometric shapes. Try putting a scarf around your neckline and create a "v" shape, then a circular shape. Which one is more appealing to you? Once you have determined your face shape, you can determine your best haircut and style for that shape.

Another test is to put on a black round collar and then a black V-neck shirt. Which one looks best? Get a friend to help you determine your best look. She will perhaps learn something about her own face shape. Eventually, as you try on various patterns near your face, you will notice there is a difference. One will make YOU look better. The other might look good, but it is not *you* but the *item* that is accentuated.

There are also certain patterns that make you look better. Either circles or geometric shapes will look better on you. Try dresses, blouses, coats, brooches, and other items of circular shape and then try them with geometric shapes. One will definitely look better on you that the other, in almost all situations. Once you determine your face shape, you will have an easier time deciding between two dresses, various accessories and even handbag shapes.

Attaining the Best Look

After much research, I have found there is no one "formula" to create the best look for every person. You can experiment with the best combination of face shape, hair color, eye color and body shape to get the right colors and styles for you, but it is personal taste that pulls it all together. This takes some work, but it could save you thousands of dollars in fashion mistakes and many frustrating hours of trying on everything in your closet before a big event. It will also create a planned approach to shopping, saving time and money, and giving you better results in purchases. You will be the "smart shopper" and friends will want to know your secret.

Refined Colors for You

One of the best investments in my wardrobe was to be analyzed for my signature colors and styles. It seemed like a daunting task to do this myself, so I hired an expert. Many women have figured it out on their own, but I wanted to have the best source of colors and shapes for my own satisfaction. There are several ways to determine your best color palette.

You can work with a personal shopper, professional image consultant, or color analyst to determine your best colors based on your skin tone, hair color, and eyes.

Along with these factors, you will want to look in your closet at those outfits that you received the most compliments when you wear them. Those outfits are typically the ones that are your best colors. From your past, you can determine what items made you feel your absolute best. Some color experts use the seasons of the year as the four basic color palettes: winter, spring, summer and autumn.

Sometimes it is the cut and fit of the outfit that is complimentary rather than the colors, but other times it is definitely the colors that are best suited to you.

A quick and easy way to determine if you look best in cool or warm colors is to use gold and silver as a determining factor. If you put gold cloth up to your face, or silver cloth – which do you prefer? Which reflects best on your skin tone? If gold, then warm, if silver, then cool.

Winter colors consist of the "jewel tones" and relate to those women who have a generally deep and vivid coloring of eyes, hair and skin (think: icy pink, rich purple, royal blue, magenta, and black). These colors brilliantly shine when worn by true brunettes with dark eyes, eyebrows and hair. Particularly wonderful is the woman with that coloring and pale milky complexion.

Every woman should have outfits with turquoise, winter white, navy and grey in her wardrobe. These will always be the "go-to" items when one is not sure what to wear.

On the warmer side, Middle Eastern, Italian and French women with their earthy brown hues of eyes, hair and skin look very good in an autumn palette. Peach, terracotta, pumpkin, and jade work well for this warm coloring. Autumn brings depth and golden undertones. Colors such as olive green, salmon, warm blue/greens, navy, warm browns and rust tones will look great on the autumn woman. (Think Ralph Lauren and the Colorado sunset colors).

Spring colors are warm and bright as the colors of spring flowers and green hues of the forest. Some of the favorites are moss green, coral, camel, and teal blue. Warm and strawberry blond/redheads will find their best looks when wearing outfits in this palette if they have a warmer tone to their skin.

Summer with its cool undertones are the colors that typify cool blondes and cool "brownettes" (not blonde and not black) who have ash undertones and shine in muted cool tones such as blue greens, soft fuchsia, lavender, soft white, raspberry, cool taupe, greys, and aqua green. This is the most delicate and coolest seasonal coloring.

Many older women can select summer as their colors because of the silver/ash undertones in their hair as they change to grey. Even if they were defined by another season earlier in life, they may find this season more flattering as they mature.

Every woman needs a bit of turquoise, navy, winter white, and gray in her wardrobe. These colors are versatile in themselves and can be paired with many of your best colors from your unique palette to create some diversion and depth to your wardrobe.

And finally, there are "universal colors," according to "Chic Fashionista." These colors will look good on almost everyone: winter white, ivory, mid-gray, stone, taupe, pewter, teal, purple, emerald, turquoise, and lavender. I have tried nearly every one of these colors and Chic knows what she is talking about.

One last hint: there are some basic colors you are sure to want to add to your wardrobe because they are found in fashion every season. These include those cool colors of navy, grey, white and silver. Annual warm colors include cream, chocolate brown, and gold.

Your Signature Color

Look at the colors of your eyes and hair. Sometimes your skin tone will also be a deciding factor on what colors are best for you. Review the information below and use some of these concepts to test what colors will work best for you. You may already be choosing these combinations and never knew why. You may have wondered why you continued to get compliments when you chose to combine these colors in your outfits, or why you continue to gravitate toward one color every time you go shopping. That just might be your signature color!

When shopping with a friend, use the time as a lesson in finding out what colors specifically make YOU look your overall best, not the clothes. Are you a "spring" or "fall" or "winter"?

Some eye and hair combination results are:

- Grey eyes and platinum blond hair. You will have a large color selection as these colors are cool and neutral.
- Brown eyes and dirty blond hair. This is a monochromatic palette. Brown, taupe, some pinks and blues. Pale pink works well if your skin is pale.
- Brown eyes and brown hair. True red is a great go-to color for you.
- Hazel eyes and ash hair. Gold is exceptional if you have a warm skin. Cool skin allows purple to be a great color as purple and green (in the hazel) work as opposites. All shades of brown work well with hazel eyes, but blue is not usually a good color for hazel eyes because it will wash out the eye color.
- Blue/green eyes and gray/silver hair. Shades of blue and white are fabulous on this combination. Your skin is usually fair if you have light blue eyes.

- Green eyes with brown hair. Purples and greens can bring out your eyes. Purple works best with cool skin, and green with warmer skin.
- Green eyes with fair hair, even strawberry blond. Go for lighter shades and pastels.
- Blue or green eyes with ginger hair. Orange-red, coral, and greens.
- Blue eyes/blond hair allow a woman to wear colors such as fuchsia, blue green, bright yellow, powder blue, periwinkle, violet, and watermelon.
- Brunettes. You can wear more intense colors and your exceptional color palette should be full of jewel tones.

Warmer skin tones, particularly with yellow undertones, can wear copper shades (think: cinnamon and ginger). Some reds are also great with warm skin: russet and strawberry.

A Color Scheme Wardrobe

We have looked at a few examples of good colors based on eye and hair color, and skin tone, but if you are still not sure about your color palette, now is a good time to enlist the help of a professional. The cost of the consultant will save you hundreds or even thousands of dollars on wrong purchases.

If you cannot find a color analyst or do not have the budget for one, do your own research and find a willing friend, treat her to lunch, and go to clothing stores to try on outfits of different colors. As you shop, remember, this is a lesson in finding out what makes YOU look your overall best, not the clothes. Are you a "spring" or "fall" or "winter"?

This concept of color palette is not new, but it is crucial to getting the best wardrobe your budget will allow. No matter how great the sale on that designer dress, if it is purple and your skin turns yellow when you wear it, you have just wasted that money. Clothing, interior decorating, even men's ties have a cycle to them. A designer color of the season changes out about every five to seven years.

Clothing designers realize that women will buy what looks good on them, so they will always carry something in each "season" of color in their collection.

Refinement in Hairstyle

Let's say you have now achieved the greatest color match to your personality, eyes and hair color, and you have the perfect outfit to suit your body type. *You still have not completed the best look for you.* Hair is really important, and it is essential to your desirable image.

Having rough, curly or frizzy hair will damage your overall look and make you appear unkempt and unruly, no matter how perfect the outfit. Your hair must appear fresh, lovely, and appropriate for you to have a truly polished look. A good cut is essential, as is a frizz-free manageable style. You are judged by your outward appearance, and your hair must be as beautiful and perfectly managed as the rest of your refined look.

Manageability and upkeep is as important as your cut and shape. If you cannot cope with your hairstyle from day to day, you will end up spending more time and effort than necessary. Start with a good cut for your face shape and your lifestyle. The best cuts are usually in the better salons, so you must consider spending some cash on that regular cut to ensure your daily routine can yield the best result.

If you cannot afford a great stylist (Ceron is the very best), look around at models' or local stylish women's hair and try to find a cut and style that will look good on you. Collect photos of that cut and the various ways that the model or person styles it. A modestly priced salon usually has some talented stylists. Find out who is best at creating your hairstyle, bring your photo research, and get the most for your money. I have received recommendations from friends who know their stylist will work well with my hair type and length. And if you color your hair, find a reputable colorist and book your appointments with that person every time to maintain the right look from a good cut, consistent coloring, and an easy-to-manage style.

Learn the tricks on management and upkeep. A container of dry shampoo is a must to have on hand, just in case; however, it never will take the place of a good shampoo and conditioner before a big meeting or big night.

Learn the types and amounts of shampoo and conditioner your hair needs and use only that amount – too much of any product is not only a waste but can also weigh your hair down and remove your natural shine.

Taking care of your hair includes:

- Brush your hair every night.
- Drink plenty of spring water.
- Air dry wet hair, when possible, to avoid heat stress on your ends.
- Use a monthly hair mask to hydrate dry ends.
- Tie hair with ribbons and covered bands that do not break ends.
- Wear a swim cap if you spend time in a pool.
- Try a product that adds shine for a fresh and youthful appearance.

The shape of your hair around your face can be a determining factor in how your overall look appears to others. Whether your face shape is angular or geometric, you will want to shape your hair to work with your face. If your face is round, you may try an angular cut to counterbalance the roundness and give your face a longer shape.

Your hair is one of the most important components of your appearance. It frames your face and is usually one of the first things people notice when they look at you (other than your gracious smile). The look, feel and cut of a hairstyle will enhance or take away from your overall look. Based on your facial shape, you can find the hairstyle that best frames your face and helps you to remain ageless. Those women who keep their hairstyle similar over a period of time appear to never age. Grace Kelly retained a similar haircut for more than forty years. The wavy blonde style that framed her beautiful features remained nearly the same length throughout her life; this kept her looking ageless in photographs over time. Jackie Kennedy did the same thing. She retained the same length and bob style that became her signature look over her lifetime.

When planning for an important event, most women schedule a haircut and color one week in advance of the event to allow the cut to "fall into shape" and the color to settle. Deep conditioning a few days before the event is important as well.

 Shiny, well-kept hair will make you appear much younger and attractive. Do not forget to get a good night's sleep – it will give a sparkle to your eyes.

Once your face is properly framed by your perfect haircut and style, your complexion and coloring are next.

Hair Care Do's

- Eat properly and drink plenty of water.
- Wash the roots and rinse thoroughly.
- Use a filter on your showerhead.
- Brush from scalp to ends every night.
- Clean your brush regularly.
- Use a good conditioner, sparingly.
- Get regular haircuts to alleviate split ends.

Hair Care Don'ts

Some factors that contribute to dull hair include:

- Nutritional deficiencies.
- Use of harsh products.
- Use of cheap conditioners.
- Overexposure to sun, wind, elements.

- Frequent hair coloring.
- Excessive stress.
- High mineral content in water.
- Use of heating tools.

Refined-Looking Skin

As part of an overall etiquette makeover, your skincare regime can always be improved; this does *not* mean throw out all the products you so lovingly purchased and tried. It means you must make skincare a priority every day and a habit. You must make skincare a ritual that you do not WANT to miss. You cannot possibly try various products from day to day, so you should choose the ones that seem to be working as a routine for you and put the others away. Too many choices is not the best way to start your day, unless you are really a morning person and like to make a lot of unnecessary decisions.

Realize that one thing in your control right now is how you take care of your skin. Wear sunscreen, moisturize dry skin and keep it pH balanced with a good toner. Light eye cream at night and regularly sloughing off dead skin cells with liquids or beads will maintain a healthy glow and reduce dark circles. Remove the old so the new can come glowing through.

There are many great ways to improve the texture, look and health of your skin. (Think: drink spring water with lemon juice every morning for benefits beyond your skin.) By the time you begin to develop your figure in your early teens, you should be ready to learn about a good skincare system; this will help your skin to become balanced against the hormone changes and various foods that can affect your skin. If you develop a routine cleanser and toner twice a day and use a non-oily sunscreen, your face will benefit from it over the years. Add a night moisturizer, and you have just kept aging at bay.

French women are taught at an early age to take care of themselves – their body (what they eat) and their skin. They learn to hydrate, eat fresh fruits and vegetables (think *organic*, especially when eating these raw), and use the best skincare products available.

If you were to purchase one new skincare product every few months and use it, you would have an arsenal in one year and most of the product (if used correctly) would still be in the jar. It is a sound but large investment to start, but the benefits far outweigh the cost. You will notice a difference in your skin. Do your research and find out what works best for your skin. Do no be afraid of asking for samples. Sales clerks know that this is the best way to get you to come back to them and are more than willing to show you their products and how to use them.

Become a student of skincare and you will see time well spent, rewarding you with a drastic improvement in your look and your happiness. You will find your skin feels silky and smooth and you need less cover up and makeup.

If you have not had a professional facial, you should invest in one. Before you go, prepare a list of things you want to know more about. Give your aesthetician the liberty to discuss the products she uses throughout the facial. Some aestheticians think you want total quiet, so make sure she understands that although you would like to relax, you are also there to learn about good skincare.

Here are suggested ideas to question your aesthetician:

- What type of skin do I have?
- What is the best kind of regimen for my skin and daily routine?
- Is my skin aging well?
- How often do I need to use a peel or dermabrasion for my skin type and age?
- What age is my skin?
- What are the biggest problems with my skin and how do I begin to correct them?

These are questions that should be asked of the professional. You are paying for her expertise, and in that relaxing atmosphere you should attempt to find out more about your skin from someone who is treating it for you. Ask her about over-the-counter products most similar to the high-end products she uses, and explain your budget. She would rather you come back to her regularly than spend lots of money to purchase expensive products. She should have some skill and knowledge of the products available online and in department stores and their merit. If you have problem skin, particularly acne, use an antibacterial body soap to clean your skin to rid it of any impurities and bacteria. The best money you can spend is for a good moisturizer and toner to balance your pH. Most skin problems are caused by an imbalance to the skin's pH. Another good product to have on hand is an exfoliator.

Skin rejuvenation starts with turning your dead cells over (removing them) to allow new skin cells to emerge and give your skin a fresh glow. From the inside out, eating anti-inflammatory foods is a good practice to keep your healthy glow.

A dear cousin of mine grew up in the 'forties and had a daily ritual of applying Oil of Olay, because that was all that was available. Her skin was lovely, and even if she inherited great skin, it was her skincare routine that kept her looking much younger well into her nineties.

At a minimum, cleanse your skin morning and evening, use a good eye cream nightly, and a moisturizing, light sunscreen daily. This brief routine will keep your skin youthful and healthy. Do not feel the need to change your skincare regime more than every six to nine months. Your skin will benefit from a regular routine. And you will never know if those products were beneficial if you change products too often.

Microdermabrasion products work very well to sluff off dead skin cells, as do acids (such as fruit acids Alpha and Beta). Glycolic acid and Retinol are used to create similar results. Turning over the skin cells is part of a good regimen for youthful-looking skin. If used in conjunction with the proper cleansing products and a good toner, your skin should be in good condition most of the time.

Choosing a good skincare regimen over costly makeup will benefit more in the long term.

You may experience routine or irregular/rare breakouts due to what you eat and as well as because of hormone changes. A lot of fatty foods, fried foods, heavy cream products and cheeses can cause breakouts, as well as food with additives and hormones. Monthly breakouts should be discussed with a dermatologist to ensure your skin does not end up scarring.

Another way to ensure your face looks its best is to make sure facial hair is removed, particularly lip and eyebrow areas. As women age, there may be "dowager" hairs that appear on the chin. Removing these and trimming nose hairs is a must in order for mature women to appear elegant.

Applying makeup and removing makeup is a technique that is acquired over time. Cosmetic counters in major department stores offer free makeovers and there are occasional offers from spas to teach women how to use cosmetics to enhance their best look. Take advantage of these offers if you have the opportunity. Otherwise, hire a professional and practice the techniques you learn.

Women do not need a lot of makeup for their daily program but they should maintain something they can manage based on their schedule. Choosing a good skincare regime over makeup will benefit more in the long term.

Some makeup can be beneficial to your skin. Many liquid foundations include sunscreen, which adds value if you forget to apply a separate sunscreen daily. Other foundations contain ingredients that support skin elasticity (or claim to) and other skin care concerns. There are new products coming into the market every year, it seems. There are all natural choices that are best suited to prevent chronic damage to your body, and are recommended by the author. We are not always as vigilant about our makeup as our food choices, however, attention to the components of beauty products can be important, as some are generally not conducive to long term optimal health. And, always remember that the idea of wearing makeup is to enhance your features, not hide them. Determine which features you want to highlight, and focus on those, while finishing the rest of your face with a fresh light look.

A woman in her thirties or older should apply some makeup before going out (the exception being to apply sunscreen and tinted lip gloss for a run in the park or early morning exercise class); this is not only appealing visually but also good for morale. When you know you look finished, you feel more confident in public.

ELEGANT POSTURE

Good posture takes effort and must be one of your strictest good habits from this day forward. Sitting tall and standing tall are permanent choices, something we decide to do every day. When we do not consider it, we tend to slip out of the good habit and replace it with a bad habit of slouching. When someone is in a poor mood, the tendency is to slouch. It is the natural reaction to how someone feels at the moment. It is very important to counteract that mood with good posture and head held high –and perhaps the mood will not linger.

We sometimes feel that standing tall is a sign of self-importance. It is really the ill postured lady who stands out and looks uncomfortable.

Balancing a book on your head is still a traditional way to "learn" how to walk and stand correctly. Finishing schools in Europe still use this technique as one of the ways to introduce proper posture to young women.

Note the photos of elegant women of today and yesterday. These women are stately, standing or sitting tall and always holding their head up high. This is not an air of pompous grandeur as much as it is the appropriate way to carry oneself. It is proper manners to have good posture. One would only wish for the highest compliment in one's own life: "elegance to the point of distraction," as Oleg Cassini stated of Jacqueline de Ribes; such a compliment would be the attainment any woman would seek if desiring a more sophisticated taste.

It is distasteful when elegant women wear flip-flops and yoga outfits in public places (other than the beach and yoga studios) and hunch their shoulders. We sometimes feel that standing tall is a sign of self-importance, but it is the poorly postured individual who stands out and looks ill-dressed and uncomfortable.

The well-postured person is always in command of the room and looks about as if to greet everything and everyone in it. She is ready for engagement with anyone because she is looking outside herself to others. She is not so introverted that she shies away from graceful elegant posture and is preoccupied with herself.

Posture is the beginning of elegance. The gowns and evening wear of today are fitted to personalities that will elegantly wear them. The gowns are made for erect shoulders and squared hips, not slouches. When trying on outfits, particularly evening wear, remember to stand erect and tall and look all the way up and down the gown to make sure it is fitted to your body. Sit in it, stand tall in it, and bend down in it. It should move with you. It should be the extension of your elegance. When alterations are required, stand as you would in a formal receiving line or elegant ballroom to make sure the gown is fitted properly.

It is always a good idea to search for an elegant woman who does these things in order to be reminded of how to sit and stand and walk gracefully. Look for role models in this area. Society news columns, online searches, YouTube videos, books and magazines are great places to find examples. Photos of models during the 1940s, '50s and '60s will exemplify the elegant look of their time. These photographs may be difficult to find at first, but once you discover where to look, there is a storehouse of good information for you to use in training your eye and taste.

If you have never taken a ballet class, there are great opportunities to learn about the ballet stance and positions and form of posture that comes from the *barre*. Some exercise classes now incorporate ballet "positions," moves, and stretches.

The biggest confidence booster for a woman who seeks to be elegant and refined is not a new designer handbag, but a tall elegant posture, gained by training herself to sit up straight and not slouch. Getting in and out of a car or limousine presents a serious test of posture and style. To enter a car, legs go in last. To exit a car, legs go out first. Keeping your knees together in every situation is a must for an elegant-looking woman.

Even airlines teach women to cross their ankles and slowly pull one leg over the other if they are going to cross their legs. It takes some practice to maneuver entering and exiting cars, lounge chairs, bar stools, and other situations where your legs are on display. It is unsightly to see a woman crossing her legs at her knees on a bar stool. This shows little elegance and class and usually ends up looking awkward and too edgy. When wearing formal attire, the best look is a slender torso where legs are always together and not crossed under the ball gown.

 Homework: Start a posture check: every hour on the hour today, check your posture – is your tummy tucked in? are you relaxed in your hips when sitting but back straight? Shoulders relaxed and not hunched? Can you put a line through your head all the way down your back?

Regular Exercise

We briefly discussed posture. Combine posture with exercise, and the two are very important to your continued good health and prevention of back problems, leg problems, and bone problems in the future. Exercise is cumulative. It improves your health as long as you do it, and if you quit it still gives you lasting benefits for the time you were diligent about maintaining your regimen. It is always beneficial, however, to continue an exercise routine.

Stretching and exercise, with its benefits of endorphins and loss of body fat, can be the best confidence booster. You can exercise a few times a week and still get the benefits of endorphins, increase your metabolism, and feel good about taking care of yourself. It can be more beneficial to your attitude about yourself than a skinny pair of jeans.

Computers and cell phones have created another dilemma over good posture. It is important to maintain your good posture even though the demand to bend your head over and cramp your hands around a small metal device while moving your fingers texting is threatening to ruin your spine's natural curve forever, not to mention cramping your finger and hand joints.

One thing that will keep you happy and help you enjoy life is being in good shape. Regular exercise will assist in this good life attitude. Joining a club or exercise or ballet class may be the best money you could spend on your overall attractiveness since your posture, grace and flexibility depend upon exercise and stretching to keep you looking your best. Endorphins (the chemicals secreted when exercising) can also give you a euphoric feeling of wellbeing and add to your overall allure.

Regular exercise also allows your metabolism to continue to run well and allows you to eat foods that would normally add weight to your overall body shape – except for the exercise that means higher burning of calories attributed to a faster metabolism.

A woman with a sense of discipline sufficient for regular exercise (aerobic), weight training (good for bone density) and stretching (helps with overall flexibility and agility) will be more calm and collected. She will exude an air of confidence, since she is investing some of her time in taking good care of herself and looking out for her own wellbeing. Her smile is genuine and friendly.

Homework: List your top five personal benefits of regular exercise, such as: reduce stress, boost self-esteem, bone density, more energy. Make these your motivational tools. Over time, regular exercise will give you a better, longer life. Just look at how sedentary people seem older than they really are.

To further instill good personal care, write a weekly plan on how and when you will incorporate exercise in your routine. With new ways to measure success such as a Fitbit, iPhone, and other tools, it is more rewarding to track your progress and stay inspired.

Wearing Your Clothing

As I mentioned earlier, *wear your clothes and do not let them wear you.* Well, it makes sense that what you wear should only be a "drape" for the real you shining through. Your posture is a key to looking great in any outfit. Training yourself to sit up and stand correctly is not a simple matter. It takes discipline and mindfulness. Stretching in bed gives you a head start to ending your day energized and relaxed.

I was in Paris one summer and walked out on a veranda overlooking one of the most prestigious lunch spots near the Louvre. I hesitated at the top of the stairs to get my bearings and find my friends at the table, and while I was doing that people turned and stared at me – they must have thought I was *somebody* the way I stood in the doorway with my head held high (the light was blinding me at the time). I was simply looking around, as I put on my dark glasses, to find my table. What a surprise to hear my friend comment that everyone was looking toward the top of the stairs.

Apparently, I must have appeared elegant and demure as I stood there, even though I was shyly looking around. I was wearing a short black sleeveless dress, great hat, and large sunglasses *a la Sabrina* in the 1940s movie. It was the look, not the person, they were staring at. You cannot plan this. After that lesson, I now walk more slowly in restaurants and try to look mysterious, just for fun.

An elegant torso is the objective of sitting tall and walking softly. If you can lift yourself out of your hips, you are elongating your rib cage and your spine. With the relaxed position of your head held high (as if a book was laid upon it) and your upper body lifted out of your hips, you will be amazed at how much better you feel – even after trying it for only a few days.

At Work and at Home

Most chairs are not conducive to sitting tall, but you can now find seats that will help you attain good posture when at a desk or table. If your day consists of sitting for long periods of time in front of a computer, the best thing to do to make sure you have good posture is to get up at least every thirty to forty-five minutes for five or ten minutes, and walk around the office. Stretches while in your chair are also a good way to ensure you are not lagging in your form. Walking and stretching will remind you to have that imaginary book on your head and also to relax muscles that have become tense by sitting in front of the computer.

When at home, a good way to make a habit of sitting and standing tall is to actually put a book on your head for a few minutes every day and walk around. It will give you a sense of how you should be walking all the time.

Pulling yourself out of your "carriage" will also make your steps lighter. You will essentially glide across a room. One etiquette teacher told us to always assume the "bistro" position, which was tucking in your derriere and squaring off your hips as if to walk between two crowded bistro tables. It worked and I still remember to do this exercise from time to time. Rather than take heavy giant steps with each foot, attempt to walk from your hips and lift each leg, and then place it down gracefully. I cannot say there are great examples of this on the runway, because those ladies weigh only eighty pounds, walk with a sway back (very bad posture) and swing their arms behind their back, while sticking their heads out making their necks strained. All of that induces a very unnatural walk and posture. It may be, however, that they are trying to create that "s" curve (Hogarth) with their body!

 Stretching exercises will help your posture more than anything else because it will elongate muscles that have become tight and contracted over time, particularly if you are stressed. Try some ballet stretches over yoga or other exercises. Any type of stretching is important, and once it becomes a habit it will assist you maintaining good posture over time.

DISTINGUISHED DRESSING

Ten benefits of being well dressed:

1. *People will take you seriously.*
2. *Your self-confidence will increase.*
3. *You will appear more trustworthy.*
4. *You will be more prepared.*
5. *Others will feel respected.*
6. *You will become more engaged in life.*
7. *You will maximize your wardrobe investment.*
8. *It increases your standards.*
9. *You will be motivated to get and stay fit.*
10. *You will be more focused on quality vs quantity.*

There are unwritten rules of elegance for women, but most women do not even attempt to understand and incorporate these rules in their everyday life. At one time, Disney Corporation required all high school senior boys to dress in suits and senior girls to dress in pantsuits when on their all-night senior trip to Disneyland (no jeans, sneakers, warm ups, cut offs). Disney executives believed that when someone wears nicer, more formal clothing, they behave differently (the dressier the clothing, the more formal behavior is expected).

Homework: Think of and list three examples when you were treated well because you were appropriately dressed. Be specific. The "ten benefits of being well dressed" are very important. List your own benefits that you feel will motivate you to dress well every day.

Because there is a certain protocol for dressing (dress codes) in specific social circles and for certain events, an overview of these types of dressing is included below. *You may have the proper type of clothing, but always consider the season you wear your clothing and make sure the fabric and colors are season-appropriate.* These events have a certain air about them and that is some of the fun of attending them.

Dressy Casual

The dressy casual look is more of an oxymoron than a real "attire" category. There is no such thing, and to pronounce this is utter foolishness. It is either dressy or casual but not both. If you receive an invitation with this attire, beware. There will be various concoctions of dressing from jeans to suits to little black dresses. My choice for this type of event is the LBD, with a bracelet or necklace but not both. It is far better to be finer dressed than to assume it is a rodeo you are attending.

Professional Casual

Pulling together a LOOK might take some trial and error, but make that error in your closet, *not* on the street. There are sufficient "Glamour Don't" personalities out there. Do not become a style victim and find your style of choice in the back of *Glamour* magazine as a "Don't." Train your eye to notice what works for your body type, coloring and hair style, and – just as important – train yourself to notice what does *not* work. Then find out WHY. It might be best to err on being too conservative and then you can experiment from there, rather than do too much radical change to your look immediately. Make the effort to do things well and do things right.

The slim, thin gray pencil skirt, white blouse, stylish animal print pump or royal blue alligator clutch really do work – for *some* women. You must realize the outfit itself is quiet, almost boring, but the shoes awaken the entire look, creating excitement toward a well-suited young aggressive talented woman who is not afraid of her own good looks. It does not work when the woman is in a profession that requires a "uniform" look to fit in and move up the corporate ladder.

An advertising agency expects "edgy" from the women who work there. A local bank does not. It is always important to select the appropriate style based on your workplace. In a bank or insurance company, for example, high-end attire is frowned upon and will ostracize you if you choose to wear labels that are inappropriately priced to your income at your current career.

There is nothing wrong with reaching higher in your look and style at work, but be aware that this may create friction among other women who may not be spending as much on their clothes, yet look as elegant and appropriate as you do. Save your special outfits for going out on the weekends and evenings. The manager may inadvertently choose someone less flashy over you for a promotion if the expensive designer, fashion-forward look is not smiled upon. *(I have not heard of any occasion where it helps you to dress more expensively than your boss)*. And besides, the best-dressed women do not necessarily wear brilliant labels or follow the latest designer fashions, but rather they find quality and fit to be the finest measure of sophistication and elegance.

Cocktail

Cocktail dressing is sophisticated chic. Some would argue that Cocktail means low-cut open-back dressing. I beg to differ. In all of the research I have found, cocktail attire *does not have as much décolleté as dinner party dressing*. The stylish woman knows the difference. When attending more than one event during the evening, the urbane woman dresses for the most elaborate occasion that night with perhaps a cloak or satin evening coat for the cocktail event, then a wrap for the dinner party.

 Cocktail is usually a short gown or long flowing pants in evening fabric. It is usually made of a luscious fabric and cut. As with every outfit designed to impress, the fit is the real thing that matters. Little black dresses are everywhere, but the woman who wears hers with confidence and elegance is the woman who is in control.

Cocktail events often include working professionals who go straight from work. Therefore, one will see a variety of dressing styles. It is important to be dressed appropriately, such as a dress suit where you can remove the jacket, add a necklace and small clutch. Adding sheer black stockings to a black work suit with black pumps and a bit of nice jewelry will take a refined woman to a cocktail party as well.

Should you find yourself included to a special event at the last minute, having one great "go-to" dress in your closet is crucial. You will appear relaxed and elegant when you are appropriately dressed.

Depending upon what is expected in the social circles you frequent, a cocktail dress is usually very simple, figure-hugging and plain, whereas a formal dress is more elaborate, brighter colored, or with more design and detail, such as beads, sequins or adornments. The cocktail dress is made of fine fabrics, usually in one bold color, or black, or sometimes brocade. The lines should flatter the figure that wears it. Shun a cocktail dress that is not fitted to your figure. The design itself should be made to accentuate your shoulders, bust, waistline, or other fabulous features. It should be one of the most elegant sheaths you own.

The simpler the design, the more effort can be made on the fine jewels and accessories worn with it. Colors such as emerald green, ruby, garnet red and sapphire blue make elegant cocktail dresses. They are nearly fashionable year 'round, although you may see the occasional pastel cocktail dress, if it has beading or other details, to distinguish it from a tea party frock. The difference in seasonal dressing is usually the fabric, rather than the color. Evening can tolerate darker colors and usually means formal attire.

Dinner Party

Dinner parties are more formal than cocktail events. They require more formality and usually begin with a cocktail hour, then a sit-down formal dinner of several courses of food and wine. For women, it requires a dressy short dress or long, depending upon the occasion; (no suits here unless made in a silk or satin evening fabric. Dinner party dressing is the most elegant in your closet other than a ball gown. Décolleté is normal for dinner parties. Jewelry usually includes a dinner ring, earrings, and necklace or brooch, but normally no more than three pieces of jewelry.

Since you are typically seated next to gentlemen on each side, your manner should be excruciatingly formal and conversation should be limited to innocuous topics such as general geo-politics, travel, bestselling books you have read or know about, and a bit of conversation about family. Manicures are essential for a polished look from ladies and gentlemen.

In dressing for cocktail and dinner parties, the older the woman, the more shoulder and arm she usually covers, but in order to be elegant, most women "bear a little skin" at cocktail and formal dinner affairs. If a woman chooses to bear her lovely back, she is most elegant with a higher neckline in front. A dress with some décolleté will typically have the back closed. If she chooses a slit in her skirt, she remains elegant by covering other areas to keep the look interesting and not too flashy.

Evening pants should be paired with an interesting top. Depending upon the age and figure, a woman will need something interesting to counterbalance the fact she is wearing pants. She can create a very elegant look depending upon the cut and fit of the top. If the pants are wide and flowing, a slightly fitted open front, with an embellished top, can make the look.

Some of the most elegant cocktail dresses are fitted sheaths with an oriental neckline. Sometimes less skin is more elegant, and the way the dress fits the figure is most essential in having a chic look.

Being seated at a table: stand in between the seat of the chair and the table and allow a gentleman to slowly push the chair against your knees, while you gently bend them and sit down about the time the chair reaches the place you need for it to be. The gentleman should never be pushing you in the chair, nor should you really have to "scoot" the chair closer to the table once you have sat in it. There is an art to it, and practice never hurts. Do not be tempted to sit back into the chair at a formal dinner party. The back of the chair is for décor, not holding up a tired body. Your elegant posture should only be exceeded by your elegant nature and conversation.

Formal or Black Tie

The formal or black tie event requires that men dress in tuxedos and women wear long dresses. The standard dress for women at a black tie is a long, straight or semi-flared dress, usually in a dark or bright color, with some detail, such as sequins, beading, or stone appliques. If the invitation says "formal," it means tuxedo for men, and long gown for women. Most invitations now state "black tie."

With the trend toward more relaxed dress codes at events, you should be prepared to see a variety at any event, but with a clear understanding of the event, *an elegant woman knows what is appropriate and chooses that over comfort*. No one will slight you if you absolutely must wear a short dress to a formal event, however, generous allowance is usually given once: The next time you arrive inappropriately dressed, you might find yourself a bit uncomfortable. Preparing in advance to attend formal events, you should have a wardrobe that includes a simple black cocktail dress and a long formal dress.

Look ahead to any formal events you plan to attend each season and find those gowns that are fitting of your personality and pocketbook, even though some of the fun of being invited to an event is to shop for that perfect outfit. The money you invest in an elegant formal gown will be worth the peace of mind to know you are ready for the season, when invited.

Should you find yourself included at the last minute, having one great "go-to" dress in your closet is a most stress-relieving situation. It is so gratifying when you can be appropriately dressed. There may be circumstances that do not allow you to do this, but the smart woman plans her wardrobe based on her lifestyle, and a great-looking versatile gown should be in her closet as a staple for formal events.

White Tie or Gala Ball

"Being well dressed is a beautiful form of politeness."Coco Chanel

When invited to a "white tie event," ball or gala, you can sense the excitement and anticipation. This event is planned months in advance and guarantees a wonderful evening to all attendees. Much planning goes into it by the chairpersons or hosts. It is an elaborate affair and you are expected to dress up. It is an event where you enjoy a beautiful venue with an evening of cocktails, dinner, dancing and entertainment. The gala ball is the event that every woman longs to attend. This is an occasion for you to "pull out all the stops" and dress "to the nines." You may have hair and makeup professionally done, and wear a beautiful gown with elaborate jewelry, such as a ring, earrings and necklace or brooch. Beading and sequins on the dress call for gentle pairing with jewels.

The event is not just about the clothing. Your radiant face (whitened teeth, perfect lip color, and smoky green, blue or brown eyes) and gentle demeanor are all the ornaments you need.

Jackie Kennedy, when entertaining at the White House, always took off one piece of jewelry right before she attended a ball. She insisted that fewer pieces gave a more elegant look. She often chose to wear a beautiful diamond brooch in her upswept hairdo, rather than on the dress.

Wearing your finest jewelry on this occasion calls for restraint if you have many beautiful jewels to select. Try various pieces with the dress until you find the most elegant look. Test your ideas with someone of taste so you are confident you have the finest outcome, then enjoy the festivities feeling beautifully dressed, groomed and accessorized.

 The refined woman wears a long full ball gown, more ornate than a black tie event. Sequins, beads, and stones are typical at white-tie events, but an elegant woman may choose a simple but exquisite ball gown in a sumptuous fabric in order to show off her beautiful jewels.

Remember, the event is not just about the clothing or jewels. If you are not able to keep up with the Joneses, your radiant face (whitened teeth, perfect lip color, and smoky green, blue or brown eyes) are all the ornaments you need.

Invitations should always include the preferred attire in a dress "code" that is common to most people. You may want to research invitation protocol if you find you are not sure about the proper way to state it. Normally, by putting 'cocktail attire' on the invitation, you are assured people will arrive well dressed. Men will be sure to wear jackets and women will wear cocktail or evening dresses. The event itself dictates the attire, but it is always proper to include the attire "code" at the bottom of the invitation.

Final thoughts:

1. Ball gowns usually have trains. Before walking in a crowded ballroom, turn and pick up the back of your dress about one yard below your waist in the back. This will allow you to walk without the train following behind. (Think: *Gigi)*
2. If you choose to wear opera gloves, wear them while dancing, but take them off at the table.
3. No matter how much jewelry you wear, it should never distract from your overall look.

Shoes

There is nothing like a great pair of shoes to make a woman feel sophisticated. Shoes definitely define the woman, and if they do not compliment her outfit, they create an off-balanced look, a type of messy-bohemian look that – admittedly – can work at times, but if your style is classic sophistication and style, the shoes should enhance the entire look. If the look is complicated and loud, the shoes should be the underpinning for the look. They may add that just right touch to make it all work together. If the look is quiet, simple and classic, the shoes can take a woman to the next level of classy style by adding a gracious elegant pointed toe, or D'Orsay pump.

Shoes should never be the glaring accessory to the entire outfit. The word "accessory" means to embellish the outfit, not be the statement piece. Using color effectively with shoes is one way to take the look up a rung or two. A simple suit is never overshadowed by a pair of classic navy or black pumps.

The Spectator has always been worn with simple monochromatic looks and will only work in that arena. Knowing how to make the shoe work with the outfit takes thought and ingenuity. It takes pulling together looks (*Think: magazine glossy photos of models with "the look" outfits). Here are a few "rules" to ponder:*

1. Shoe must be darker or same color as stockings or hosiery worn, and darker or same color as "hemline." It is difficult to wear red shoes with black stockings and look elegant.
2. Black stockings should only be worn with a black hemline dress or skirt. All other colored outfits should wear neutral stockings, exceptions being navy with navy, or brown with brown.
3. Strappy high-heeled sandals are for evening wear.
4. Loud, busy shoes are never elegant. They may be fun, but never elegant.
5. It is difficult to look elegant with shoes covered with rhinestones. These embellished shoes are difficult to consider appropriate even for a Ball.
6. Shoes with buckles and bows and tie strings up the leg are not elegant. They are sporty, at best.
7. Exotic skins and suede are sporty, but never evening wear.
8. Stilettos have their place, rarely in the board room.
9. Spectators do not go in or out of style. They are timeless, but always worn "sparingly."
10. Your taste in shoes exemplifies your taste. Do not exaggerate by wearing outlandish shoes – this only screams "no taste."
11. Shoes that look worn ruin the entire outfit.
12. Always polish shoes before wearing them.
13. Recycle or give away shoes that are outdated or worn out.
14. Knee-high boots must fit your calf to look elegant.
15. Learn to walk gracefully in high heels.
16. Wear in your new shoes on carpeted surfaces. The leather will begin to fit your feet better, but the soles will not be worn out.
17. Your new favorite shoes should be the ones that look best with your look.

Neutral (beige, taupe) pumps are a staple in every woman's closet because they go with nearly every look. Try ballerina pink instead of beige for a nice refreshing nude look. Grey and navy, when the shoe is D'Orsay pump or sling-back heel, can also be considered neutral as well as give the effect of lengthening your legs, leaving everyone to observe your dress or gorgeous jacket.

Shoes should fit perfectly so that you are comfortable in them for a duration of time. If they have a heel, it should hit the sole at a place that supports your foot. That is a good-fitting shoe. Because lower-end shoes are manufactured with less detail in the engineered design, they are not always the best fitting shoes.

It is important to know the appropriate place and time to wear certain shoes. To the well-groomed woman, every fashion choice is just that obvious.

If you cannot afford the better quality shoes, make sure you find those brands that fit your foot well. Sizing and fit usually varies by brand, and your salesperson should know which brands work for what type of foot. You can also shop end of season sales on higher priced shoes and get a fabulous find for next year's wardrobe. Make sure you try them on when your feet are not swollen. Sometimes the end-of-season sale shoes have a fault or flaw or are stretched from being on display.

The size means nothing in the world of shoes because each designer has their own way of manufacturing. Like dress sizes, shoe sizes vary in Italy, France and the United States. It is important to learn about the designers and shoes you like, then you can invest in good quality and find the best prices.

Remember, if you are just learning about dressing tastefully, you may not have "arrived" in all your choices, so it is better to stay with the basics.

An unforgettable ("wow") outfit is easier to match up with a well-designed quiet shoe. Only in rare instances should the shoe be the focal point. Make sure your other items are well made of quality fabric and equal to the shoe, subtle in comparison. The shoe can make the outfit or compete with it, depending on the way you combine them.

Shoe Sense

- Know heel sizes and shoe types that are most flattering to your outfit and general appearance. As you get older, it is better to find a more elegant style shoe with a lower heel.
- Flats are now worn all the time, day and evening, but they were originally designed for day wear. Most flats have little or no support and should not be worn all the time.
- Wearing a shoe with support will be better for you over many years. With the many shoe designers, you do not have to give up comfort and support for style.
- Kitten heels are less dressy than pumps or full heels, and are often worn with dressy walking shorts.
- Closed toe slingbacks are beautiful on the foot and considered very chic. They are more feminine than pumps and go just as well with suits and dresses.
- High-heeled sandals (particularly with some sparkle or pearl enhancements) are dressiest when worn with ball gowns and other formal dressing.
- Dressing for evening can mean accessorizing with fabric shoes and clutches.
- Suede, crocodile and lizard shoes ("exotics") are sportier than buttery lambskin, calfskin and classy patent leather.
- Style matters but so does the leather or fabric of the shoe.
- Pointed toe shoes and loafers with a long tongue will usually crease at some point. You should be aware these styles will not look new for any length of time.

Shoe Dictionary

Examples of shoe types (some taken from Steve Madden's Shoe Glossary)

- Ankle Strap – A strip of cloth or leather that wraps around the leg where it meets the foot in order to secure the shoe to the foot.
- Ballet Flat – A soft, slipper-like, closed-toe shoe with no heel height, modeled after the shoes worn by ballet dancers.

- Bootie – A shoe that resembles a boot in style but does not have a shaft; it ends at the ankle.
- Boots – Footwear that cover the entire foot and extends at least to the height of the anklebone and possibly as high as the thigh.
- Cap Toe – A decorative layer of leather adorning and reinforcing the toe of certain dress shoes, often highlighted by a line of decorative stitching.
- D'Orsay pump – A heeled shoe that is closed at the toe and heel with open side or sides. It is very flattering to the foot and usually runs one half-size large.
- Espadrille – A shoe or sandal with a woven rope or similar material covering the wedge or sole.
- Flats – Shoes that do not have any heel height.
- Flip Flops – Flat sandals held to the foot solely by a strap that runs over and between the toes.
- Kitten Heel – A low-heeled stiletto shoe, often between 1 and 2 inches in heel height.
- Loafer – A low step-in shoe without shoelaces or buckles.
- Moccasin – A slip-on shoe with visible stitching around the perimeter of the toe box, creating a gathered effect.
- Mules – Shoes or sandals characterized by a closed, or nearly closed, toe and a backless heel of any height.
- Peep toe – A shoe with a narrow opening in the front that exposes the toes.
- Platforms – High-heeled shoes with a thick sole under the front part of the foot.
- Pumps – Women's dress shoes that are typically characterized by a medium or high heel. Styles are typically completely enclosed.
- Riding boots – Boots designed for the purpose of riding horses. Styles typically include a low heel and knee-high shaft. The term may also describe fashion boots that resemble riding boots in style.
- Sandals – An exposed shoe that includes an open toe and open back. This shoe slips on and is held in place with leather or fabric straps across the foot.

- Sling back – A backless shoe that is held in place with a strap at the back of the foot. The strap is typically elastic or buckled for adjustment.
- Slipper – A flat, casual shoe that slips on and is typically meant for use indoors. May be lined for added comfort.
- Sneaker – A rubber-soled casual shoe made of soft, often man-made, materials, and used often for casual wear and sporting events.
- Stacked Heel – A heel comprised of many layers of leather, laid one on top of another, in order to resemble a wood-grain appearance.
- Stiletto – A very thin, very high heeled shoe, the heel of which tapers nearly to a point where it comes into contact with the ground.
- Wedge Heel –A heel that extends from the back to the ball of the shoe, lying flat on the ground.

Shoe Care

It is better to spend your budget on one good pair of beige pumps that will take you nearly everywhere than to purchase two or three pairs of odd-colored shoes that only enhance one or two outfits in your closet – even if they are on sale, which is always a temptation!

Avoid shoe purchases when your feet might be swollen (late afternoons, too much salt in your food, or after long flights).

The choice of toe shape (pointed, rounded or "almond") is a matter of personal style and taste. Each design will go in and out of fashion but you can weather the storms of the season with simple lines and designs of a good-fitting and well-kept shoe more than trying to follow the latest fad in shoes.

Shoes can scream or they can whisper. Sometimes a whisper is more interesting. I have been to some beautiful homes for dinner parties and socials, and I've observed that women may find a rare, unusual pair of shoes to wear for fun . . . but simple, tasteful is *always* elegant, and with an unusual pair of shoes you run the risk of looking and feeling out of place with too daring a deviation from accepted style. The exception, of course, is if you are a shoe designer. Then you will want to show off your latest designs and create a beautiful palette whereby your clothes are simple and elegant to make the shoe the center of attention.

 Homework: Go through your closet and list the shoe types and number of pairs you own – do you have the right types of shoes for your lifestyle? What are you missing? Espadrilles for summer date night? Ballet flats? Make a list and keep it in your Look Book for future purchases.

Here are a few ideas for maintaining your shoes in perfect quality and readiness:

- Check for any smudges and marks on shoes after wearing them and set them aside for professional care if you find the heel is worn or something else needs maintenance.
- Wipe your shoes when you take them off or before you put them away in a box, shoe bag, or on the shelf. This will save time and they will be ready at any time for another wonderful day or night on your feet.
- Be sure to use shoe trees (the better brands are made of good solid cedar) for your more expensive and exotic shoes. Remember to put your exotics in shoe trees and then in shoe bags, if you have them; this will keep them from drying out, although you should have your exotics on a professional shoe care maintenance program with your other shoes and boots.
- Keep shoes smelling fresh with powder, spray or inserts as necessary, particularly your golf, tennis, yoga and running shoes.
- Try some of the latest shoe inserts (gels are great) if you wear heels all day. These inserts are wonderful and really make a

difference. After eight hours on your feet, you will still have a relaxed expression and be able enjoy your busy day.

Avoid shoe purchases when your feet might be swollen (late afternoons or after long flights) or when you have consumed too much salt or alcohol. In shopping for new shoes, look for classics with a fresh twist. Know which heel sizes work for you best as well as which type of toe and strap (if any). Suede and exotic leathers (crocodile, lizard, alligator and ostrich) are sportier than lambskin, calfskin and patent.

Shoes do not last forever, although our favorite pair has sometimes gone way beyond its normal lifetime. Bring your Look Book to pair outfits with great shoes. This might keep you on course when looking at the extensive selection of shoes each season. Great purchases take discipline, time and planning. Your Look Book will save you thousands of dollars of mistakes over time and will help you every day in dressing for the occasion. Set aside Sunday evenings or one hour each week to go through your closet to organize your Look Book. Creating a Look Book is as simple as obtaining a binder with sheet protectors to hold photos of your clothing *on you,* or similar clothing on pages from catalogs and magazines.

Once your Look Book is well organized, you can determine your next purchases based on what you already love, what you need and what your lifestyle is. You will soon rely on it to determine what you want to wear to work, board meetings, charity events, on weekends, evenings and galas. This will help reduce clutter in your closet. A closet makeover professional can create your Look Book, if you do not have time or if you prefer to invest in this service.

Stockings and Hosiery

To wear or not to wear hosiery. Stockings (hosiery) complete an elegant look for evening and business. Consider men who do not wear dark socks to work. They appear unfinished, unsightly, and unacceptable. This is the same effect women create when they dress appropriately but forego wearing hosiery. Stockings may be outdated for the casual and sporty look, but for business and formal occasions, they are a must.

Being elegant and refined is the result of attending to your manner in all you do and say. It is about a lifestyle.

Dark-colored stockings are unsightly when worn with lighter dresses and skirts, but they enhance the appearance of the legs when worn appropriately. Tights are sporty and never worn with evening apparel. Opaque stockings and sheer nude hosiery are normally worn during the day. Sheer stockings (nude or dark) are usually designated for evening wear or more formal occasions during the day. Some women will argue that warm weather allows one to forego stockings, but good fashion sense must dictate in all occasions. What is decidedly elegant should always trump the weather.

FASHIONABLE LIFESTYLE

Making your fashion statement takes work, diligence, and creativity. Below are a few ideas to incorporate as you go through your closet and begin to determine your best looks for a fashionable lifestyle.

- Design your own fashion show of the clothes you love: Host a closet party with your best friend, a bottle of good champagne, your ten favorite outfits, and video each other walking down the hallway once a year.
- Look through magazines for the new colors of the upcoming season and incorporate some of those colors in your outfits.
- Search and read about the lives of icons you follow.
- Ask people you trust how you look in an outfit you are unsure of. Get their honest feedback even if it is negative, and thank them for their comments. and rethink some of your outfits and how you wear them.

- If you have an outfit that you are unsure of, be creative with ways to wear it. Add great accessories, change the hemline, add trim or buttons, or find some way to "rescue" it so that it at least works this season.

- Spend normally down time while waiting at an office or spa to look through fashion magazines, e-magazines, Pinterest and Instagram, particularly the high fashion ones, for "looks" or portions of looks that might work for you. Take a photo and consider adding them, with perhaps a few variations, to your Look Book.

- Discover a signature color that makes you look your best. When you wear the correct colors that complement your hair color and skin color, you are subtly accentuating your best overall look. People may not remember the outfit, but they will remember how great you looked on that occasion.

Becoming elegant and refined is the result of determining to pay attention to your manner in all you do and say. It is about a lifestyle. The benefits of having some knowledge of this lifestyle can make a permanent change you will appreciate and like. The most compelling reason to continue is because you "are worth it."

CHAPTER 4 – A REFINED IMAGE

Dress shabbily and they remember the dress; dress impeccably and they remember the woman. Coco Chanel

Your Image

First Impressions: There is no such thing as a second first impression. We only get one chance at a first appearance and first glance. A single opportunity when someone sizes you up for the first time. You could say they are looking at the image of us that we present to them or portray at that moment. *However . . .*

First impressions can be daunting if there has been no planning beforehand. It takes only a quick glance, maybe three seconds, for someone to evaluate you when you meet for the first time. We are only as good as the sum of our parts, and we are who we are at our worst, as well as our best. In order to make the best first impression, we should look at ourselves as we appear anytime, anyplace, be it the marketplace, the Metro, or the gym. Observe who we normally are when driving, but who we are when making a presentation to a Board of Directors.

A smart, well-educated young woman who shows up at an interview with noisy jewelry, a nose ring, and a few indiscreet tattoos on her arms can ruin her chances of the opportunity to prove how smart, skillful and talented she really is. It is that first impression that is hard to change in someone's mind.

We must take account of our appearance and attitude in all aspects. Based on the score, we can choose to improve those areas that are lacking, even given our best effort. This calls for attention and effort to our overall appearance. In this short time, the other person forms an opinion about you based on your overall appearance: your body language, your demeanor, your mannerisms, and how you are dressed.

A smart, well-educated young woman who shows up at an interview with noisy jewelry, a nose ring, and a few indiscreet tattoos on her arms can ruin her chances of the opportunity to prove how smart and skillful she really is. It is that first impression that will kill the interview before it even has a chance. A young woman should consider where she is heading in her lifetime before she chooses to detract her overall look with such a permanent ornament as a tattoo. Although tattoos are commonplace and accepted in some career paths, most businesses are still restricted to a more conservative look. Dark lipstick and makeup, dark nail polish and dark clothing will define the woman as being a dark, moody person, unable to get along with the rest of the staff in most business establishments. Odors can also be a deterrent. Good grooming, little or no perfume (and no lingering smoke smells) are important to that overall first impression. A woman must be very critical of her overall appearance as it comes on the scene in order to have that advantage of the choice and best jobs in a company. She must prove herself a leader and team player in order to be accepted by management and become a part of the team. Hiring a new employee is a daunting task to any employer. It is costly to make a mistake. The the very first impression will tell the employer much about the potential hire. Most women think that good looks sell a woman, but actually that is sometimes a deterrant. The observer is looking for that overall healthy look that says: "I take care of myself, and I can do the job, I can be the right person for that project or client". We must remember that it is an overall appearance that makes us who we really are, and face it: we really want to be our best selves all the time.

To maximize your chances of landing the greatest jobs during your career, you must truly "dress the part" and become willing to prove your worth through the interview process, without distractions that will cause you to be discounted and stereotyped, allowing others to get those sought-after positions. Healthy, shiny hair and polished, straight teeth go a long way farther than a blond bombshell with no aura.

First impression negatives:

- Wrinkled clothing
- No eye contact
- Chewing gum
- Smoke or body odor
- Too much makeup
- No smile
- Fidgeting
- Poor overall grooming
- Wearing dark lipstick, makeup, and nails will label you
- Weak handshake

- Too much perfume
- Noisy jewelry, too many rings and bracelets
- Piercings, tattoos should be hidden: they stereotype you
- Open-toed shoes or flip flops – disregard for authority
- Low blouse/open blouse, tight /short skirt – stereotype (unless you are applying for a cocktail waitress job, possibly the ONLY exception).

These negatives are things that you must decide if the job is worth giving them up. If you just love wearing flip flops and will not give that up, then you probably need a job putting out umbrellas on a beach. Other than that, you should be thinking about the career of your dreams and how to get your foot in the door of a company that can get you there.

There are various ways to prepare yourself for the moment you meet someone for the first time: this is the time to be at your best: at ease, confident, professional and elegant.

In making good first impressions, if this is your very first job interview, or meeting your husband's new boss and his wife, or having a date that a friend set up for you, it might be important for you to obtain professional coaching for that situation. Whether it be an online course, YouTube video, friend, mentor or professional coach, whatever your ability to obtain some help, do it. You will find that this list is not all-inclusive and your coach may go even farther in developing criteria for your appearance for the best opportunity to present yourself in the best light, and remain true to your core.

In discussing jobs and careers, once you are established, it might be all right to wear some of your favored items, while continuing to gain the respect of your peers and managers. Technology firms are very liberal but banking officers dress conservatively. You must learn how to dress for success in order to showcase your talent, skill ability, and teamwork attitude.

Dressing to distract from the overall standard of any office protocol is not only disrespectful to the company but shows that woman is not a team player. This will not fare well for the future of her career. It is important to note: We stress that actual lifestyle changes must take place from the inside first, before a woman can radiate her true worth to a potential employer.

So here is a test to determine if you want to make a good first impression. Is this meeting/interview/event important to you? Why? How can you prepare for a first good impression?

There are many ways you can prepare yourself for the moment you are engaged with someone for the first time: this is the time to be at your best, at ease, confident, and looking professional and elegant. You may wonder, why so much attention on this? The less you have to think about yourself, the more focused you can be on the situation at hand, which is a good first impression.

Being prepared as much as possible is the easiest way to relieve the stress of the situation. This is the beginning of how you are always at your finest and how you can be prepared anytime and anywhere for anything that may come up. This is not simply a Boy Scout motto, it is an elegant woman's ideal. If you have prepared to your best ability, given the time frame allowed to prepare, you are as ready as you can possibly be. Relax and enjoy the experience and you will portray a confident and easy-going woman. You are ready for anything, but particularly for making a good first impression.

 Homework: Think of a poor first impression you might have made in the past. List four things you will specifically do differently to get a better result from a first impression. Think specifically of things that could have gone better, and make simple corrections to those things first.

The Elements of Impressing

We do not initially think about "impressing" someone at a first meeting. We generally just think, "Oh, I'm meeting this or that person." But you are starting contact with someone who could become important to you for the rest of your life. The daunting idea of a best first impression is way beyond the scope of any book or podcast. The reason for the initiation may be social, business or family, but the initiation is there, looming in the foreground. You may never have given it much thought, but now that you think of it, there are many times in the past where you could have crafted a better meeting in order to have a better outcome.

If you are confident in who you are, and ready to meet, then there is nothing daunting, stressful or impending about the first meeting. There is no formula for impressing someone if you are *genuine.* You can not put on airs or pretend to be someone else if you have integrity and want to be yourself. You can prepare for any day of the year as if it included a first meeting, since you may chance upon a first meeting any day of the year! This is not any special day; it is every day.

It is the idea of being the real, genuine *you*, the most content *you*, the happiest *you*, and the smartest *you* every day. Breaking it down to the image you portray, you must begin with the inner *you,* and believe in yourself that you are equal to the task and that no one is above or beneath you. You treat everyone the same so you have respect and courtesy in every situation.

We have acknowledged that, first and foremost, a refined woman must be genuine and caring. Her gentleness must surpass anything about her exterior in such a way that the exterior should only advance her into the category of refined womanhood she belongs and is living in. A comfortableness settles over the refined woman as she finds herself in various situations, but in particular the first meeting. It is a refined woman who is most at ease in awkward social settings, of which the *first encounter* is probably the highest ranking awkward social situation to the inattentive.

First Meeting Tips

Be Punctual

First impressions are based on your respect for someone else's time. Plan to arrive a few minutes earlier than the meeting time. Arriving a few minutes early, rather than late, is the first step in creating a great first impression. You will definitely be more prepared and relaxed in those few extra moments before the meeting. Allow for flexibility due to traffic or taking a wrong turn. Being on time for any appointment, whether it may be to see your new boss, colleague, first date, or meet with a college professor allows you to begin the meeting strong and finish strong. Be on time. This should be a habit. If you have trouble being on time, give yourself more time to prepare, travel or park, if necessary.

I often plan "backwards" from the appointment to make sure I can be where I say I will be when I say I will be there. If I am late, I know I must politely and sincerely apologize and ask those in the meeting to "Please forgive me for my tardiness today. I sincerely apologize for causing delays in this meeting." or "I am truly sorry for your having to wait for me today." This is the one true elegant and sincere statement I need to say.

Despite excuses, no matter how honorable the reason, I was late. This not only wasted the ten minutes of the meeting I was late for, but ten minutes of each attendee's time. I was once reminded that I wasted sixty minutes of time when I was five minutes late for a meeting with eleven individuals. I had never thought of it that way, but it left an impression with me, and ever since that meeting years ago I strive to be on time for any meeting. Do not make your meeting people more uneasy by throwing out personal excuses they do not need to know.

REFINEMENT *of* MANNER
Becoming an Elegant, Distinguished, Twenty-First Century Woman

Greeting & Introduction

First impressions are based on your first few gestures and speech. If you stumble over your own name or their names, it is very unbecoming. It shows a lack of confidence, concentration, and poise. You should smile, stand tall, and introduce yourself with a firm handshake – firmly and with a two-shake grip (one, two, let go of their hand – this is the most becoming handshake for a woman and shows equality as well as confidence, with a slight touch of femininity. You are not hand-wrestling with them. Let go of their hand after a brief encounter. Be positive and have a gracious demeanor as you learn their name, and begin a conversation.

Appropriate Behavior

First impressions are based on the first thing you say and do, including how you sit or stand. Properly introducing yourself together with your body language will create one of the most lasting impression, even more than what you wore at the meeting. If you are late, the first thing you should say is "I am sorry." If you are on time, you are anticipating this meeting, and a slight forward lean toward the person shows friendly poise. How you present yourself will show either confidence and poise, or uneasy nervousness.

Be Yourself

Using your body language and easy confidence can put everyone else at ease. If you are trying to be someone you are not, it will be detected and your first impression will be marred with an uneasiness that will translate as "uncomfortable" or "fake."

Being calm and confident puts the other person at ease and provides a better opportunity to create a great first impression. Relax, breathe deeply and smile. Listen wholeheartedly. Make sure you have calmed yourself before you step on the "stage." Be aware of your nervous habits and make sure you have curbed them for the meeting. Focus on the other person and refrain from fidgeting and tapping toes, pencils, or your nails. Show a positive attitude.

Present Yourself Fittingly

First impressions begin with sight. You are in front of that person for the first time, so they will immediately look at you. Pay attention to good posture and body language. Be open and engaging. That person does not know you. He/she can only go by what he sees, then hears.

The key to a successful first impression is to appear presentable and appropriate for the occasion and for the person you are about to meet.

Start with your dress. Is it suitable for the occasion? Do you feel comfortable and does it present you in the best light? A picture is worth a thousand words. The picture of yourself as you step into that room or in front of that person gives them a first impression of who you are. Ask yourself what that person might be wearing and try to suit your attire to the occasion.

Impeccable grooming is essential. An overall healthy appearance makes everyone feel you take care of yourself and have a professional and grounded nature. Neat shiny hair is a must. Makeup should highlight your best features. Clothing must be ironed and well-fitting to look polished. Unkempt and frizzy hair will be the first thing they see, even if you are wearing designer clothes. The key is to look and present yourself appropriately for the occasion and for the person you are about to meet. Your grooming is probably the most important thing about your overall appearance for a good first impression. If you took the time to care enough to be properly and well groomed, they will be impressed that you care about yourself and made the effort to look your best. All these things combined will boost your confidence, which brings us to the next point.

Be Courteous and Attentive

It goes without saying that good manners and polite, attentive, courteous behavior helps make a good first impression. In fact, anything less can ruin the one chance you have at making that first impression. Be on your best behavior.

One good habit worth mentioning is *turn off your mobile phone*. Do *not* take any calls in the waiting room when you suspect you will be called in to the meeting at any moment. What first impression will you create if you are speaking to someone other than the person you are meeting for the first time? Your new acquaintance deserves one hundred percent of your attention. Anything less diminishes your chances of attaining the impression you desire.

A Winning Smile

There is nothing like a sincere smile when you greet someone for the first time. This is not only polite, but warming to the heart of that individual and puts them immediately at ease. Make sure your smile is warm and genuine, or it will come across as fake.

A false smile can actually work against you. Take time to check your teeth, dispose of any gum (gum chewing in public is frowned upon by all professionals), and review your overall look in a public restroom or steal away and check your reflection in any glass window or door, if possible then as you smile, place all your attention on this moment and the person with whom you are meeting.

Conversation

Conversations are based on verbal give and take. If appropriate, prepare questions for the person you are meeting. Research and learn something interesting or noble about that person before you get together. For instance, does he play golf? Does she work with a local charitable foundation? Have you found anything in common with the person you are meeting? If so, this can be a great way to open the conversation and to keep it flowing.

Be Positive

Your attitude shows through in everything you do. Project a positive attitude, especially in the face of criticism or in the case of nervousness. Show a sense of learning and understanding, and be sure to contribute appropriately. Maintain an upbeat manner and smile. Remember, you only have a few seconds to make a great first impression. Review the headings in this chapter and make them your checklist before any initial encounter. You can win anyone over with your timeless elegance and friendliness.

Ensure a Good Impression

If you improve your planning for any encounter, it will inevitably go better because you will be more relaxed, having prepared for it. You may choose to create a pre-meeting checklist to ensure a good impression. Your list might include some of the following concepts and ideas.

Giving your outfit a thorough review the night before is an important step in making sure you are confident when you walk out the door. You then know that you have created a look that states who you are in the best light. It is also vital to make sure your facial features are given the same attention as the rest of you.

THE POLISHED, GENUINE LOOK

Other than your face, your overall look is what people observe about you before you have an opportunity to captivate them with your personality. This is why the first "look" is important in social circles as well as business circles.

We can only possess (long term) the manner with which we are most comfortable. This book is not a book of rules but of concepts to assist you in the personal changes you choose for yourself.

What is the first thing you believe people notice about you? Is it your sparkling personality, or your smile? Or your warm brown eyes? Not surprisingly, survey after survey shows that healthy looks are good looks, and people notice your overall look before they speak to you. Bright eyes, white teeth, nice smile, feminine voice, minimal makeup, and healthy hair are the things that evoke a genuine good-natured person.

A refined woman's manner is an integral part of her and should be the same whether in her dressing room or in a ballroom, whether speaking with the countess or with the laundress. That person whose manners are only put on in public is a veneered lady, not a real one. A refined woman never takes advantage of another's helplessness or ignorance, and assumes that no woman will take advantage of her.

Anything that is not genuine is pretentious and egotistical. One does herself a discourtesy by being false and vain. It is better that ill-bred people go on being what they are while the well-bred excuse the formers' behavior and show extreme benevolence toward them. They do not know what they do not know. It is the same with you and with me.

We can only possess (long term) the manner with which we are most comfortable. This book is not a book of rules but of concepts to assist you in the personal changes you choose for yourself. And as you take your place in society, you will continually find the comfort level of social graces that you have practiced on a daily basis and embraced day by day and year by year. It is not a put-on affair but an exchange of ideas whereby one might find the truer, more fragile and tender self that will always consider others and try to find the most pleasant road with someone, no matter how grievous they may be.

The genteel, well-bred person understands this because they were taught how to behave throughout their early years and later in their public lives. You and I can desire to become more accepting of others, while setting our own standards for ourselves higher. We will become more satisfied that we are people of goodness inside, which comes out in public naturally. As an article in *Vogue* stated on the subject of etiquette: "The greatest rule of the greatest code is: Observe and be considerate!"

The issue here is not to force your values and standards on anyone else without their specific request for assistance in this matter. The well-bred are tender, and careful not to hurt others. Their social life is one of the fine arts and demands good will, tact, intelligence, knowledge, energy and patience with others.

Never give up. It may take the rest of your life to be satisfied with your refined way of life. Begin today and enjoy the benefits now as well as later. Continue your research and experiment with this refined lifestyle, the style of a refined woman who is elegant, tasteful and charming. The highest compliment you can give someone is to dress appropriately when with that person.

There is still a need for etiquette manuals and classes because, for most of us, refreshers are critical to remaining refined individuals among crassly behaving persons.

 In spite of what has been written in nearly condemning the "etiquette rules" of *do this* and *don't do that,* a certain amount of direction is lacking in our twenty-first century casual culture – where farm clothes are considered good enough for the opera, and gym outfits are worn to department stores, meetings and social events. The new society has quite forgotten appropriateness and consideration of others.

Your Choice of Words

Nothing reveals your integrity, communication skills and class more than your choice of words. It has become acceptable to use curse words in normal daily discussions and conversations. It has become acceptable to many people to slur and use slang instead of selecting one's words carefully in order to convey a precise idea.

It is not how much you say but how you say it that truly conveys the message.

There are many languages today that cannot be translated word for word into English. Sometimes I find myself using a French word that has a much richer meaning when I really want to get an idea or concept across to someone. It is, however, a futile gesture when the other person to whom I am speaking does not understand French.

It is not how much you say but how you say it that truly conveys the message. Think of the "tweets" in social media usage. Sometimes the more concise the statement, the more powerful the impact. It is important because everyone seems so busy and caught up with themselves that you barely get any to focus on what you are saying. When you do, it is very short-lived. It is important to speak wisely, concisely and precisely to convey your idea or message correctly.

When writing letters or emails to someone, it is convenient to experiment with synonyms in order to better express your desired message. In earlier times, a proper refined woman had a thesaurus next to her desk to use for such a purpose. If you could not think of the exact word or wanted to stress a particular meaning, a thesaurus was exactly what was needed to assist the good writer.

There are other ways to express your sincere distaste for something other than a blast of four-letter words. Cursing shows lack of control, a limited vocabulary, and lack of respect, as well as labeling you as a follower with no independent structure in your soul.

I am a firm believer that a person will be successful in life to the extent she properly and appropriately uses select words in communicating with others. A person's income and career path are directly linked to their vocabulary. People who tend to read books often have a broader and more extensive vocabulary than those who read periodicals and newspapers or who watch hours of television, or indulge in social media as a pastime or hobby. These media (periodicals and television) typically use a sixth-grade vocabulary.

Normally, smaller words are expressed with emotion to make them seem large and dramatic. This is why some people choose crudeness and curse words to express their emotions. They seem to think that a selective word is not strong or violent enough to explain their rage, anger, happiness, jealousy, or whatever emotion they are feeling at the moment. The careful use of words gives you much more power than using the small, vulgar words that surface from your emotional turmoil. This exemplifies an out-of-control person who is hard to deal with – and definitely anything but elegant and refined.

There are other ways to express your sincere distaste for something other than a blast of four-letter words. Cursing shows lack of control and lack of respect, as well as labeling you as a follower with no independent structure in your soul.

It is important to review your feelings and understanding of how you want to communicate with others. If you choose to speak kindly and firmly when necessary, you will gain the respect of others and they will take you seriously when you speak. By contrast, others speak so vainly and with so little content that the only way they feel they can make a point is through violent obtuse words to make a point. If you have established yourself as a good speaker, you will have no trouble engaging in conversation with others and make your opinion heard just by presenting it logically.

 Homework: Make a list of the five "choice" words you always regret saying. Post them somewhere and begin writing more appropriate and fitting elegant words next to them so that you are prepared next time that word comes to mind.

Class and Style

For the sake of your own social happiness, it is of paramount importance that you cultivate a sense of the true values in people.

That is one of the first duties to yourself, if you want to live this truly wholesome philosophy.

Courtesy radiates good cheer, and good cheer is contagious. People cannot be rude or unkind to you if you have the habit of courtesy. A courteous man or woman at a party can make everyone feel comfortable and at ease.

All through time, some memorable women have had a way about them, even though they were not as beautiful as others. They had an edge, or a look, or some sort of aura that set them apart. We might call that "class" now, but it has been a factor all through time. Some beautiful women did not possess this quality, but some did. Some had a rare quality that caused them to carry themselves differently; it was not accomplished just through training but an inner confidence that carried to the outside and translated as "class."

Class, classy, classic could be defined as:

1. Judged over a period of time to be of the highest quality and outstanding of its kind,
2. Of a simple elegant style not greatly subject to changes in fashion,
3. A thing that is memorable and a very good example of its kind,
4. Showing stylish excellence, and impressive stylishness in appearance or behavior.

Class has a formality, a femininity, and an absolute "edge." Style, on the other hand, has to do with how one appears in public. One woman can have style while another beautiful woman does not possess any style at all.

Other adjectives that might describe someone with class could be attractive, striking, demure, stylish, elegant, chic, sophisticated, tasteful, excellent and refined.

Having class is that certain innate ability to be yourself in any situation appropriately engaged in the situation yet possessing a minute ethereal quality that seems you are untouchable. Class is that certain air about you that does not come with money or fame or any outside force that attempts to make you out to be something different from who you are.

Class has a formality, a femininity, and an absolute "edge." It is obvious when you see someone with class: she may appear not quite real, yet she is being absolutely true to herself. Most of the classy women in our day are the most generous and giving women. They hold themselves to a higher standard, sensing a true responsibility to others' welfare. They hold to a certain unspoken code that makes them desire to improve the society they live in, and their world in general.

Style, on the other hand, has to do with how one appears in public. One woman can have style while another does not possess any style at all. She is not necessarily improperly dressed, but it appears that the clothing and appointments and other things are standing out rather than the woman – the dress is what is standing out, not the woman. With style, a woman can use a washcloth as an ascot and pull it off with her coat, simply because she does it with style. She reaches for the accessories that will finish her look rather than take away from it or distract from it. As you go through these chapters, you will discover your own taste, ideas, charms and talents for being able to come through with a complete etiquette makeover.

In order to succeed at anything, you must put effort into it. You must want to accomplish the work that will help you attain your goal, which is, in this case, a more confident and proper you.

IMAGE DEVELOPMENT

The purpose of a mentor or "life coach" is to assist you in discovering your own character, skills and goals. A mentor or coach can also be helpful as you integrate ideas and concepts that will make you more refined. This coaching can be a way you become accountable for your goals and aspirations and develop your own image. The idea here is to have the finest support to go from point A to B successfully. This quest is about *your* improvement; therefore, the mentor or coach should have the following qualities in order to help you advance.

1.   One with no agenda
2.   A good listener
3.   Well read, educated, traveled
4.   Developed in diverse friendships
5.   Spending time with you on a limited basis
6.   Admirable, a bit adventurous, and interesting
7.   Open-minded
8.   Older (but more importantly, wiser) than you
9.   Discreet

Good Mentors can be those persons you trust and admire, but are more than just allies. They are another trusted pair of eyes, but they do not make key decisions for you. They are non-competitive, but challenge you to attain your goals and be your best

A mentor is an incredible support to you – day in and day out. I do not recommend more than one or two. Your mentors should be genuinely concerned about your success, and should honestly and wholeheartedly desire your advancement in society. Those are the two mentors a woman needs in her life: a professional mentor, and a social mentor. If she has found one special mentor who is incredible and up to the task, she may be *both* social and business mentor.

Have you utilized a mentor? I do not mean the person who kindly tells you that you are wonderful from time to time. We all need those friends, but a true mentor watches out for you at times when you do not realize you need someone to "watch your back" and is up front and honest in helping you achieve your goals.

 Homework: The best way to learn from a mentor is to become one yourself. Think of someone who could benefit from your experience, and offer to meet with that person. You will learn more about yourself and you will realize quickly what type of mentor you want to have.

I realized quite early that I needed some help in all areas of my life. Even at an early stage in my life (six years old) I chose not to wear little white frilly ankle socks, probably because I had a high-spirited older sister, and whatever she did I thought I could do as well. Although that might have made for a weak follower type, I actually became stronger in my own convictions by watching someone ahead of me learn to navigate through life. She was my first mentor. Later, I looked to our high school girls when I was in the fifth grade; it was convenient that two of them were my ballet teachers, so I had a lot of time with them. I wanted their opinion and also wanted their attention. We were separated from the high school students at our school by a playground, but I would sneak over to the high school area from time to time to see what they did at recess. My next few years lacked real mentorship and I faltered a bit in college. I was an art history/art major and there was little inspiration among my peers for any social aspiration.

I became a mentor to a few young girls along the way, particularly in my junior and senior years in college. As I started my career, however, I knew I needed someone, and I found her, in the best place: society. She became my inspiration and go-to for so many ideas and questions. Even though I characteristically learned from many other self-taught avenues, I still look to her for class, inspiration, sophistication and wisdom. In my opinion, she is unparalleled as a mentor and a gracious person. She is involved in business, society, and philanthropies. She works every day, yet seems to have sufficient time for people and their individual needs. Although I studied and poured over etiquette books, I learned the most about refinement by observation.

I have worked putting into practice what I have always loved, which is appropriateness. I was shy growing up, and actually faked stomach aches in my grade school years when I knew that my best friends would not be at school that day. I was timid, so knowing the appropriate thing to do and say was my trusted ally and safeguard from total embarrassment. I believed I might do the wrong thing at the wrong time and be embarrassed beyond repair. It took much time and learning to develop sufficient self-confidence to really steer my life in a sure direction. It is still formidable for me to face unforeseen and unknown territory in social settings. Being prepared ahead of time allows me to have more confidence when faced with conversations and meeting new individuals in formal settings. Whether in social settings, informal activities or business, practicing good manners encourages a more relaxed, peaceful atmosphere for all of us.

As a modern woman, you can be whoever you want to be and yet, if there is a certain desire to be the best you can be, in taste, in manner, in style, you must give up certain old habits and certain old ways for a finer manner in all you do and become. The royals are a good example of living appropriately to how they are perceived. Royalty is quite different from being rich or famous. It is exchanging who you are for who you must be…. *(Remember Audrey Hepburn's character in <u>Roman Holiday</u>?)*

I do not advocate taking an etiquette manual and memorizing the contents. It is disingenuous for someone to tell you that you will have lasting changes and become more elegant just by reading a book, including this book. But if the book challenges you to think, to analyze, and to act on the offering, it is a book that has content and form and instills in you the desire to become an elegant person.

Some of the finest manuals and resource books on etiquette and manners were written one to two generations ago. They were always intended to be resources for anyone who was uncertain how to handle a specific situation, such as a funeral, wedding, or dinner party. All of these occasions matter to the classy and refined woman. She realizes that her proper use of the manuals to build her understanding on how to behave is just like using cookbooks, as opposed to the actual feast of being elegant and knowing how to live as a refined woman.

The first editions of some etiquette manuals are difficult to find, but I always recommend the initial printing. It contains the more intimate thoughts of the author before she was edited and commented away. The ideas in those older versions are full of jewels that I have made into my "go-to" lists.

I am a huge proponent of lists. Throughout the book you will see challenges to make lists of many sorts. You will also see some of my own lists. My lists are my aids, or more positively, my desires and wish lists to change from the inside and get a good result outside. It can be as simple as a way to approach people, or a new habit on the weekends. They are a way for me to continue to be creative in life and creative in my own sphere (which may or may not influence or enlighten others). This is my way of staying focused on who I really want to be and how I want to become that person who is developing over time, the person I enjoy being around. Then the rest is history. Our life legacy is made up of moments. Life is not simply a matter of days, weeks or months, but those moments in time, moments when you have an epiphany over something that puzzled you, a moment when you realize it is more fun to smile and laugh than be somber, a moment when you find out something about yourself that is truly endearing and then embrace it as your personality.

As some human beings struggle in the rat race, they forget about those moments that will never be offered to them again. What are the benefits of such a way of thinking? Others will want to be around us if we live filled with liveliness. We easily get bored with boring people. So if we are boring, then we will only attract boring people who can relate to our pitiful boring lives. Trite, but true, the saying: live with no regrets is probably a paradigm of having the best life.

I truly enjoy being around the sort of people who are quirky, a bit different, intelligent, and "interesting" to me. They do not even have to say anything to be interesting. It is about their person, persona, and their presence (*think: good vibe*). It is fun to live this way and it is a good life. It is probably the best life because it does not totally focus on "me" but on what is all around me, with discovery and enjoyment and contentment.

MAKING CHANGES IN YOUR LIFE

Many people attempt to make modifications to their lives but fail miserably. They either did not decide to continue once they made the initial change or it was superficial and they went back to being the person they always were.

If you desire to make any good changes in your life you will need to contemplate focusing on the following:

i. Your integrity and ethical values. Make sure you have your values and integrity intact before making any changes. Otherwise, you might not change the way you really feel about something and you will end up a fake. Or possibly those changes will not last if they were not for the betterment of who you are.

ii. Your knowledge and understanding. You must focus on your own understanding of things and not do something that someone else suggests just because it sounds good. If the idea does not resonate with you, you either did not grasp it, or you do not believe in the concept sufficiently to have an understanding of how it will fit into the way you want to live. You may have some knowledge of the idea but you must also have a deeper understanding in order to implement it into your life and genuinely change.

iii. Your decisions and goals. If the idea or concept is not honestly in your best interest or does not create value for you in your life, it will go against your overall personal goals. If the idea is in line with your goals and is something you have desired to incorporate into your life, the change becomes a part of you that already parallels who you are. It will become a challenge you are willing to take on.

 *Homework: If you want to make some changes in your life, you need to be accountable. Write your list of changes for this year and give to someone trustworthy. Ask them to meet you quarterly to see how you are advancing. She can help you stay on track with your goals.*

CHAPTER 5 – REFINED CONFIDENCE

Elegance is not standing out, but being remembered. Giorgio Armani

You are confident and full of self-esteem when you are no longer self-conscious of all you do and say. Confidence is a trait of all refined women. Self-assurance and poise are characteristic of women who have nothing to prove. Once you have sufficient character to live your life to the best of your ability, the next goal is to be available to others. Your confidence will make room for you to be a team player as an honest schoolmate, dependable co-worker, smart mother at home, and wise wife to your husband. You will no longer be consumed in taking care of your needs and wants and desires. You will now see the great big world around you.

A refined woman has the ability to take care of what she must take care of, and she possesses the necessary confidence and assurance to do so. She finds a way to become skilled in what is expected of her. She will educate herself, if necessary. She will always be a student of diverse subjects because she is a diverse person, always seeking to improve her mind and soul and maintain her body.

The confident woman lives in the present, not in a dream world where everything is nebulous and shifting. She lives in the real world with both feet planted on the ground.

The confident woman has a sense of optimism based on her belief that she can make a difference not only in her own life but the lives of others – just by being herself. She lives in the present, not in a dream world where everything is nebulous and shifting. She lives in the real world with both feet planted on the ground. This confidence gives her courage to reach out and be a leader within her family, her community, and her world. She is organized sufficiently to handle her own life, and she possesses the additional energy to share her confident nature with others through common courtesy.

Being genuinely courteous means treating others the way you want to be treated. Courtesy also sets the standard of how you will behave, treating everyone from every walk of life with equal respect. It is the insecure woman who has to disrespect others to make herself feel important and worthy.

The confident woman has nothing to prove and can be herself everywhere, showering courtesy to all and being the refined woman she wants to be. She is benevolent and honest with everyone and shows kindness at all times.

Generous honesty is the basis of tact. The well-mannered woman has empathy to find the positive truth and tells or acts on it, without causing embarrassment or pain to someone else. Honesty is about being authentic and genuine with others. No one likes insincere, *lip-service* politeness, which can be as bad as outright rudeness.

Lillian Eichler wrote *Etiquette* in 1924. She defined *etiquette* as having French and German origin, meaning "the stamp or ticket describing the contents of a package" – this would show forth your etiquette or trained manner as your behavior, look, and charm; how you act displays what is inside the package. The Greek beginnings of *etiquette* meant to have an order or rank. We are more civil and organized in our refinement as we attend to our protocol on how to behave.

Courtesy is not the license to lower yourself to make someone feel better.

No matter the origin, etiquette is understood universally as a code of behavior that delineates expectations for social conduct according to contemporary conventional norms within a society, social class or group.

Homework: Confidence is a fragile thing. It must begin inside from a contentment in who you are. Determine today to find out what is keeping you from being content and work on that first, then confidence will naturally follow.

YOUR MANNER AND COMMON COURTESY

Being courteous is not a thing to be put on and off like an overcoat. It should be a manner or style of life. As you are feeling comfortable about yourself, you can actually radiate this courteousness to others. It is a sense of easiness. Making others feel at ease is a big part of it.

Courtesy is overlooking rudeness from other people and never making others feel ridiculous by what we say or how we act toward them. It is about being aware of others' feelings to the point that we would not injure them intentionally by what we say or do when around them, even when we are *not* around them (gossip). Courtesy is not, however, the license to lower yourself to make someone feel better.

Little Courtesies of Daily Life

The old things are not always good simply because they are old. But there are some old things that will never be old-fashioned or out of date. Some things will never belong to one generation alone. One of these is courtesy. Even in this highly liberated, unconventional society, courtesy and politeness are essential traits of a refined woman.

The distinguished woman strives for *like companionship*, but is comfortable in all situations. Class, sophistication and elegance go with her out into the world through her life. The polished woman is far from being rigid. She is adventurous, engaging, interesting, and full of vitality to accomplish the things she desires in her life and on behalf of others, but never caters to others or loses who she is.

Refinement is challenging and always a step ahead of the status quo. It cannot be fully attained over a lifetime, but it is worth striving for. It is a journey, not a destination. It is that sought-after quality that is contagious among women who desire to better themselves in any way. It is for the woman who desires to do well in all she does, and has an eager anticipation of good things in her life.

The refined woman maintains the little courtesies that have become entrenched in her personality.

Acknowledging the Invitation

A courtesy often overlooked is the response to an invitation. Every invitation brings with it a responsibility of the guest attending the event. It includes an obligation to be an active participant at the event. This might mean bringing one of your favorite recipes outfitted with beautiful garnish if it is a neighborhood *covered dish* party, or a bottle of special olive oil or arrangement of flowers, small box of the best chocolates, or some other gift for the host.

The host is the one doing all the work to provide a wonderful time for you and all of her guests. Assist her by coming well prepared. You might consider reading up on current events to be a good conversationalist at the sit-down dinner or cocktail party. You could learn a few phrases in a foreign language to greet the guest of honor who has returned from a year abroad when you have been included in a friend's celebratory dinner party. Put some thought into being an "active" participant, which will make the event more enjoyable for you and others.

When there is an invitation, there is certainly the need for a response. The RSVP at the bottom of an invitation is not an option. Consider if you did not respond to a traffic ticket, or to a summons by the Queen. Well, do you not consider your friends, who deem you worthy of a written or emailed invitation, also worthy of at least the same courtesy to respond? When pondering if you can attend or not, you should determine the last date to respond and make a decision prior to that date. It is fair and reasonable to tell your friend (who considers you enough to send an invitation) that you honestly cannot commit to the event at this time, but do not want to miss the event. In doing so, you have told her you would love to attend, but honor the deadline and will let her know prior to the deadline, so she can continue to invite guests to her quota. Relating a good, sound reason why you cannot commit to the event at this time is reasonable among acquaintances.

If you cannot commit to the event once the deadline arrives, you must decline and hope that you will continue to be included in other events from these lovely people. The person who does not RSVP at all should not expect another invitation from the host. The disrespect given to the host by not responding is sufficient in itself for the host to remove the invitee from future invitations.

Let us consider the options for responding to an invitation. A "no" in advance is a welcome response by any host because that allows him/her to plan the event with the appropriate number of attendees, or include other persons in their place. A "yes" is even more favorable because you are clearing your schedule for that date and time and consider this invitation a pleasurable event that you desire to attend. There is no "maybe" on the invitation. Some invitations request "regrets only" – this means that if you do not regret within a socially acceptable amount of time after receiving the invitation, the host expects you to be there.

When there is a "regrets only" request at the end of an invitation, it is very important that all "maybes" call the host or contact the host in his /her preferred communication method. They may leave a phone number or email address. Think about your response before calling this person so that you know exactly what you want to say. This saves the host valuable time. It is proper to have a prepared response rather than stumbling and perhaps accepting when you actually called to regret. Because the host is very excited about the event, she may encourage you to change your mind and change your schedule. Be prepared to respond politely with a firm no, if you cannot attend. This will prevent you from calling days later and regretting, once you have accepted.

Post-event politeness: This next suggestion is regarded as the best way to show your manners. Thank the host within three days of the event. If you had a nice time, let the host know this by a brief, clever, and personal note, fresh flower delivery, fruit basket or chocolates, or whatever the occasion equals. When thanking for a bar-b-que at your neighbors, perhaps a plate of chocolate chip cookies the next day would be the best thank you ever.

    If it was a party in your honor, the thank-you would undoubtedly be more sophisticated, keeping in mind the best thank-you comes from a consideration of the host and a warmness in the giver's heart.

Thank You Notes

A general outline to writing memorable thank you notes: Timely – Beautiful – Sincere – Personal - Elegant

    Make sure the thank-you note is timely. The proper response is within three days. Learn to write beautifully, whether script or block print; your hand-written notes with pleasing words and beautiful penmanship are genuinely the finest display of your gesture of thanks and good will. Make an effort to be truly sincere in what you say, and write on fine letterhead or note paper. The finest stationery I have found was from Dempsey & Carroll in New York, (recommended in one of the Emily Post editions). Pricey yet elegant, it is fitting for any required formal letter. The paper is fine and thinly pressed, the engraved details are matchless. Several types of stationery are important to the elegant woman. Crane stationery is well crafted and the cotton is of good quality; it allows various pens to write on the paper smoothly. Small thank-you notes with beautiful details and lined envelopes from specialty shops are perfectly suited for some writing purposes.

It is essential to let the host know how much you enjoyed the event and how grateful you were to be included. The body of the note should include something clever, such as how impressed you were with her collection of antique cocktail napkins, or how delighted you were to be sitting next to the Administrator of the Junior College where your son is enrolled to attend next semester. When you find a connection to the extreme thought and care your host put into your enjoyment of the event, you will discover several things to write in gratitude to her. It is that simple. Making a statement of how nice the party was does not equal true elegance in a memorable thank-you note. Strive to find something unique that you enjoyed specifically about the evening, day or weekend that will tell the host you enjoyed yourself, as that was her aim at inviting you in the first place. To make the note memorable, use the best stationery you can afford. Draft your note before you write it on your stationery.

When you ponder the wonderful planning and care your host put into your enjoyment of the event, you will discover several things to write in gratitude to her.

Make it beautiful through your unique, legible handwriting. Make it personal with something you particularly noticed or liked about the event, gift, or purpose. Make it elegant by taking your time in composing and executing the writing of the sentiment.

Saying "No" to a Request

There are many ways to redirect a request that you do not solicit or want. If this is in person, you might act like you did not hear the person, or state you cannot do it, and reluctantly you both part. There is, however, an art to saying *no*, meaning it, and retaining that relationship with the requestor. While you will be approached to change your mind, you can stand your ground graciously. There seems to be a stigma to saying "no" firmly. It is as if you are a mean person if you say *no* to a request, particularly if the person asking expects a *yes* from you, as so many times before. You now have the option to say *no* gently and firmly and mean it and stick to it, by giving a reasonable response along with the *no*, or a *no* along with a reasonable response.

You can reasonably say *no* while letting someone know she is important to you and you wish you could accommodate. You can always suggest other resources besides yourself, which may soften the blow of your saying *no*. Any other *no* to any other request must be deliberate in telling the truth (in kindness and sincerity); it could trail with the saying, "I am unable to say yes at this time."

Practice makes perfect, and if you practice how you say *no*, it will sound more and more genuine as you tell them politely. You must realize the fact you have priorities that do not include them as your number one reason to live. They will respect you for standing up to your needs and ambitions and schedule, if you gently explain that you wish you could help. Never say, "I am sorry I cannot. "This is self-inflicted guilt. You should state that you cannot do this or that and you still support them in whatever they are doing, but you cannot help them at this time. Being kind and being nice are two different worlds. Being kind to them by letting them down gently is being polite. It is not always nice, particularly if they are insistent. Always being nice is saying *yes* all the time, and you will die doing this.

 Homework: Thank you notes can be daunting. We usually put off things that are difficult or uncomfortable. Make an outline of a thank you note, keep it with your stationery, and beautiful stamps, and favorite pen. Using your outline, draft your note with specific details, and you will succeed at making every gracious letter personal and special.

You must remember your priorities and your time. We all have the same amount of time and given that and the many things asked of you, you simply cannot do everything. You do not have the time or resources to accommodate everyone's wishes. If there is a real need for a bag of groceries, you should accommodate that *need*; otherwise you can say *no!*

You can pre-empt the request if you know it is coming by explaining ahead of time that you are very busy this week or month, and you do not have the luxury to do anything for anyone right now. Be sincere in saying *no*. Firmly saying *no* will stop any whining and begging, which will eventually ensue if you do not make your position clear.

A Politeness in Attitude

Being polite is not a Southern thing, although Southerners have one up on the rest of us, most of the time in being polite. The way of a gentle refined woman is to say "please" and "thank you," "sir" and "ma'am," and really have a distinctive tone of respect for everyone she comes in contact with. The appreciative nature of the Southern refined woman is commendable and she is raised to have this gentility in her breeding. Saying "thank you" is like breathing. It is a mark of understanding that someone has done something for you and should be commended for so doing.

A refined woman may observe and glance at something or someone of interest but her face does not reveal any dramatic surprise or horror or disdain. She retains her standard of courtesy in all areas of her life.

The common courtesy of kindness and manners requires you to say "please" and "thank you," yet these words have nearly become extinct in society today. The appropriate response to someone filling your water glass, or bringing your entrée, or bringing your car out of valet, is usually to say *thank you*. When requesting something, saying *"please"* is appropriate since you are asking someone to do or say something based upon your personal appeal. There is a hierarchical system where one does not speak to anyone that is in service to them until after the entire event, however, there are very few of these highly formal occasions anymore.

All rude behavior begins with an attitude. Actions such as staring too long or using your finger to point at something or someone is considered rude in all languages. Both are unattractive and create a dramatic effect – both of which the refined woman is not interested in displaying. A refined woman may observe and glance at something or someone of interest but her face does not reveal any dramatic surprise or horror or disdain, nor does she point out something or someone using her arms and hands and fingers to become a human sign pointing something out to everyone who is within audible range.

Refinement demands the standard of courtesy in all areas of life. A calm demeanor does not mean a woman does not show emotion, however, she is tempered in how she shows it in public. That calmness is the refined woman's way of being kind to all and overlooking the crude behavior of others.

We all want to appear refined in manner and actions. How we behave tells everyone who we are. Refraining from embarrassing someone or pointing out someone's faults is the way of the refined. Nervous gestures are also perceived as unrefined. If you have a very outgoing personality, when you tone down your gestures, you show more grace and poise in the situation. Awkwardness usually displays unpreparedness for the situation. Again, sometimes gestures and mannerisms are a sign of nerves, yet when you are comfortable in your surroundings, you do not need to show any apprehension or overly exaggerated mannerisms.

You probably have your own list of things that are definitely awkward. Here are a few examples of inelegant gestures.

1. Fidgeting
2. Talking or laughing too loudly
3. Constantly adjusting your outfit
4. Chewing gum, popping bubble gum

5. Biting or fidgeting with fingernails
6. Sluggishly dragging feet in walking
7. Wiping teeth with the tongue
8. Folding arms rather than lowering them to sides
9. Resting head or chin on hands and elbows
10. Combing or running hands through your hair

You are most kind and civil when you take time to research and determine the most appropriate outfit for the occasion; this not only compliments the host, but it maintains your status that you fit in and are aware of proper protocol, which should also lead to proper conversation and behavior. It is important to dress correctly. When you dress for the event, you show an appreciation for the occasion. Most day occasions warrant a suit or day dress with no décolleté. When you are carefully and appropriately dressed, you can forget about yourself and concentrate on the activity, event or people present.

Other small courtesies that will always be in fashion include such things characteristic of a truly refined person. The refined woman does not act rude, boorish, unbecoming or insensitive. She is at her best when there is pressure around her. It does not affect her courteous way of manner. She continues to be herself and does not let any emergency cause her to lose her composure; this behavior sets her apart and shows her essence of true gentleness.

It is important to give compliments genuinely and accept them sincerely. The elegant woman does not gush, nor is she so cold to never compliment a kindness or graciousness to her. There must also be courtesy in apologies given and accepted.

Many persons have declined to observe the small courtesy of proper and appropriate gestures such as compliments. It is important to give them genuinely and accept them sincerely. There must also be courtesy in apologies given and accepted. Rudeness in all forms has no place in a refined woman's repertoire.

There is no good reason to harm someone in public (or in private). An apology is standard protocol when a refined woman with standards has belittled or caused harm to someone by what she says or does. On the other hand, acceptance of an apology does not necessarily mean the harm is relinquished entirely when one believes it was intentional.

Small courtesies may be lacking in our conversations and interactions in everyday life, but it may be due to impartiality and impersonal behavior of busy, self-important people. People who are so busy with what they think is important may have forgotten the common courtesies. Elevators, doors, seats on planes, all seem to have an impertinence attached to the use of them. Should we demand our way in all of these shared spaces with others?

The refined woman does not place herself above or below someone else but understands the importance of common courtesies in her character. She continues in her own manner and overcomes the rude company of others by acting in the interest of those who are worthy of her attention, such as the elderly, blind or disrespected. She shows respect where it is due and disregards those around her who do not deserve nor appreciate her kindness and demeanor.

Small common courtesies make up most of what we do each day. It is a decision to live properly that will set you apart and actually show the refinement of character and behavior that becomes you. You are refined in manner as you perform daily duties and disregard the rudeness in all forms. You endure to act ladylike and with integrity in all situations, no matter how you are perceived or treated. It is not a reaction that your manner will show forth; the best reply to rudeness is by maintaining your high standards of conduct.

With many basic common courtesies, we distinguish ourselves from "the crowd." What is most important is your sincerity to be polished and refined in all you do. How you begin your journey to be more refined is your decision. You can take things that you have learned over the years, and add new ideas to refine your manner toward others but, more important, within yourself. It is not educating yourself intellectually, but rather something that comes from the heart. It is the desire to be more refined and elegant in your life.

When confronted with a person who might have a colorful lifestyle, it is kind and courteous to avoid personal questions. This allows the person to feel comfortable and accepted by you and your party, no matter what that person's reputation might be. The idea of purposely making someone uncomfortable in front of others is rude and vulgar. A refined woman does not confront anyone with personal or prying questions. This power tactic is popular in more recent years and there is an air of cynicism among females in particular that does not allow for a gracious woman to enter the conversation because she is not willing to discuss gossip, nor is she willing to embarrass someone with personal information or questions. She treats everyone the same, and yet does not put herself down or lower herself to such behavior.

Homework: List a few common courtesies you may have forgotten or are not doing anymore. Determine to get back to the habit if being courteous in every way. You will become an amazing example to many people.

GENUINE ELEGANCE

You must not think that because your face is pretty and your personality appealing you can be rude. You cannot escape being disliked if you whisper among your peers, giggle together in a clique, and show no consideration for others' feelings. Every time you act this way, you are losing admiration from people who previously respected you.

It is wonderful to be cheerful and have an enjoyable nature, but the extra mile is to be kind and courteous, too. You can be self-reliant and elegant. You can be bold and firm but not overbearing. You can be strong and fearless but feminine. Everyone admires the woman who can take care of herself, but few admire the woman who bullies her way around.

When we operate in and demonstrate etiquette and social grace, we are operating from a place of poise and self-assurance.

It would be a simple matter to fill these pages with generalities and tell you what you must do and what you must not do. Such advice would be futile. Refinement is not a written formula, but an outlook, an attitude. It shapes the way you handle yourself. You are your own best judge of what you shall do and what you shall not do. Nothing, no one, can tell you better than your own conscience and your own good sense what is correct and what is incorrect. Etiquette does not attempt to "lay down the law," it merely offers suggestions that are based on modern tendencies that are subject to changing conditions and circumstances. When following a refined manner, it always guides us with civility and fairness in mind. Treating everyone the same and understanding the weakness of all causes us to be more lenient in our assumptions and more gracious concerning any criticism. The most gracious of all persons is that person who has truly loved and is loved.

"The young man and woman who have found love have found life's richest treasure. They need no book of etiquette to teach them courtesy and politeness, for kindness dwells in their hearts – and when kindness dwells in the heart, one is pleasant, courteous, and considerate toward everyone." Lillian Eichler

It is a simple thing to relate to loving someone dearly and then feeling benevolence toward all. It is the rose-colored glasses of being in love. It is impossible for anyone to give rules and regulations to lovers. Etiquette is unable to standardize the conduct of those in love. They act on the spontaneity of benevolence and respect toward others.

Those in love have an impulse of kindness and desire to treat everyone tenderly and gently as they are being treated by the one who loves them. They reciprocate to everyone what they have received and even gush over simple wonderful things to the delight of anyone in their presence. They seem to have the poise and grace of manner and elegance in their gait as they float through life, caring for the things of importance and letting the petty fall at their feet.

Think about a time when you have seen someone walk into a room and command the space. They are not trying to intimidate anyone, but they are themselves through and through. Immediately they caused heads to turn and were able to capture the focus of the entire room. What they do is narrowed down to one thing – they were operating from a place of *self-confidence*. They had that inner knowing: how to properly carry themselves, how to communicate effectively, and how to get what they want out of life.

There is no greater personal harm than to be condescending toward someone and in doing this forget your own standards of conduct or behavior for the sake of someone else. They will begrudge your attitude, and you will be regarded as a fake, since your manner was not genuine to begin with. A process of refinement takes place in all of us, whether we are aware of it or not. When we are aware and an active participant in its usefulness in our life, we obtain much benefit from its cutting and grating to make us well-rounded rather than rough edged. It is better to continue to be yourself, whether you can help someone or not, than to go beyond your sincere desire to be kind.

Busy people actually do get things done. They accomplish things that are important to them and choose to do what they do, and say *no* to the rest. Does that sound rude to you? Are you letting your time slip away? Do you wonder where the days went, where the months went? Busy people require a lot of themselves to prioritize and reduce all time wasters in order to achieve the things that matter to them. They understand accountability. They are, for the most part, either highly organized, or they have someone in their life to assist on this matter. The big question is, what really matters to you today, tomorrow, next week, next year, twenty years from now? Is becoming more elegant something that is interesting to you?

Refining means going through a process of culling out all the "dross" or unrefined parts and oddities of character, looks and lifestyle that really are not important, whether tangible or intangible.

Refinement means being gentle and kind, sincere in actions, simple in tastes. Being refined distinguishes you as having a fine character. Refinement is the epitome of sophistication and elegant behavior, because, you might have tangible possessions that make you feel important and obtain the observation of others, but that alone is essentially vulgar. Vulgarity is the low behavior of a person who is striving to attain something other than a good nature and benevolence toward others. The two natures can be compared to a flashy designer handbag and a demure well-designed ordered purse with features inside that keep a woman feeling in charge and organized. A handbag can contain pockets and slits and additional extras that do not show up on the outside, but when you open it, it appears to be in order and classy. That is also how I feel inside, orderly and classy when everything is properly arranged and my character is intact, and eventually shows on the outside.

A REFINED LIFESTYLE – DAILY QUALITY

Manner is the lifestyle and way you live your life every day. It is not the set of rules defined as "etiquette" (although we should know those rules) and it is not a fixed way of doing things. There *are* standards of protocol for some activities such as the Symphony or the Opera. Such events require participants be punctual, maintain a quiet, relaxed posture during the performances, and show kind acknowledgment of a performance well done at the end.

REFINEMENT *of* MANNER
Becoming an Elegant, Distinguished, Twenty-First Century Woman

It is the manner by which you live around beauty that makes you a distinguishably refined woman. Learning to appreciate quality over quantity and being surrounded with a few beautiful things is the key. It does not depend upon your budget, but your sense of finding a few precious items to own, appreciate and enjoy throughout your life. This makes each day special.

 I purchased a Mont Blanc Pen probably before I could actually afford it. This pen has given me much enjoyment in writing personal notes, and other correspondence. It is pleasurable for me to use this pen even though it is now sixteen years old. It is one of the small, beautiful things I appreciate almost every day.

CHAPTER 6 – REFINED SELECTION

"I tried to live like Grace Kelly." Grace Kelly
"If you want to be original, be ready to be copied." Coco Chanel

Being a selective person means much more than just being *original,* or *finicky.* I am very picky about the foods I eat and the clothes I wear. Being selective is about refining your overall "taste" to the point of desiring the elegant, simple, finer things of *quality* over *quantity.* In this regard, the elegant woman always makes it look easy. She simply chooses quality every time.

Selectiveness applies to how we run our lives in general as well as in detail. Being selective is saying *no* to certain requests and performing what we agree to perform. You, as a discerning woman, decide your word will be good, and you know for what reasons you make your commitment.

The selective woman is a not a pushover, but is determined, driven and elegant all at the same time.

Being selective is choosing all the time to do the best thing possible based on all the information you have at the time. You decide to choose the right thing for you, the elegant thing, and the reputable thing. This is what sets you apart from most women. You are selective and precise in your decisions about your life, what you do, what you say, and how you act. You are selective in who you spend your time with, who influences you, and who you desire to be, day in and day out. Selectivity is *quality over quantity*, choosing a higher path rather than lowering yourself to the demands of others.

A Selective Woman:
1. Gives others the benefit of the doubt.
2. Manages expectations in a gracious way.
3. Speaks in a gentle way to all persons.
4. Is never in a hurry.
5. Is careful in showing disapproval without judgment.
6. Has opinions based on well-researched facts.
7. Tempers decisions with sense and restraint.
8. Uses emotion and influence to make a point.
9. Is thoughtful but moderate in discussions and debates.

None of the above suggests that the selective woman is a pushover. On the contrary, she is determined, driven and elegant all at the same time. She balances her passions with tempered classiness. The discerning woman is purposeful and organized. She can be spontaneous in those areas of her life that will create a wonderful, amazing lifestyle, yet never careless. Her motto is "no one wins unless everybody wins"[3] and she strives to live up to that in all she does. She selects the greater long-term good for herself and others over trivial, short-lived, fleeting desires and wants, and never skimps on quality anywhere. She is disciplined, but spontaneous because she understands her standards, and she maintains boundaries. Setting standards and boundaries are the ways she gains respect from others and herself. She leaves things better than she finds them. She leaves her mark as a refined person, able to control herself and depart at the appropriate time.

Her time is important to her. She is selective in her choices of how her time is invested. She chooses to devote her time to worthwhile endeavors, such as educating herself on subjects that interest her, and maintaining a balance between her personal desires and her responsibilities in the world around her.

She is deeply rooted in kindness and fairness. She lives in the moment but plans for the future. She chooses to control her emotions, avoiding any situation that is irreparable. She is civil with all persons but does not belittle herself by succumbing to maliciousness. She is selective in her friendships but is fair and pleasant to all persons, particularly in business. She is selective in how she deals with her career choices and commitments. She chooses to keep her life simple, organized, and free of clutter in actions and possessions.

The gracious woman appreciates even the smallest gesture of love toward her. She is noble and content, not keeping score with others. Holding grudges and acting poorly are actions she cannot afford to participate in. This refined woman goes the additional mile because it is her duty and, even more it is her manner. The mannerly woman can focus on meaningful projects that are worth her attention, while discounting and refusing to succumb to the temptation of being all things to all people. She pursues what is worthy of her.

---

3 *A favorite quote of Bruce Springsteen, and life motto of Jack Blanton, American oil industry executive, civic leader and philanthropist.*

Homework: Spend the rest of this week observing little niceties that are done toward you. You will be surprised how many little things others generously give to you. Then remember this when the rude truck driver cuts in front of you. He does not have refinement – do you?

DAY TO DAY AFFAIRS

Taking time to select the perfect gift for someone special, selecting a delicate dress to wear to high tea, or choosing a book that will challenge you are some of the ways you, as a refined woman, can be selective day to day. These choices or ones like them occur daily. As you become tasteful in all you do, you also become selective in your decisions.

Your refined taste might include selecting reading material that will develop your ideas, enrich your vocabulary, or increase your knowledge of history, geography, science, art, or influential people. It might include selecting the proper stationery for letter writing, or the most elegant purse for those special events. Whatever your decisions may be, as your taste is refined, you will be more selective in your decisions and choices. "Just anything" will no longer suffice.

Selective women do not waste their time on things that do not enhance or enrich their lives or the lives of others. They live in a world where they are active participants and decision makers. They do not live vicariously through other peoples' lives. They do not have time for it, and they do not have time or energy for gossip.

If you are watching other people live the life you have always wanted for yourself, that is living vicariously. As you choose the refined life, you choose to live your life as it was meant to be: interesting, adventurous, fun, exciting, daring, and definitely selective. It is your life to live. You are a selective refined woman if you are genuine in your thinking and outward behavior. Be brave enough to live your own life and be responsible for your own actions. Respect yourself, and be accountable for your own actions.

You might make mistakes, but accept the consequences of them, learn from them, and move on. Bitterness is your worst enemy and no refined person can afford to be bitter over previous experiences or people. If someone hurt you, admit this as being very painful, but do not hold everyone else liable for your happiness or lack thereof due to one treacherous person or incident that was out of your control.

The sad and empty life is one of bitterness. A bitter heart robs you of your time, your pleasures, and your future happiness. It robs no one else but you. Very few friends will be able to stand by you unless you actively seek resolution and healing from the harm and hurt you have incurred. It might take some time for you to recover, but recover you will, for you are far better than the unfortunate situation. You choose to "move on."

Living a selective lifestyle is finding a routine that will keep you at your best. It will allow you to be relaxed and rested, regardless of your busy schedule, limited wardrobe, or life circumstances.

Another trait of the selective woman is her ability to nurture true friendships. Her wisdom is based on knowing who to trust, or *not* trust until proven trustworthy. This is the refined woman's defense system. Her desire to include and be civil to everyone, no matter how they treat her, is balanced in her wise understanding of human nature. She knows that not everyone is out to protect and love her the way she loves and treats others. She is absolutely selective in the development of her friendships, including relationships with the opposite sex. She understands that there are vast differences in thoughts and she strives to communicate clearly with everyone so as not to have false expectations nor instill false hopes or thinking on the other person. Selective behavior is a refined trait that takes an understanding heart and an understanding mind. She develops a keen sense of knowing people and knowing herself, her strengths, weaknesses, and how she relates to others. She is not slothful in her wit or intellect and is willing to share her opinions, yet softens them as necessary depending on the person she is with.

The refined woman's qualities lend to exemplary fine living with its fine attention to detail. This finesse, or discretion, is what every elegant woman is about. There are no shortcuts to refined elegance. It is a discipline, but far more, it is a heightened experience, a movement toward a better-quality lifestyle.

EXTRAVAGANT LUXURY

Extravagant luxury is truly an oxymoron, for real luxury is practiced subtly. The greater the luxury, the more discreet it must be. Overindulgence in anything is never elegant and always appears audacious and gaudy.

Being prodigal or extravagant is not necessarily practicing elegance. Impulsive, wasteful excessive extravagance can ruin one's attempts to become elegant. The truly elegant woman is decisively simple with discriminating taste. Elegance is a selective process. It is made of high quality choices based on value (possessions, time commitments, family, friendships), and not necessarily based on outside pressures (such as cost, time constraints, or peers).

Living a selective lifestyle is finding a routine that will keep you at your best. It will allow you to be relaxed and rested, regardless of your busy schedule, limited wardrobe, or life circumstances. You are open to changes in your ideas that might provide more refined elegance and less hype or extravagance.

Here are a few ideas on becoming more refined and selective:

1. Simplify your life by saying *no* when you cannot really commit to the request, and when you say *yes*, do it whole-heartedly.
2. Love what you have and enjoy others, not their possessions.
3. Accept compliments gracefully, and give them sincerely without *gushing* or embarrassing the recipient.
4. Do not complain. Take responsibility for your own happiness.
5. Retain your sense of humor. Never take yourself or life too seriously.
6. Have boundaries. Gracefully stand against people who do not offer you the respect you deserve.
7. Rid your life of bad habits, poor grammar and ill words. Enrich your life with good reading, people, and social events. This will allow you to practice good manners often.
8. Stroll through the day as if you had a book on your head. This will maintain your good posture and cause you to slow down, and observe your surroundings.
9. Sit, stand and walk elegantly. Be truly happy. Do not be jealous of anyone but love who you are becoming each day.
10. Speak articulately. Whisper occasionally.

CULTIVATING AN ENJOYABLE LIFE

There are many areas where you can become more *selective*. This allows you more time for enjoyment. I have listed some ideas below based on a lifestyle blog for developing your standard of living and character with more refined selective amusement and *flair*[4]:

1. Write thank you notes on great stationary.
2. Be kind with your words about others. If you're going to talk about someone behind his or her back, say something good.
3. Have a signature meal that you can prepare on the spur of the moment (be a spontaneous host). Keep interesting foods in your pantry.

---

[4] *Inspired by: 100 ways to be more elegant; www.livecharmed.com*

4. Dine, don't feed. Slow down and savor your meal.
5. Do not smack chewing gum in public. Limit your use of gum to private consumption or to open your ears on an airplane.
6. Decide to do more of what comes naturally to you. Where there is ease, there is elegance.
7. Be a discreet woman. Cultivate your secret garden. It's not necessary to share your entire life story with a complete stranger.
8. Prefer to be silent at opportune moments. It will make you stunning.
9. Eat beautiful foods moderately. Observe the food intently and savor the flavors, colors and textures to find true enjoyment beyond satisfaction of your hunger.
10. Choose a signature scent that expresses your feminine essence.
11. Move gracefully through life. Select comfortable and elegant heels and ballet flats.
12. Study the arts. Bring intelligent and refined conversation to the table.
13. Dress for your destiny, even if you are merely taking a trip to the grocery store.
14. Sip your drink. It shows a delicate demureness like nothing else.
15. Choose elegance always. Wear your tennis shoes to work out, your flip flops on the beach, and choose wonderful shoes for every other occasion.
16. Decide that you really do not need a lot of expendable income to be elegant. It is a mindset, not a shopping budget.
17. Choose quality over quantity, and enjoy anything you have. If you do not love it, give it to someone who will.
18. Travel. It does wonders for your personal enrichment.
19. Select a one-on-one time to play scrabble or chess with someone special. It will make you laugh together

Cultivating Joie de Vivre

How do they do it, you ask? The idea of a lasting, elegant French woman's wardrobe consists of fewer high-quality pieces – and *great* accessories. The French women spend more per item than Americans on the whole, but they end up with fewer – but amazing – purchases on a smaller budget. Their selections are to be admired and emulated. They choose to do without and find versatility in their wardrobe. They even find ways to revitalize the same dress for longer periods of time. The same black dress will be worn for perhaps ten years, with the hemline changing or the skirt remade, but it it always the "woman" who makes the dress.

Here are a few tips I learned while living in Paris. I realized that these ideas are easy to infuse in my day-to-day life at home. It made me feel like a finer, more selective person as I practiced these. French women are known for their selectiveness and a culture of being discriminating. Their closets are a mere fraction of our American counterparts, yet they always look smart, elegant and tasteful.

1. Dress the part.

Paris is known for its fashion and beauty. Being chic, stylish, and using your fashion sense as a form of self-expression makes clothing more than just a fashion choice, it is an *art form.* Try different variations of the same old thing you usually reach for. Add something new to the "uniform." Even a scarf can dress up the most mundane grey suit or navy dress.

 Dressing your best (regardless if you are going to the corner *"boucherie"* or out for a night on the town) means having excellent basics that will always be in style, looking effortless yet chic, and putting energy into the small things (*such as shoes, handbag, a great wrap, scarf, tights, gloves, or sweater, and other accessories*). Wear something that says, "I am refined and easygoing."

2. Enjoy your down time.

Go to a café and savor an espresso or a rare English tea. It does not make sense to be on a strict budget and not have a bit of fun.

A five-dollar cup of coffee means you are treating yourself to a simple luxury of elegance and pleasure.

Take part of your day to sit, relax, people watch, and savor the moment while sipping a delicious drink. The Parisian way is to slow down and appreciate life as it passes, not run through it like you are on a marathon. Sit outside whenever possible.

Invite someone you would like to catch up with to tea at your home. It only takes a teapot, some interesting tea, tea cups and a small tray of petite sandwiches, cookies or pastry to host a tea. It also gives you a chance to put out your nicest napkins, plates, cups, and some fresh flowers.

3. Plant and enjoy flowers.

It is about smelling the roses in life, and enjoying your very own garden. This will allow you to have freshly cut flowers or herbs for cooking. You will learn about the plants that are indigenous to your area. You will have local color and fragrance at your doorstep. Take it from the French – they love their gardens, even if it consists of a hanging basket on the kitchen windowsill. There truly is something relaxing and beautiful about watching your own flowers grow.

4. Commit to one leisurely meal a day.

Slow down and enjoy your meal, even if it is cereal in the morning. Be seated, put the napkin on your lap and enjoy each spoonful. You will realize that it takes only a few more minutes to dine than to eat. Evening meals should be relaxing and pleasurable and truly enjoyed, as you have arrived at the end of the day. Unwinding is, after all, an American pastime, but the French love their evening aperitifs. Try having antipasto (cured meats, fresh cheeses, olives, herbs and crackers) in the evening instead of a meal. Sparkling water or wine, baguettes, cheese and fine conversation are all key components to embodying a French lifestyle.

5. Read a novel.

Self-help books have their place, but Parisians relish their time with an excellent, enthralling novel. Your favorite choice might be a romance, a thriller, or whatever you may find takes you out of your element. Change up your reading habits. Keep several different books handy on your night table. Escape with a classic book, magazine, or poetry from the romantics.

6. Get outside.

Each season there is so much happening in Paris, the French are rarely found indoors. Play outside and experience nature. Read or people watch at a sidewalk cafe. Your own little spot on the globe has wonderful attractions that you may have forgotten.

Find those little niceties in your town or a nearby city where you can experience new adventures and old, comfortable times again. A great way to enjoy the outdoors is to go to your local zoo. You can sit on a bench and wonder at the delight of a small child seeing an exotic animal for the first time.

If you find yourself tied to your desk in the office, head outdoors to enjoy a bag lunch. You might work with a small team to collect sufficient donations to purchase picnic benches for an outdoor common area. The sun-given dose of Vitamin D will boost your mood, and the camaraderie will boost morale. You will become a real leader among your peers.

7. Kiss.

When greeting friends, trade in the hugs and handshakes for *faire la bise* (giving a kiss). This is clearly a fundamental of living more French than American, and is much healthier than a handshake. To do it as the French do, tilt your head *to the left first*, and go for their right cheek, while they go for your right cheek.

Kissing your lover for sixty seconds or more is also healthy. Do it in public, if you want to be scandalous. Kissing reduces stress and boosts your immunity.

8. Open your eyes and be curious.

There is so much around you to learn from and experience. You may have lived in the same sleepy town all your life. Try to see it with a new set of eyes, as if it is your first time as a visitor. Take a trip around your hometown with the type of excitement that you would experience in Paris.

9. Showcase and delight in your femininity.

Margaret Thatcher said: "Power is like being a lady . . . If you have to tell people you are, you aren't." Enjoy being a lady, Mademoiselle or Madame. It is following that hint of intuition and allowing life to flow that is feminine. Opening your soul to love, and having that childlike wonder exudes a feminine glow that is contagious. You can charm a room by being authentic and genuine, yet always a bit mysterious.

10. Truly Parisian.

If you desire to bring Paris to you personally, there are two words that say it: beautiful lingerie. There's nothing quite like wrapping your body in lace and silk to get your femininity flowing. The French women purchase only a few fine lingerie items at a time and trade them out when they show some wear. Fewer sumptuous, glamorous, and extremely feminine items will cause you to admire them more, and enjoy the delicate features that makes them so unique and beautiful. They are meant to create an aura about you that makes *you* feel sensual and special. Lavish in the silk bows, lace insets, and beautiful design. You will notice the feeling of luxury simply for the pleasure of wearing them.

Cultivating an Eye for Beauty

If you plan to move forward in cultivating a selective lifestyle, one of your areas of learning should be appreciation for the arts. This includes all types of art. Painting, sculpture, architecture, music (symphony, opera, jazz), along with poetry are considered "the arts," and today the arts also include additional forms, such as dance, theatre, film, photography and conceptual art.

Homework: Look up three of the top Italian or Dutch Masters of the Renaissance, and three popular Impressionsist Painters. You will be surprised how familiar their names will be to you.

The arts are expressive and are intended to bring out our emotion. What we do not understand about the arts is that they are expressive attempts at opening the window of our soul to another. The music of Brahms is German and Austrian influenced with Beethoven, Mozart and Haydn as his mentors. When you listen to Brahms, you get a sense of geographical culture and value and a serene beauty that permeates the nerves inside you and calms your mind. Looking at a Rembrandt painting can absolve all hunger for beauty and mystery as the dark paintings take your full attention to delve into before walking away satisfied. It takes cultivating your senses and taste to comprehend the deepness of the arts. Artworks are intended to astonish and amaze you, to get down to the emotions and power of your soul so that you experience the thoughts of the artist and it affects you permanently.

Once you study Michelangelo's *Pieta* in St. Peter's Basilica, you shake your head in disbelief that a human can carve a creation of such warmth and moving love from a cold stone. Standing before the marble figures evokes one's deepest emotion. The Italian Renaissance sculptor Bellini also moves me in a similar way. It takes a selective eye to feel the presence of greatness and to sense a passionate moving of one's soul from a simple statue created hundreds of years ago. These things take a cultivation of time, patience, and most of all, the cultivation of a desire to experience beauty with all of your senses.

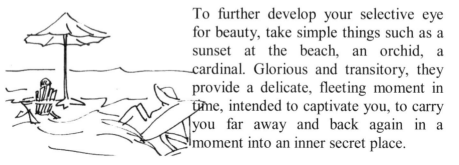

To further develop your selective eye for beauty, take simple things such as a sunset at the beach, an orchid, a cardinal. Glorious and transitory, they provide a delicate, fleeting moment in time, intended to captivate you, to carry you far away and back again in a moment into an inner secret place.

This is the selective, cultivated place of beauty. Reading Lord Byron's poetry can bring you to a very lost place of beauty and elegance. I once read George Washington's letter to the Hebrew Congregation at Newport. It was stately, presumptive, poignant, and full of grace and elegance in words and intent. It moved me with emotion and longing to be able to communicate so exquisitely.

CHAPTER 7 - EFFORTLESSNESS

"It's not money that makes you well dressed. It's understanding."
Chrisian Dior

I have decided I am going to live well. Always, no matter where I am and what I am doing, I will continue to have a well-lived existence. No matter who I am with or not with, what I own, or do not own, I know that *living well is the best life*. The blogger who wrote *100 ways to be elegant* also wrote about owning only 100 great possessions. You may own more than one hundred great items or much less, but her brilliant idea was to love those things that you have saved up to purchase, or chanced upon and thought were too lovely to pass up and you would find a "use" for them.

I found seven red cut glass goblets from France tucked away in an antique shop vitrine. They were beautiful and rare-looking but through the glass they seemed lost, dusty and tired. After relinquishing a small amount of cash, I took them home and made them prized possessions by using them for my favorite recipe of panna cotta, fruit compotes, and even small brownie *a la mode* dessert cups. They are so beautiful! And because I love them, I find ways to promote them at parties, when unexpected neighbors or guests stop by, or even late at night for a quick granola and milk fix.

I realized I had been living among items that were not special to me at all. They were impersonal items others thought I would enjoy.

As time goes by, we accumulate so many items that we lose sight of what we love about them unless we use them or display them in a special place. This was the idea behind the great *one hundred*. We all too often become slaves of what we own, so it then owns us. We have to dust it, maintain it, store it, move it, or get rid of it.

It comes down to the question: Are all of my possessions considered wonderful and beautiful by me? The answer is not always financially based. Some items may be more expensive, perhaps, but not elegant, such as your expensive mustard yellow wool coat that swallows you up and has no elegant lines at all, or Aunt Mary's rock crystal elephant lamp stashed in the back of the attic.

You will never wear the coat because it is not beautiful or elegant nor does it even fit you. You ignore the elephant lamp in favor of your favorite antique Japanese imari vase lamp because it is much finer and more elegant.

After careful consideration of these things, I began to think that I wanted to exercise my eye in selective ownership, and began looking at my possessions as items that I either loved or as items I was just storing. It began with my busy travel schedule, where I was away from my home as much as I was there. I soon realized I was living with much less most of the time, either at the home of a friend or a hotel, and so I wondered what I really wanted surrounding me at my home that made me want to be there – the items that made it my *home*. It was a good exercise for me to eliminate over the months the unrefined items I had around my house, either by donating them, offering them to others who would love them, or just tossing them.

Over a period of time, I have replaced many of my less wonderful possessions with wonderful, beautiful items that are now considered my treasures and make me love coming home and being encircled by them. I enjoy being at home among this ambience and it is the ease of it – the effortless yet elegant look and feel of my home that seems to draw me.

Eventually, I realized that the things I possessed were not the things I truly enjoyed and loved to use or admire.

My home is my cocoon. It is not a matter of anti-materialism, but a matter of refining my taste so that I realized I had been living among items that were not special to me at all. They were impersonal items others thought I would enjoy, or mass-produced items that did not serve me well anymore. As you think about it, you will find a few items that no longer seem tasteful to you. You are refining your taste and you are exposing yourself to fine beautiful things, such as art and music. You have perhaps outgrown those items that are collecting dust in your home. Your refined taste will inevitably result in simple, fine discrimination, less clutter, and fewer but nicer belongings, even in your closet.

The average American owns so much "stuff" – but not wonderful, delightful possessions that make you want to dance among them. I questioned how many T-shirts the average American owns, and the first website I found (Answers.com) stated that it was thirty-five. I doubt that this was an actual survey of a cross-section of Americans, but it supports my point.

One hundred items sound like a lot when you first think of it, but over the years you accumulate things that may be given to you, not selected through your own discriminatory taste and never given away or returned or discarded. I realized that the things I possessed were not the things I truly enjoyed and loved to use or admire. Sprinkled among my treasures were things that were merely belongings.

Those things we choose to live among, use, and enjoy should be what we love, cherish, and always makes us happy. Those items should reflect who we are or who we are becoming when we glance at them.

In keeping with the idea of owning just a few great items, I developed my own 100 list a few years ago. Below is an excerpt.

- Russian antique ring box from my older sister on return from her first trip to Russia.
- An original oil by Lindy Bruggink, a friend and painter of Supreme Court justices.
- Madame de Rothschild demitasse set (the cups with the little birds hanging jewelry on the branches).
- Kings silver flatware found in an obscure New Orleans antique shop.
- 18th century French armoire from a Loire Valley estate.
- Etiquette book collection of first editions.
- Copper pots from France (I truly love cooking with them).
- Graduation gift of pearl earrings from my mother (they always make me smile).

- Game table from a French chateau discovered in a small furniture shop.
- Oriental cabinet from old Chinese hotel lobby bought from a store with unclaimed containers from China.
- Murano glass tray from my first trip to Venice where I fell in love with the people, culture and art.

Homework: List the top fifteen things you wish to acquire that would bring you closer to that lavish quality of being content with what you own. What current possessions would you exchange for those new fifteen items?

Purchasing wonderful, rare, one-of-a-kind items to enjoy and appreciate should make you more selective in how you determine gifts for others. The giving of appropriate and wonderful gifts is in itself part of the giving process. When thinking of someone special and what to bequeath to them, the criteria could be determined through questions such as:

- Does she have everything she wants and will this burden her or make her happy?

- What was the last thing I heard her say that indicates what she likes or dislikes passionately?

- Should I give her something ethereal instead of practical?

- What about something that is temporary, like an unusual plant, flowers, food, magazine subscription or notecards?

I was reminded recently that it is only worth a refined woman's time to give great gifts, or none at all. Poorly chosen gifts with very little or no thought are destined for the closet or worse fate, and the poor choice inevitably reflects on your taste.

Being too commercial in our gift giving results in the recipient thinking of the gift in ambivalence or perhaps disdain. I believe this is because we put too little effort in the selection process, or in the purchase, or the wrapping. My sister found some beautiful items for her friend's daughters who live in Paris. They were beautiful gifts but she placed them in gift bags with tissue. The eldest child (gregarious and forthright) asked why the gifts were not "wrapped". We often think so little of the recipient's awareness of elegance that we may choose to cut corners to save some time and not put as much thought into the "presentation" as in the gift itself.

Giving or receiving gifts and cards and the gracefulness with which we give and receive them is a wonderful custom.

Remembering birthdays and anniversaries with thoughtful gifts is a distinguished and gracious thing to do. Once you choose to do this, however, you must maintain it, even if it is a card every year to someone special for his or her birthday anniversary. Think of the anticipation of the recipient waiting to see what you have selected for them, particularly if yours becomes their favorite gift to open. You have set a precedent and cannot let that person down.

It must become your way of life to select wisely and find that perfectly elegant gift for those you love. With electronic calendars, it is easier than ever to put all your special dates in recurring mode and add reminders in advance of the occasion to allow sufficient time and thought for selection of the gift or card.

Wedding anniversaries are always fun and meaningful when you choose to purchase traditional gifts. How delightful for the bride of one year to receive something special from you made of paper for her very first anniversary, or for her husband to celebrate their *leather* anniversary with her favorite designer handbag to his wife of twelve years. The thoughtfulness behind the gift is what will ring true to people you love. Giving or receiving gifts and cards and the gracefulness with which we give and receive them is a wonderful custom.

Traditional anniversary gift categories:

    1st Paper /Clocks

    2nd Cotton /China

    3rd Crystal/Glass

    4th Fruit/Flowers /Appliances

    5th Wood /Silverware

    6th Candy/Iron /Wood

    7th Wool/Copper /Desk Sets

    8th Pottery/Bronze /Linens/Lace

    9th Willow/Pottery /Leather

    10th Tin/Aluminum /Diamond Jewelry

    15th Crystal /Watches

    20th China /Platinum

    25th Silver

    30th Pearl /Diamond

    40th Ruby

    50th Gold

    60th Diamond

The Sincere Thank You

There is a way to say *thank you* that has merit and weight to it. It is a genuine gesture of kindness, appreciation, and reciprocating honor. Saying *please* and *thank you* is the common courtesy spoken among all refined women and gentlemen, but the formal *thank you* upon receiving something of value (whether it is a delightful evening at someone's home, two tickets to the ballet, a beautiful gift, or a thoughtful visit when you are down) is far more complicated.

The thank-you note is often misunderstood and sometimes avoided. The *thank you* serves as a gesture of good will and appreciation for the time, thought and means spent by the giver. Once you truly understand this, you will always consider the feelings and enjoyment of someone receiving your gesture of thanks, be it a card, note, email, flowers or phone call.

This places you in a heartfelt mood capable of writing the most endearing note, or relaying the warmest gratitude. Depending on the occasion and cause, you should choose the transport of the thank you in a manner equal to the gift received. If you should receive a gift in person, warm thanks and a few words about how meaningful the gift is would be sufficient. If the gift was sent to you, a written thank-you note, or personal call if you are unable to send a note, is expected. If you are the guest at a party or dinner or special occasion, a written thank-you note, personal phone call, flowers, or small gift is appropriate within three days of the event.

Bringing gifts to a party is also a nice gesture, as long as you, the guest, are thinking of the host when choosing the gift. If you choose flowers wrapped in paper, this is most unthoughtful because the host has to leave her guests to put the flowers in a vase to show her appreciation of your gesture.

The French consider superfluous gifts given to hosts discourteous and in poor taste. Your French host is not expecting anything in return for her graciousness except your wonderful presence at her home or event. Your warmest thoughts in a thank-you note afterward are considered in taste and sufficient to satisfy her.

Weekends and holidays at someone's home requires a thoughtful gift such as specialty items from your part of the country, something that you know they like or need, a wonderful novel, or something to suit their lifestyle. Be wary of selecting anything too specific to a style or decorator fashion that may not be in keeping with their taste.

It may be better to purchase an item that is more in line with their personality. If you have been invited to stay at a home, it is expected you know them fairly well. Specialty foods are always a welcome treat as they are temporal in lieu of an item that must be found a home.

Giving of gifts in person is sometimes a difficult thing for a shy person. The fact that the recipient will dote on you and your gift is sometimes as daunting as finding that perfect gift for someone special. But the recipient should always be aware of your uneasiness at the attention, and will manage to find the place where you both have an enjoyable experience.

It is normally the case that someone who is a thoughtful gift giver is also a very clever thank-you note writer because the thoughtfulness appears in both the giving and receiving of a gift. Wrapping is also an indication of the honor and respect and love you have for the recipient of the gift. If it is thrown in a used gift bag, although the gift itself is perfect in every way, the first impression is less than beautiful and perfect and may spoil the luxury of the surprise inside; this could reduce the consideration of a rare and exceptional gift. Your wrapping helps with the anticipation of the special quality of the gift and the recipient.

Giving money as a gift is not particularly tasteful or personal, however, sometimes it is the only gift you are invited to give.

Graduation, funeral memorial, retirement, office group gift, or other events often just want "donations" of cash for certain reasons. When you personally give money, remember that the recipient has particularly requested it for a purpose. You should mention that purpose in the envelope or gift card. If it is your decision to give money for a specific purpose, or if the recipient does not note a purpose when asking for money, mention that you hope that the money is useful for their intended purpose or that it becomes useful and timely in their upcoming endeavors.

THE LOST ART OF ELEGANCE

Everyone wants a bit more glamour and elegance in their life, and that is why we often turn to Hollywood. The glamour actors represent in their roles and real lives seems to transport us from our mundane jobs, homes and lives.

But what if we could actually add a bit of Hollywood's mystique and glamour in our own lives rather than live vicariously through those people? What if we decided to eat dinner by candlelight and whisper sweet poetry wearing a satin robe and red lipstick? Is this something that matters to you? Do you long for and want the glamourous life from time to time? Is that why we as women turn to beautiful shoes and handbags to exemplify a sense of style and fashion that raises us up into an echelon of taste and class, getting a sense of "stardom" from time to time?

I have seen women purchase designer items to feel like they are elevating their status in society, only to be disappointed that they are still the same women when they look in the mirror – and now perhaps with a huge credit card bill. The issue here is that women believe social status will give them class. It actually works against a woman to move up in society but not have the core ethical values that are required to mingle with all of society, or to take up her responsibilities toward others without being dissuaded from compromising or falling into scandal.

Values such as trustworthiness, respect, responsibility, fairness, caring, and citizenship are what really matter in life – these are the core values of a woman of integrity and class. Integrity is something we all want, and either fight to retain or give up for a price. Unfortunately, it is (as the old proverb says) like "putting lipstick on a pig" – unless there has been an internal makeover, the person is the same as before, and just because she has changed the outside, there is no guarantee of a lasting benefit to her. Even if her choosing this lifestyle gave her a few weeks, months or years of feeling better about herself, without a real change in her attitude, she is still the same person.

It is better for a woman to respect her state and be the best she can be within her means, realizing that most people see through a facade to her genuine temperament.

The underlying issue is that we must respect ourselves first to change our outer habits and ways of manner. We must become content but never satisfied; this is the challenge of every woman who is looking for the best life for herself and the ones she loves.

It is better for a woman to respect her state and be the best she can be within her means, realizing that most people see through a facade to her genuine temperament and her substance, which is her character. I am friends with women in all walks of life who have embraced their position in society with dignity and grace. Making their own way in life is admirable, given the education and opportunities they have been given.

A clean, well-pressed dress from the bargain basement worn with shoulders back and head held high is statelier than a woman who has clawed her way up the social ladder and does not know how to behave properly. Respect for who you are inside comes first. That woman who clawed her way, if she still has any conscience left at all, will not stand tall next to the housekeeper or dishwasher who has remained true to herself. Remember, the more you have, the more is required of you, in society and in life.

 Homework: List 15 things that you would like to do to become a more interesting person to YOU. After each item on the list, give reasons why this will benefit you. Once you have finished this book, go back and review the list and see if you have incorporated some of your ideas – make them actionable items.

I make my list every January and keep it handy through the year. I check off what I have accomplished, and add ideas that come to mind. The idea is for me to think beyond what I normally do that would open doors to a bigger life than what I have presently. Some of the items on my list are very small and some are great tasks I hope to achieve. Here are a few examples:

- Take a class or read a book about stocks and bonds (what is a bull and what is a bear?!)
- Brown bag lunch at a nearby art museum. Listen to the lecturer or guide or take a docent tour (I love the fascinating information about the artists and their works)
- Use herbs in cooking (I will even learn about those edible flowers)
- Frequent the local library; check out the art history books (it will keep me loving art and remind me why I do)
- Listen to a different kind of music (oh, do I really have to?)
- Join a book club (or start one once I know how to do it)
- Smile when talking on the phone (it will actually make me listen more intently and friendly)

So, you get the idea: there must be reason and cause for doing these new ventures – what is in it for *you?*!

- Take a night class on music, or listen to podcasts. Find a favorite composer and learn all about him/her.
- Light a candle at dinner time.
- Wear a dress instead of jeans.

- Purchase a three-way mirror.
- Stop wearing jogging clothes and jogging shoes unless you are jogging or going directly to or from exercise class.
- Have a glowing complexion by observing the weekend Dr. Perricone diet.
- Update your Look Book.
- Spend more time and attention on your hair and makeup before going out.
- Create a "maintenance corner" in your closet and begin to put things there that need your attention. Keep the tools handy that might be necessary to maintain your wardrobe, including a dry-cleaning bag, lint roller and clothes brush, shoe polish/brush kit, skirt clips, and good hangers.
- Choose to wear things that do not have designer labels on them.

Once you make your list and begin to review and revise it, you will see how enjoyable it is to do some of these things, and you will find the time to do them, since they are now a priority and you have listed the reasons you want to incorporate them into your day to day routine. You will begin to enjoy a more sophisticated and elegant life.

GRACE AND MANNER

Conversation

The first skill in gracefulness and good manners is to be yourself wherever you are and whoever you are with. Mastering this is not simply *hanging out* with everyone. Your refined manner should be naturally pleasant and agreeable.

The objective in developing your conversational skills is to bring your personality into its own *flowering* of richness and beauty. The opposite of this would be to develop specific singular idiosyncrasies that make you stand out. In *The Body Book*, Cameron Diaz mentions the value of spending time with people, and how important community is. She touts cooking with others, and spending time laughing with them. Being social has many health benefits, and will enhance your conversation skills as well.

Most people do not spend much of their time with uninspiring people, so your stylishness must balance your kind nature if you are going to practice being yourself with everyone, particularly in conversing. No one likes to be catered to. Temper *sweet* with a little *salty* – that is what makes you an interesting, intriguing, and fun person to be around. In social circles, the same faces and same people result in the same event. People desire differences of opinion and personality. You can manage this by being a great conversationalist, maybe conservative at first, then adding more of your sparkly personality and opinions as you get to know others.

A good conversationalist is a good listener: unselfish, focused, attentive and inquisitive. She has worked on her speech, her voice, and her vocabulary, constantly improving them to become pleasant to be around. She whispers when necessary to get her point across.

There is a relatively new manner of speech that is not only annoying, but seems to have taken over the entire world: the "sing-song" list. This occurs when a person is listing several things in conversation, and seems to go up in pitch and sing the last few items of the list. This dialect has taken over America and I have even heard British anchorwomen with this horrid habit. The tone and pitch changes used to be indicative of *valley girl speech,* but now appears in formal and serious newscasts and programs. This type of swing of the voice is unattractive and only indicates a type of slang in the song-like nature of the speaker's inflections. Although it is now an epidemic among conversers, it is something that is to be considered as unrefined, and unconventional. We should consider this lack of formal word formation and intonation of speech a disappointment and misuse of how conversational talk should sound. Not only the sing-song but vulgarity in speech and misuse of the English language makes one wonder where it will go from here.

In practicing your voice inflections, avoid the following:

- Loud, high-pitched voice.
- Too fast or too slow speech.
- Monotone with no variation at all.
- Mumbling and trailing words at the end of a sentence.

Whispering is a separate category of good speech. It can be the very best tool to get someone's attention, and is useful in interesting private conversation. (*Think: whisper = personal, serious, special information*).

Controlling the volume of your speech, and pitch variation is a way of making your conversation more interesting. So do the following:

- A smooth cadence – not too fast, and not too slow
- No major accent, try to enunciate words in the simplest of fashion.
- Use words that fully describe your thoughts to the best of your vocabulary, as your intentions are always to avoid being misunderstood (or misquoted, or mis-*tweeted*).
- A low comfortable pitch. An abrasive pitch causes the listener to tune it out. The important conversation may be indifferently received due to the pitch of the voice.

Prior to stating something that might be harmful or painful or disagreeable to someone, ask yourself: *is this absolutely necessary?*

As a good conversationalist, you should attempt to be somewhat pleasing to everyone, even when sacrificing your own self-interest. It is important in social settings to be yourself within reason, but also to be able to conform to the social standards of doing things without giving up who you are in doing so. There is a fine line between following social graces and being totally yourself. Seek to find that balance that creates an elegant air about you, and make sure you are following a certain amount of social protocol to be included among persons of refinement.

Remember when conversing to tone down your opinion *soapbox*. The proper way to express your personality is a fine line between being yourself and making sure you are not too judgmental and opposed to everything and everyone. Some people seek to speak with charm and ease, while others tend to disarm, disagree, and debate the subject matter until all have relinquished their sword. Crossing swords when speaking to someone on a matter where there are differences of opinion is a delicate matter between the personalities of the speakers.

It is great sport to the French to debate in conversing, and they will purposely take the opposite side of your opinion to do so. This is great fun to some people, and the art of doing it well and playing within the rules of engagement in such activities is beyond most of us. We would rather have a debate and come to a conclusion than dance around the subject in a sort of rhetorical tennis volley.

In a social setting, you might ask yourself prior to stating something that might be harmful or painful or disagreeable to someone, *is there a necessity in stating this?* If there is not, you might want to refrain from saying it. This is a sort of *tact* that most people do not possess anymore. They speak without thought about what they say and how it will affect anyone within ears' reach.

A refined woman's manner is never aggressive, blunt or rude. She is sincere, but fair and tempered about all things she speaks about. She knows the proper things to say that are acceptable and appropriate. Even when there is a bit of political debate involved in the discussion, statements are made with charm and grace, at times persuasive, perhaps, but never with the intent of strong-arming or being bullish in mentioning these matters.

A great conversationalist knows how to "give and take" in the art of speaking, conversing, and debating with someone else. She seeks and desires *a gentle eloquence* in her speech and discussion that is becoming, rather than vulgar and overbearing.

Being unique is sometimes a distraction, but you must be ready to take your position if you purposely and quietly let your thoughts and opinions be known, especially if your position may be counter to the other person's opinion. It is most refined that you always remain true to yourself, with a simple healthy self-respect along with a respect for others; this attitude will benefit you greatly in conversation and life in general.

If you are a person who would rather shy away from conversation, try *proactive listening.*

Pretense for the objective of impressing others is essentially unrefined. The tasteful do not show any pretense, they are well-mannered and show gracefulness, not strained or forced formality. It is better to be yourself until you have acquired the tasteful eloquence of a well-bred person, having exercised those essential skills of respect for others and self. No socially adept person pretends he or she is more than they are. They are accepting of themselves and put that secondary to their position in society and responsibilities.

If you are placed in a position of authority or management over others, your placement there is a great test of your social graces, and how you treat others. There is a hierarchy in business as well as society, but knowing your position and becoming the best person in that placement is your duty, responsibility and privilege.

If you are a person who would rather shy away from conversation, try proactive listening. This involves all of your perceptiveness and sensory skills in actively hearing what the speaker is saying, with the idea that you comprehend it, and process it, wondering what has not been said. This can lead to good questions and answers and right away you are one of the conversationalists in the group because you are continuing the subject with the speaker and enjoying it more than you are aware of yourself (shy people are tremendously self-aware). This results in a great time by all involved.

Small talk, as defined by one author, is "amiable, unhurried communication," and can be very important in the formation of friendly acquaintances as well as forging business agreements. Both kinds of introductory "meetings" necessitate small talk as an introduction to the real delicate, formal, and interesting conversations that lie ahead in both cases (forging friendships and business contracts).

 Small talk is encouraged in all business lunches, social events and dinners, as well as grocery lines, airports, and neighborhoods. It is one of the areas of speech that very few understand and give import. Small talk does not preclude the use of a solid, extensive vocabulary but will highlight it, when used appropriately in a friendly tone.

Be aware that there are certain times that small talk will not be invited. Such times might include when someone is seriously engaged in their business and small talk would be an interruption. Another time would be when there is a meeting of two people and you attempt to join in with small talk. Unless you understand the conversation you are interrupting, it is not wise to speak at all until acknowledged by the two people conversing.

Topics of Conversation

1. Overview of recent performance at symphony, ballet, or opera
2. Synopsis of new book that might be of interest
3. Highlights of a new movie or television series
4. Upcoming program, movie or performance you have heard about
5. Good news about someone familiar to group
6. Sports information, news, or highlights
7. Facts on health, exercise and nutrition recently learned or tried
8. Items of interest from that day's newspaper or e-journal

   Not suggested:

1. Your own wealth or that of anyone else
2. Ongoing rhetoric on a depressing story in that day's newspaper

3. Injury or death of someone popular
4. Asking or discussing overly personal information
5. Asking or discussing details of a surgery, injury, accident
6. Criticism of major and eminent persons, including the President of a country or the United States
7. Hot political debates (they could backfire on you, so steer away unless challenged)

Greetings - the Beginning

The way you handle greetings will set you apart as someone who is capable of ease in any situation. You should always be prepared with a formal, yet warm greeting for all occasions.

How do you do is a proper greeting, but a genuine, *hello, how are you* may be the proper greeting in some circumstances. Decide on the personal greeting that you will use in general conversation and stay with that. When you have a genuine greeting that you use all the time, it will seem real and genuine and never fake or false.

The simple *how do you do* rings true with all people and it is really a statement, not a question. The response should simply be *how do you do*. In America, we are adjusted to the ease of *hello* – that, however, does not set a person apart from anyone else because anyone can reasonably state the word *hello* in a gentle fashion. What are the terms of your greeting? Do you want to continue the conversation or just say *hello* and move on? Your intention should be noted in your very first words of greeting. If you appear rushed and just say *hello*, and move on, you will appear annoyed and stressed, which is the opposite of the appearance you want to give to others. You should face them straight on, greet them, wait to be greeted back, and then, based on both body languages, either begin a conversation or move on.

REFINEMENT *of* MANNER
Becoming an Elegant, Distinguished, Twenty-First Century Woman

You should always be prepared to introduce your companions or be introduced to (and be able to recall) your greeter's companion(s), if any. Remember, a greeting sets the stage for the rest of your time in front of this person or persons. Make it genuinely warm and friendly, yet formal enough to show class so that it becomes your *signature*.

It has been said that an appropriate and proper greeting will make a good first impression. This is the beginning of how you choose to refine your *manner*, in small, selective ways that will make a difference in how you feel and the reaction you get from others.

Homework: Determine to speak only half as much as you listen this week. You will have plenty to say after hearing much information from others during the week. You will also appear more mysterious for not talking so much. Memorize the great people of our generation: The Nobel prize winner, the presidents, prime ministers, heads of state in other countries, but particularly become familiar with the names of the Chiefs of Staff of the President, the vice president and leading persons in Congress. You should also know your own governor and important political figures of your state. This will always come up on conversation and just knowing their names and titles will help you in conversing.

CHAPTER 8 – A REFINED TASTE

"My tastes are simple: I am easily satisfied with the best." Churchill

DISTINCTIVELY RARE

Refined taste is always paired with distinctive simplicity. Once you have developed taste, all the mediocre items you own will no longer seem discriminating enough for you. I purchased a great vintage Chanel coat a few years ago, and I found I was reaching for it over all of my other choices. It was not necessarily because of the label but because of the craftsmanship and fit, unique design and detail, colors, and best of all, how I felt when I wore it. I knew I would wear it for many years, and would reach for it instead of other coats. That is when I realized other less elegant items I had purchased were just taking up space in my closet. Those items became stepping stones in my journey and quest for elegance and refinement. Some of them were purchased on a whim, others were thoughtful purchases that I wore for years. I truly enjoyed wearing them until I acquired the demure and sophisticated coat with the princess lines, pink and blue threads woven throughout a sea of squid ink boucle that made me look and feel fabulously chic and elegant. I don it often and never realize how many times I reach for it. I do not need a lot of coats living in the South, so it makes sense to have one or two great coats I will love for the next ten years and never tire of wearing.

The great ink colored coat is one example of wearing what you love. It is the way of fewer and simpler wardrobe choices but *great* ones, where anything you pull out of the closet should: 1. fit you, 2. be clean and pressed, 3. suit your unique elegant style, and, 4. make you look and feel great. *(What was I doing with all those extra garments just taking up space in my closet?!)*

Here was a lesson in how I wanted my entire life to be: simple, uncluttered by frivolities and non-useful items and, best of all, elegant. I really mean my *entire* life, including my dishes, flatware, glassware, furniture, linens, and even my front porch. It has been an evolution, and the quest is still shaping and influencing my identity and love for beauty.

I credit my art background, good books, and a few truly sophisticated and elegant friends over the years who have inspired me and influenced my taste. The experiences have taught me to surround myself with beauty, beautiful things, beautiful experiences and places, and honest, inspiring people. Growing up in the South, with its slower pace and people-oriented atmosphere, also caused me to live my life simpler, finer, quieter, and with more sophistication and style. Yet you can aspire to this no matter where you were raised, and you can find inspiration everywhere.

YOUR DECORATING STYLE

If you have chosen to have people around you, you will eventually open up your home to them (whether it be a dorm room or a castle). Whether inviting a few guests or entertaining lavishly, your distinctive possessions and beautiful objects will be on display for others to admire (and scrutinize). Entertaining is not for the faint of heart. Therefore it is important to perform a quiet, slow, full walk-through of your home. Look for items and areas that are not as elegant as you desire them to be. This gives you the opportunity to attempt to look at your home as others would when they visit you.

Professionals can also review your style and décor and accessories, and offer suggestions and advice on how to make it elegant and people-friendly. They can offer ideas on how to create a flow for guests throughout your home. Sometimes a new set of eyes can be more objective in how to display your favorite things than you can, who live among those items day in and day out.

Whether inviting a few guests or entertaining lavishly, your distinctive possessions and beautiful objects will be on display for others to admire (and scrutinize). Entertaining is not for the faint of heart.

The objective of elegant entertaining is to have an ease and sophistication about your place so that it shows who you are and how you live. It should be impeccably clean and clutter-free, while being warm and inviting with a personal touch throughout.

Entertaining at home is nearly forgotten in our hectic world. It may be due to a lack of confidence in their taste and sophistication that has deterred many women from inviting guests to their homes. The idea of others inspecting your living space is pretty daunting. Because of the audacity of some guests, it is relentlessly stressful. Several years ago dinner parties became popular among young couples. This seemed like a great idea, until you find yourself committed to the weekend that your family chose to have a reunion, or committed eleven months ago to the evening that just happened to be your best friend's wedding. It goes on and on why we seldom plan far in advance and commit ourselves and our home to a group of individuals we may barely know.

So the best way to become more comfortable in entertaining at home is to entertain on your terms. Perhaps having an outdoor party is most comfortable, as guests only return into the house to freshen up.

Another idea is to have a cocktail hour in the living area, and dinner in the dining room, with the rest of the home closed off. This allows you to have private areas but entertain in some of your loveliest and most interesting rooms.

And finally, if you just love entertaining and enjoying your friends but your home is not an option, host a luncheon or tea at a great restaurant or other public venue. You get the best of both worlds: you can concentrate completely on the enjoyment factor, and let the restaurant staff or caterer do the rest.

To cater or not to cater. It is always a nice touch when you, as host, have prepared something personally to serve your guests. If that is too stressful, your caterer can prepare your favorite recipes to your specifications, leaving you the role of entertaining your guests.

Home entertaining begins with a welcome atmosphere and order. No one feels comfortable when they are in a home that is a patchwork of styles, colors and ideas – it's too busy to relax and enjoy conversation. The eye moves around the room and cannot relax or focus on the people.

A home is best when it is completely one decorating style or something that flows from room to room and is invitingly charming and elegant, whether it is modern, contemporary, French/Italian, English, Oriental or a stylish mixture. The idea is to create a master painting, creating a space where you place items of various interest to move your guests' eyes around the room in a sort of "order" to create a delightful setting for companionship and conversation.

Your goal is to have a place that is beautiful but quiet, not screaming for attention but rather invitingly calm. Comfort, ease and style are essential, so what is your decorator style? There are many ways to define a mood, expression, or feeling with décor. Whether you are a student, a single woman, married, divorced or widowed, you can create a home that is fun and elegant for having friends over. Even the simplest table can be elegant, if the surroundings are not distracting or so eclectic they disrupt the ambience you wish for your guests.

 Fresh flowers, linen napkins, candles, and other accoutrements will add your signature to the event, and will always exude a generous and luxurious mood for you.

Remember to serve coffee, tea and dessert after the meal. It is a gracious way to allow everyone more time together, yet control the end of a beautiful evening or luncheon.

Not everyone has acquired or even desired to own silver flatware, china, crystal and formal serving trays. It is not as important to have the finest of these if you create the formality of elegance in another way. If you are hosting a dinner party on a limited budget, one way to make your pasta and salad entrée appear more elegant is with candles, garnish, and a color theme. These are key ingredients to showing your talent for "dressing up" the meal.

Social Elegance

The Echelon of Events – THE GALA

One of the finest social events you may attend is the Ball or Gala Ball. Cinderella and her stepsisters might have been your first introduction to the Ball, but hopefully not your last. A Gala Ball is synonymous with lavishness and splendor. If the event is not up to this category, it should not be considered a Gala Ball. This wonderfully elegant event is in a separate category of entertaining altogether. It should be anticipated with much expectancy and preparation as it is the epitome of sophistication and decorum. From music to menu to entertainment to décor, it is fashioned as the highest echelon of social parties and must be taken for such (*Think: Debutante Ball, Opera Ball, Metropolitan Museum Ball*).

 The most important thing about ita Gala is *the quality,* from setting the mood at the entrance, to greetings and preludes, to the table, the menu, the entertainment and music, and finally to the people in all their finery – elegant quality prevails. It is either to be the finest of everything available, or it should not be attempted. If there is a budget that is not capable of supporting the event to its expected standard, it should not be undertaken.

The very words "Gala Ball" exude grandeur in all facets. If circumstances prevent having premium food, elegant decorations, gracious and spaciously elegant tables and dance floor, and exquisite music, it is not to be endeavored. It is never to be undertaken with economy in mind. If the Gala is designed as a charity event or fundraiser, it should not be considered the type of Ball that is equal to the balls I am referring to. If a fundraiser is going to be considered an elegant ball where excessive luxury is the key component, the very idea of raising money for charity must be quite hidden from the guests. The table price should be taken care of months before the event, but the event itself is designed for pure enjoyment, excessive extravagance, and unequivocal ambience.

Invitations of engraved quality are sent out months in advance of the event. Great suspense is created through the invitation with additional expectancy leading up to the special evening through contact from the chairpersons or hosts. The expectation is heightened through the wonder at how this ball will be even greater than previous ones. Women procure the finest hairdressers, makeup artists, jewels, and elaborate and beautiful ball gowns (*Think: long full skirt, elegant, and definitely extravagant fabric and details*). Men prepare for the event through expert grooming and donning impeccable white-tie attire. The ballroom is transformed by the finest floral companies and designers. Elaborate table settings and menus are scrutinized by the best catering firms obtainable. Budgets are not always followed when planning a gala ball of any consequence.

Should a private event be planned, the word *ball* is never used on the invitation. "White Tie" signifies to both men and women how to dress for the occasion, and white tie always signifies the finest occasion.

More should be written on the importance of knowing how to properly attend a Gala Ball. Pomp and circumstance are required. There are certain understood manners meticulously followed. It should be clear that accepting an invitation to a Gala is ensuring your host you are prepared to conduct yourself formally and tastefully in all aspects at the occasion. Once you understand how to conduct yourself at a Gala, your demeanor at any event has forever improved.

TASTE IN POSSESSIONS

Everyone has their own idea of *taste* and there is no such thing as good or bad taste. There is only *taste*. Each possession you own is either tasteful or not tasteful. It should reflect your elegance, fineness, quality, and what is pleasing to the eye (beautiful).

Our belongings are those things of material value or intrinsic value that we attain, use, sometimes adore, and maintain. As you become refined in taste, you will see your possessions in a different light and adjust accordingly.

Timing Your Purchases

Here are the best months to purchase certain items; in addition, the intelligent woman of the twentieth-first century knows the best times to purchase items according to local cycles, special discounts, and other information.

Possessions should be our own choices and what we possess usually defines who we are.

She is savvy in how to purchase, and can wait for an item she knows will be reduced during certain times of the year. She plans her budget and purchases accordingly as well as reviewing her list of gifts to ensure she can obtain the very best items she can afford. Possessions should be our own choices and what we possess usually defines who we are.

- January – clothing, Broadway tickets, carpeting, furniture, gift cards, linens, motorcycles, suits, video games
- February – Broadway tickets, television and home theatres.
- March – chocolate, frozen foods, golf clubs, luggage
- April – cruises, sneakers
- May – refrigerators, mattresses, office furniture
- June – dishware, gym memberships and equipment, tools
- July – furniture, home décor, tools, video games
- August – linens and storage, office furniture, kids clothing, office supplies, swimsuits
- September – appliances, bicycles, Broadway tickets, cars, lawnmowers, holiday airfare, office supplies, wine
- October – appliances, jeans, patio furniture
- November – appliances, candy, televisions and other electronics, tools

- December – champagne, golf clubs, pools, televisions & other electronics, tools

Refined Taste in Clothing

You have read ideas on how to elevate your wardrobe with some style and taste, how to find those pieces that look best on your body type, skin coloring, eyes, and hair color. You have been reminded of ideas to improve your choice and selections to find the best quality you can afford and love your clothes and how they look on you, making you look tasteful, elegant, and selective.

Other women may not have found this in their own lives yet, and for those who have trouble putting their outfits together to look great, I would suggest starting with a type of *uniform* that you look well in. Try a certain type of dress or suit and wear that for some period of time, adding different pieces with it until you look like someone out of Vogue or Glamour. We think that changing our look everyday will make us happy. Nothing is further from the truth. Selective choices added to a basic wardrobe will add order and calmness to your dressing habits, rather than more stress in having too many choices.

It is important to feel good in what you are wearing, and that comes with refining your taste until you feel like no one else could wear your outfit better than you. This is the kind of feeling of happiness in your clothes, knowing you have developed taste in your own style and type of clothing for your life.

We could discuss all the women who fall short of this ideal. They seem to be everywhere, wearing running tights and crop tops to the grocery, donning skimpy shorts with low-cut tops to shop at department stores, or even to local restaurants for lunch, and flip flops to church. It is a disgrace that a woman does not care enough about her appearance to be well put together and elegant in these scenarios. Thankfully, most of us learn by example. By continuing to refine your taste in clothes, others will see how confident you are and perhaps seek refined changes in their own lives. They will perhaps determine to work at developing a better look. As it is with everything, they have to desire it.

CULTIVATING FRIENDSHIPS

There are many types of friends we can have, but the premise remains the same for all friendships: ***they must be cultivated, or developed, over time***. Your friends are your support group, whether they all know each other or not, whether you have friends from varying walks of life and groups.

The friends you cherish are the ones with whom you invest time. Those persons you find interesting and have some like-mindedness in some areas of life are those friends that you will nurture the best relationships with. The persons who mean the most to you for specific reasons are the ones you seem to gravitate to in good times and in bad. There are days when you just want to spend time with someone easy to be with, someone who knows you, and will be there to listen to you about anything or nothing. Those are the individuals you foster friendships with, giving no thought to the effort or expenditure.

In developing your selective friendships keep in mind the following:

1. *Fast-paced life.* Life is fast-paced and we all have responsibilities and commitments. This pressure can cause friends to be less accessible, and it may require a decision to actively develop and work at finding mutually beneficial times to be together.
2. *Life changes us.* We all go through changes in our lifetime, and therefore are not always in the "same place" as our friends. Understanding this can assist in retaining friendships over the years.
3. *Common bond of trust and respect.* When friendships are based on caring, respecting, and trusting, you have a mutual bond that becomes an inner sanctum. You can have *inside the*

vault talks that you cherish and look forward to with a close friend you may not get to see very often but you always pick up where you left off.

4. *Endeavor to savor.* Determination to be with a person for a specific time period is a commitment to be available and to make an effort to get together even when inconvenient. The lasting friendship of a few close people is something that takes an effort but reaps the lifetime benefits of development of a wholeness of character. You are a better person for having friends and keeping friends through the years. Petty jealousies, misunderstandings, and scandalous gossip do not separate or alienate real friends. These friendships can be strengthened through facing conditions that would attempt to break up a lasting bond.

Refined Friendships

We have already discussed the importance of cultivating friendships: keeping true old friends, and making new friends over your lifetime. Now we want to delve into the idea of refining your lifestyle and allowing your true friends to get to know you through the process.

True friends are often rare to find and even more difficult to keep. The only way to nurture a friendship is to be a friend. Once there is mutual understanding, and you both have developed a mutual respect for each other, you can truly rely on this person to be there for you, as you assure her/him you will be there for her/him.

We are so caught up in our own busy worlds that when we have a friend, we assume they understand how busy we are, and expect them to make the effort to be with us. This is not a way to develop or maintain a friendship. Mutual respect is not there, neither is the mutual affection. Friendships are based on commonality in some senses, and refined friendships are all the more respectful of each other and time constraints. It is a give and take, and the refined woman understands her place in this role and truly has understanding in how to cultivate her friendships through time with them, allowing access to her life.

A real friend can cushion any blow to us, keep us sane during times of an insane world, and always seem to know what to say when we need it.

You may be the one to initiate the meetings, conversations, phone calls, and letters or emails most of the time with your friend, but if this is an important person in your life and you know she desires the friendship, the elegant woman is willing to put in a bit more time and energy into the relationship, knowing that her leadership and desire will either take root with her friend and grow their friendship into something valuable to both, or she will eventually have to reduce her efforts to allow her friend to step into the role of initiating more of the visits and phone calls.

You may be the one to initiate the meetings, conversations, phone calls, and letters or emails most of the time with your friend, but if this is an important person in your life and you know she desires the friendship, the elegant woman is willing to put in a bit more time and energy into the relationship, knowing that her leadership and desire will either take root with her friend and grow their friendship into something valuable to both, or she will eventually have to reduce her efforts to allow her friend to step into the role of initiating more of the visits and phone calls.

If there is absolutely no reciprocation, request a meeting and find out if something has placed a wedge between you. Be honest and find out where you both are in your lives, so that you can either resume, or rebuild the friendship, or let it cool for a season. As nice as it seems that you will always have your good friends from your childhood or high school, it is not always the case. We go through so many changes in our lives that having old and dear friends sounds wonderful, but if older friendships begin to wane, it may just be the natural cycle of a friendship that may end at some point. Make sure that it is not something that you caused or created, but insist that you both are honest and open. The elegant woman is honest when she is terminating or cooling off a relationship of any kind. She honors that person sufficiently to give them the respect of an explanation. You have then created a proper acquaintance from a friend, and perhaps time will bring the two of you together again. It needs to be about two adult individuals understanding any differences. You want to determine if your lives have drifted apart, if this is a new chapter for both of you as continued friends or not. You may desire to maintain a friendship and your friend is feeling like it is not valuable anymore. A parting of the minds and hearts occurs and is more painful for the party who wanted to maintain the friendship.

When you respect someone, you hold them in high regard, as you should with your dearest friends.

Sometimes the best friendships are our oldest friends. There was no agenda "back then" and the friendship was based on honest care for each other's best. As you get older, new friends can have agendas in why they want to be friends with you. It will take a longer time to decide if that person has an agenda, or is going to be loyal to you. This will determine the depth of the friendship. No matter how long it has been between visits with some of my dearest friends, we just *pick up where we left off*, and that makes for a comfortable relationship.

Is there everlasting loyalty between friends no matter what? We all change, but your integrity and soul want to believe in lasting friendships. Parting ways with old friends is a part of life, but not the easiest to accept. New friends may replace those old trusted ones, and life goes on, but tragically, the history between the old friends is buried.

A real friend can cushion any blow to us, keep us sane during times of an insane world, and always seem to know what to say when we need it. , Still, although a friendship is based on trust and affection and mutual benefit, friendships are *not* based on need, but on commonality, honesty, trust and respect.

When you respect someone, you hold them in high regard, as you should with your dearest friends. If you are attempting to make new friends with someone, be patient and remember that you must reach out to them and get to know them before really engaging and trusting them as a dear friend.

Many women go in and out of friendships during their twenties and thirties. They realize that the differences in their lives are bigger than the likenesses (single vs. married with children). What commonality do they share except their desire to remain friends and share their differences with each other? And yet, there are many women who have retained a sisterly friendship with women they met at a very early age. The study of the lives of two friends is beautifully portrayed in the movie *Beaches*. The two women's upbringings and life philosophies were very different, yet they worked to make sure the friendship stayed alive. Hollywood's twists and turns made sure it was a classic *chick flick* (bring your handkerchief).

Girlfriends often meet to resolve each other's problems (guy friends bond on a more social level). This problem-solving is not always the case with women, but we do have our moments when we are our best friend's biggest cheerleader, ready to defend her against her critics who would try to harm her or make her cry.

There is nothing as dear and tender as a true girlfriend. It is not like any other relationship. The elegant woman is selective in who she shares her life with, who she deems worthy and willing to invest as much as she herself does. You must discover who is willing to devote her time with you and you with her.

There is a test of friendships that must be determined as you grow apart over the years. Friends are forever, we naïvely expect, but we also hopefully believe that some *really are* forever. Some friends may have moved away or you may have lost touch with them for a while. It is never too late to start up a dormant friendship again, if she is willing. You might need to remind her of how much you value her friendship before she gives in and meets or talks to you over the phone. Often, persistence will pay off and she will recall how you maintained the friendship because it was important to you. She *is* important to you.

Everyone needs to know they are important to someone, particularly old friends. If either of you have changed a lot since your last visit together, there is sufficient history with that old friend to bring it back to the forefront and choose to continue to stay in contact, no matter how often or seldom it is for both of you. Friends are a part of your soul, and you cannot live without soul.

Refined Activities

As our taste changes, so does our desire for certain activities. You may have liked drag races or swim meets growing up, but now they seem loud and boring to you. You have expanded your horizons to take in the arts, music, and other endeavors that may suit you better.

As your taste changes you may find more enjoyment from other activities. And finding more leisure time in your life, you may choose to take up new pastimes and activities. I learned to play golf one summer when I was on a part-time project and had my afternoons free, and I still enjoy it tremendously. I have made great friends through the sport. The people I have met through golf are intelligent and interesting. When you spend four hours on a Saturday morning with three other people, hopefully, all four of you become interesting to each other. Golf is very social, as is Polo. Other good social events are tennis, exercise classes, Sunday teas, charities, clubs, and other organizations –all are great ways to experience new and interesting activities with nice people. Remember the selective process and make sure that you are passionate about these activities. You will reap more enjoyment through events and activities that motivate you.

Refined Living Space

There are many "decorator styles" to choose from, but to get you thinking toward your own distinctive style and comfort of stylishness for your home, here are three basic types of decorating views.

1. Formal –You have a flair for putting formal pieces together to look cosmopolitan and classy. You use dark and light, with white spaces and very little clutter. *Spacious, youthful* and *elegant* are the keywords you live by. You gravitate toward items considered masterpieces of beauty and function and you use all of your best pieces in entertaining. You are not afraid of formality and love to sit down to a formal dinner party. You adhere to rich color and contrast wooden antiques with more modern pieces. You think formal in all you do, from the silver cup where your toothbrush rests to the posh pillow cases you have acquired to get the highest-quality sleep.

2. Country French /Italian –You love the idea of an outdoor kitchen where you can entertain on a lawn beside the rows of grapes in a wine village. *Think: all things blue, white and lavender.* You create the illusion of stepping out of a French foreign film, and pay special attention to the details that give that feeling. A combination of comfort and class is your shining glory in entertaining and you want everyone to feel at home in your elegant lifestyle of outdoor luxurious landscaping. You utilize all those things you have acquired and have on display for use and admiration. You seem a bit old-fashioned in that you are not high-minded about your entertaining, yet you have an ease and elegance that states: "I love the finer things and so does my company." You go all out. Your motto is: Everyone welcome! You strive to make the seating family style yet do not shy away from collecting the best of everything that you want to own and entertain with. You love to travel and enjoy lively discussions on a variety of topics. You invite an eclectic group to dine with you for the company and great conversations. You want your guests to feel like they are entering a chateau and vineyard because, in your opinion, it is the most pleasant place to be!

3. Vintage Chic – This third category can be termed the least formal of the group. This is the eclectic collection of various beautiful "misfits" that are adored by you. You simply cannot part with these items so you have integrated them into your lifestyle and customs and décor. This is the type of home and entertaining fashion that is always a surprise and wonder to guests, who feel so honored just to be a part of the celebration. You love fresh-cut flowers everywhere in vases, buckets and odd containers that make your friends smile and feel welcome and treated well. You choose beautiful patterns to mix and match, creating a haven of good cheer and well wishes to all who enter.

There is no common thread between these three ideas for decorating, just as there will be no common thread for your decorating and someone else's. These ideas are just a way to get you to think about how you want to entertain, your lifestyle, where you are most comfortable, and what ambience makes you feel the loveliest as a host. You can create a beautiful palette of color and texture and wellbeing as you create the warmth of your home and make it entertainment-ready.

Homework: This month, invest some time at the library or bookstore looking through decorator books and magazines. Take photos of those things that seem to be your taste or could enhance your home. Subscribe to interior design magazines that you are attracted to. Search websites for ideas. Research is a great way to find your very own personal touch to enhance your lovely home. List the top ideas you find and put these on an annual "to purchase list" and keep handy when tempted to buy another dress, coat, or pair of shoes – budget for home items instead. Make it personal: add a "Welcome Home" mat at your back doorstep.

This is not a book devoted to entertaining or decorating, however the idea of your home environment is particularly important since you are becoming a refined woman and have developed desires to entertain and be around other interesting people. A review of your home will also make you feel more in charge of your living space and perhaps see it as the haven it should be to you.

REFINED DINING

The dining experience can be daunting and but extremely satisfying on many levels. The food, the ambience, the company, and the service are all elements that must come together correctly to experience fine dining. Once you have enjoyed this, you realize what you have been missing. As you become more refined, you will want to experience this type of dining preference rather than just "eating out."

The refined woman is comfortable in the most formal settings for dining as well as the local bistro. She understands that her actions are the same everywhere she dines. However, the experience is never the same twice, not even in the same restaurant. All the elements of a successful dining experience do not depend completely on her, but there is a part she must play correctly for it to be the most enjoyable. She focuses on her demure nature, fixed attention to her host and his lead in ordering, her knowledge of acceptable table conversation and, finally, the proper use of table utensils and dining protocol for a fine dining experience. The refined woman is at ease in the part she plays and is in attendance for the delight and companionship of her host, who is in charge of the evening, his only concern being pleasing her.

Dining features include things such as taste, presentation and aroma of the foods that are brought to the table. Other elements include the wait staff and their professional behavior, including how they bring the dishes, explain them to the woman, take away dishes, fill glasses, and handle napkins. It is enjoyable to know they pay attention to details without appearing they are even there at all.

I was dining with a dear couple recently in a long booth against a wall. The lady opposite me was a refined, gracious woman. We were seated across from each other closest to the wall. When she noticed the server wondering if he could quietly reach across the long booth for her plate, she graciously handed it to him with a light smile. She had timed it perfectly with no effort at all, as if it had been planned all along. (Remember, being gracious and refined is about making everyone feel comfortable by your graciousness). It was a ballet of sorts how she managed to time it. In a matter of a few seconds, what could have been a disruption of our wonderful conversation was barely noticed by all (except my being amazed and delighted to see the *portiousness*[5] of my friend).

All the personal touches from the staff are very important for a refined dining experience: how they manage the table, respond to a small gesture by you or your host, ensure that you are comfortable and enjoying yourself. These niceties will all make a difference, and such excellent serving is a focused job and expected of finer wait staff.

Your manner and refined attitude toward everyone in the restaurant should remain formal, yet friendly, and you should be able to enjoy yourself even if you are dining alone.

Your role in the evening is to relax, enjoy yourself and your host or companion, and be delightful company. Men invite interesting beautiful women to dine with them because they love the company and they also love to "show off" a bit of what they know, their taste in restaurants and fine dining, and they generally desire the attention.

---

[5] *A rare word meaning the perfect graciousness of a woman in a difficult situation.*

The way you handle yourself with the staff, your companion, and even the *maître d'* is one indication of your refinement. If you are there with a gentleman, he always takes the lead and speaks to the host or maître d. You stand next to him, looking elegant, refined and demure in your great outfit. You then follow the *maître d'* to the table followed by your date or companion. He pulls the chair out for you or the *maître d'* does, and you stand in front of your place at the table as the person holding the back of the chair gently glides the seat to your knees as you bend your knees and gently sit in the front of your chair. The *maître d'* then takes the napkin and places it on your lap, while the gentleman usually sits to your right. (That is not a steadfast rule, but it is nice to have him to your right if you are right-handed.)

You are handed a menu without pricing, while your male host is handed the same menu with prices. You are not to be bothered with the price of anything on the menu. This is a dining experience your host wants you to totally enjoy and experience, bar any notion of expense. If this is your first time with the person, you should order something from the middle price range. (We all know that veal would be more expensive than chicken or fish, and aged beef more expensive than both of these). You can be safe ordering the veal and know you will enjoy it if you like tender meat and a small portion (which is usually the case with veal).

When selecting your order, tell your host what you would like, or discuss the options with him. He will then order all of the courses on your behalf and then orders his after yours, course by course. This is one way it is expected in the nicer establishments and in European Michelin star restaurants, because the expectation when arriving is that everyone there is involved with your dining experience, from the chef to the staff to the busboy, to you and your host – everyone wants the evening to be the best in fine dining.

Restaurants, and chefs in particular, are very competitive with other comparable restaurants and know that the best advertisement for them is word of mouth. Your experience, when perfect, guarantees them other fine dining guests.

Bistros have a more casual approach to seating and ordering. No matter where you dine, it is always proper to discuss your choices and tell your host what you would like. He then can acknowledge that *this* is a good dish, or he will suggest something he thinks you would might prefer more than the dish you mentioned. This is common courtesy of a gentleman. He is taking you to a restaurant where he has already dined, or knows the best dishes this restaurant offers, and he wants you to be pleased. He will suggest a dish he believes is the best the chef offers in hopes you will be impressed at the wonderful food and evening as a whole. Men take women to fine restaurants to impress them and to enjoy their company as the women enjoy themselves. This is pleasing to a man of fine taste and he receives more enjoyment watching you have a pleasurable experience. His payback is your wonderful company and conversation and your overall delightful companionship for the evening.

When the dining experience is less than pleasurable, you are to make a good show of enjoying yourself, but allow him to let the *maître d'* know –in a gentle way – that everything was not up to his standards. This is standard protocol because the gentleman wants you to know that he did everything in his power to make the evening unforgettable for you. If there were things beyond his control, he may want to point this out politely so that you understand his intention was to totally please you in inviting you to dine with him.

When dining alone in a good restaurant, the staff is sensitive to your situation and will want to please you and be prompt in taking care of you, knowing that your time might be limited. They understand your goal may not be an elaborate evening of dining. The staff usually spend more time conversing with a single diner, if it appears the diner prefers talking, and they will usually be punctual in bringing each dish and drink, as soon as they notice you are ready for it. Your manner and refined attitude toward everyone in the restaurant should remain formal, yet friendly, and you should be able to enjoy yourself even if you are dining alone.

REFINED TRAVEL

Traveling has become more and more of an annoyance. Even though you are a refined person and can handle tough situations, let's face it: Traveling can try anyone's patience. Being civil to airline personnel (if you can get one to talk to) and other people at the airport is a test of your true refinement. Whereas you would normally be kind to all persons, it is a stressful thing to even make sense of some of the events you must endure at an airport when traveling.

If you have the pleasure of traveling by private plane, railway, or limousine, travel can be a pleasing experience from start to finish, very refined and enjoyable. The pleasure and extravagance of traveling the Orient Express is an experience like no other.

When traveling with the general public, there are many things to consider. Plans must be confirmed earlier than ever before. Packing and handling luggage is more daunting now with security measures and luggage restrictions. When planning a trip abroad or within your own country, many things must be considered. Connections need to be longer than they were a few years ago due to airplane maintenance delays or cancellations.

If you are savvy enough to download the airline "app" and can get to the website, you can check for any delays before leaving for the airport; likewise, you can arrange for the airline to text you regarding any delay.

Once at the airport, while waiting for your flight you will receive real time updates on the status of your flight, and although you are not really in control, you will feel like you are. Another option is to ship your suitcase in advance, bothering only with a carryon at the airport; this is becoming a viable option, given the fees now for taking large, heavy luggage.

The airport staff notoriously prolong announcing any delays or late arrivals or departures, knowing that confusion ensues once they do announce. This can be particularly important when a flight has been cancelled. The first people to know about the cancellation are certainly capable of booking the next available flight but after more travelers find out, there will no longer be alternate flights with any seats left.

Although this all sounds depressing to travel, it is the greatest experience we can afford ourselves – to go somewhere different and experience the culture, museums, restaurants, shopping, and people of another city. Find out more about the major cities of the world and what they have to offer. You will be surprised at the delightful things that avail the savvy tourist.

The entire travel experience can definitely be a huge exertion of energy, but the rewards are fabulous. It is an education in itself to visit another place and experience the culture there. It is especially important to be in a proper frame of mind that is understanding, patient, and above all, direct and alert.

People who travel are usually well suited and flexible to change, since they are accustomed to different ways of life and different people they have discovered. Although we are not all travel agents, you should consider learning more about bookings and how flights are priced by comparing websites and knowing as much as you can about your travel arrangements and alternate ways to travel.

Homework: Date night idea: rent a travel film or movie filmed in another country. This will inform you of other areas of the world, the cultures, and perhaps make you more interesting since you will know about a foreign country. There are many wonderful films about all of the US National Parks.

If you know the places you want to visit, it might be important to be: 1. Flexible on dates to go to that destination, 2. Available to book if the opportunity arises, and 3. Willing to cancel if there are safety risks.

Security and safety are the most important concerns for anyone who travels. With flexibility and readiness, you can change your destination to a more tourist-friendly place when it seems there are too many places under siege or watch by terrorist activity, or uneasy economies, or other valid reasons to avoid that destination.

CHAPTER 9 – REFINED EXPERIENCE

"Nothing is less important than which fork you use. Etiquette is the science of living. It embraces everything. It is ethics. It is honor. Emily Post

Experience is the greatest teacher. You will have to *live and learn* as you go with the ideas captured in this book. Refer to those thoughts that resonated with you from reading through *Refinement* and find a way to incorporate the more elegant lifestyle into your daily routine. You will enjoy the experience and see some changes in your life just by exposing yourself to these ideas.

It is reasonable to believe that we retain only 25 percent of what we hear or read. Perhaps you have captured only about one-fourth of the contents of this book; this means as you re-read the book, you will see something new each time. Let the book be a reference, a place to be reminded of who you can be and a place where you can reinforce your self-respect and self-confidence. Let it instill in you the truth that you can do whatever it is you set your heart and mind to do, in the world, in society, in your town or city, and within smaller groups of friends, family, and neighbors.

As you become more serious about introducing elegance in your life, you must begin to *think* more elegantly and diversified.

Ten areas of focus that you might want to research for more integration into your life:

1. Respect for others
2. Social grace
3. Integrity
4. Arts
5. Sciences
6. Politics and history
7. Geography, cultures and travel
8. Compassion
9. Finances, investments
10. Philanthropy

As you become more serious about introducing elegance in your life, you must begin to *think* more elegantly and diversified. Areas you turn your attention to will begin to develop in elegant behavior and social grace.

Along with the grace it takes to become elegantly social, your attention to others must be sincere and from a gentle heart. This allows you to admire and respect others and have true compassion for them. With this newfound benevolence, your integrity will begin to shine forth as someone who is delighted in her life and wants to make the most of it while caring for others and never intentionally stepping over others. You will become more interested in things such as the arts, and perhaps become involved in philanthropy or charities that have to do with science and research. You might begin to believe that giving back to education is a great way to invest some of your free time.

Attending book club lectures, or supporting a current event speaker series, might become a part of your passion to be more aware and influence the world. To round out your life, you will want to ensure you are doing the most with your finances and financial goals. Through these changes and adjustments your life becomes more sophisticated and you should know more about investing and stocks, bonds, and annuities.

Some other more practical ways for your personal improvement of your elegance might include: refined speech, learning a foreign language, the pursuit of quality, nurturing your friendships and connections, education on food and wine, interest in culture, travel expertise, financial intelligence, home living standards, and manner of dress. You can be the best-dressed, best-suited socialite in town, but there is always room for improvement. Here are a few ways to display a refined lifestyle:

Refinement Rules

1. Treat everyone the same – be kind
2. Have integrity
3. Always try to leave something better than you found it
4. Dress well
5. Live well
6. Speak intelligently, softly and sincerely
7. Be prepared
8. Follow up
9. Make your word good even when it costs you dearly
10. Class is not money and money does not bring you class

Homework: Review your Mission Statement. Look at your goals and break them down into smaller achievable ones. Put them on your calendar or make them a monthly reminder on your phone or personal device. Reward yourself when your reach some of these goals that seemed unachievable months ago.

It is not too early to write down goals. You might want to look ahead to five, ten and twenty-five year goals. This will sharpen your focus on what is important to you in your life. This is a way you can determine not to lose years of your life wandering and floating around. Find out what really makes you tick, what you are passionate about – then get to the bottom of it. Even if you start one hobby today and pursue it slowly, in ten years that hobby could be turned into a garage business or philanthropy affecting many people.

An Interesting Person

One of the best ways to become refined is to broaden your interests and look for opportunities to better yourself. Interesting people are attractive to others and desired to be around. Refined people listen to other people and take their lead. They often look to others as they expand their horizons and find themselves more and more in the presence of interesting people. These are the individuals invited to cocktail parties, and written up in the local gossip columns (although that is not elegant, at all, it gets your name circulated). With that advantage, you then are able to broaden your circle of friends even more.

You can begin by just finding a small portion of your potential, but if you truly want this life of refinement for the remainder of your life, you have to commit and become that person you believe in – in all areas of your life.

It has been said that men marry interesting women. They observe and are attracted to women who can bring them forward in society and can carry them toward a higher successful social circle (this is part of the "it takes an entire house to keep a man" philosophy). Men will expect their wives to be able to entertain, host dinners and events, and socialize with persons who might make a difference in their career and social life.

The refined woman has the innate ability to multi-task, particularly within society, and certain women flourish at it. The ones that flourish at it have some commonalities:

1. She is self-disciplined.
2. She pays attention to every detail in all matters: her own impeccable manners, taste in clothes, makeup, hair and conversation and, generally, everything she does and says and is involved in.
3. She does not volunteer herself to just any cause, but is selective in what she chooses to put her name on and spend her time doing.
4. She is well-read and usually well-traveled and overall very interesting in her own right.
5. She carries herself well and is well-bred or self-taught to be well-bred.
6. She knows how to entertain well.
7. She will research and become familiar with the matters concerning current events and can speak intelligently about them.
8. She has opinions based on factual research and not just hearsay or gossip.
9. She is the perfect combination of "salty & sweet" – she is her own person and not afraid of being that person, yet she treats everyone with respect and dignity and gives place to others' opinions, personalities, and manner.

Areas that a refined woman will seek to improve include her travel experience, reading, speaking, leadership, social graces, and philanthropy.

TRAVEL - Just how important is foreign travel to a woman of elegance? Everyone I interviewed stated that travel is the best education for a woman to understand cultures, foods and people. The experiences gained in traveling allow a woman to understand the larger world that may have been previously abstract to her. This is a welcome addition to the woman who desires to be capable and savvy in social camaraderie with various types of people of differing backgrounds and race. She is far more capable of understanding and communicating with others if she has experienced various lifestyles in foreign countries, with their cultures and traditions. Travel experience is a necessity, given the world economy and society in which we live.

READING - If you are an avid reader, you understand how enriching books are to your life, to your vocabulary, and to your overall outlook on the world. You should also be subscribing to good e-newspapers daily as well as doing your own research across the board (conservative to liberal) of news websites that will temper what you hear on television newscasts.

Reading is a key to learning and understanding more words and concepts. The books you choose should parallel your interests but you should mix them up with novels, best sellers, documentaries, biographies of great people, and even stray outside the lines with books written about electronics, the financial world, or any sector that would be interesting to learn more about.

LEADERSHIP - Your ability to navigate through the social circles of men and women who are powerful and opinionated and cynical may not get you very far, however, the refined woman is not concerned with making her mark with those people. She is concerned only with a quality of life she can be proud of and hold her head high and know her integrity got her where she is and will keep her on the correct road to an elegant life. Social popularity does not necessarily equal elegance or refinement. It is her role as a leader and pacesetter that will remain in the hearts and minds of others long after she is gone. Her elegant statements of word and deed will leave an indelible mark on people who will desire to attain a higher level of kindness and graciousness after having met her and been with her. This is her legacy of leadership by example.

SOCIAL GRACE - No matter how well traveled or how well read you are, even if you are the best speaker in your city, unless you temper it with social grace, you will be considered a "know-it-all" and have very little agility around society.

The absence of grace in a woman is not fondly accepted, and the elegance of social grace in a woman should be her "calling card" to get anywhere she wants to be and with anyone she wishes. Aside from just being interesting, a woman must be fresh and cool and tender-spirited. She should be tempered with a social grace that permeates all she is and does. This comes with a price. She can no longer be brassy and intolerant of others, thinking that they are beneath her or for her to squash. She must be sincerely full of benevolent grace that makes her feminine and have the type of kindness that is respectful of all. This combination makes an elegant woman of substance. She has something between her ears and she has something in her heart. She is never insulting or unkind, because she is tolerant of others and their differences and is realistic in what she believes – and believes it to the core – such that she is comfortable in what she believes and does not have to defend it in a rambunctious way.

Social grace encompasses the ability to be yourself while attending the most prestigious ball or event and able to converse with the Queen, if necessary, in fashion and ability because you are not overtly self-conscious but simply conscious of the proper time and attitude of where you are, and thus you behave accordingly.

Shy people are very self-conscious. An elegant woman must counterbalance her shyness by being fully prepared and able to calmly be where she is and create no fuss about it.

Elegance and grace abound in the woman who is kind and caring of others and does not really think about her own situation or her lack of confidence, but only of the others that she is placed with and their comfort, ease, and situation by which she actively engages with them for a perfectly normal, relaxing and enjoyable experience.

Becoming socially graceful means you are preparing yourself to be comfortable in all situations with all types of persons. To do this, you must first of all have something to say and know how to listen actively. This will allow you to be quiet and attentive yet not have to be the center of attention by speaking. Your directed questions can create an atmosphere of fun and lively conversation without having to say very much. You can direct questions back to the speaker in a way that creates more interest in what the speaker is saying encouraging him or her to say more on the matter at hand. When you are put on the spot with a question about your opinion or knowledge of something, particularly current events, the only way you can give a presentable answer is if you have to put some time and research into the subject matter. This is necessary before you can truly have solid responses to anyone asking you for your opinion. Unless you do not want to form an opinion on a subject, you should at least know the basic facts – a bit about the truth of the subject – so that you can listen attentively to someone as they discuss a recent matter (perhaps highly ignited by the mainstream press) and yet not be caught up in the emotion of a "side" that someone takes.

During every Miss USA pageant, the contestants are presented questions that may or may not suit them. How they answer the question is sometimes comical, but always comes down to one thing: did they prepare sufficiently?

In preparing for the questions asked the contestants in any beauty pageant, the staff or entourage always try to prepare the contestant based on who the judges are, or what the political and media frenzy is that month. The questions will inevitably be controversial in nature. Why? Because the idea is to determine if the contestant is capable of thinking under pressure and able to handle the immediate celebrity status she may attain within a few hours after the competition. This is only to prove that our young ladies, as beautiful and talented and educated as they are, may lack one quality: intelligent elegance under pressure.

After viewing a few of these contests, I wondered if I would be able to respond any better than these women who have prepared for a period of time to be on that stage at that moment answering that question. This proves that your elegance is not immediately won or immediately innate within you – it will take dedication and work to change any rough edges you may have and ingrain within your heart the desire to be kindly, courteous, and mannerly at all times and in all situations.

The contestants proved time and time again that no matter how much your "team" tries to prepare you by asking you fake questions, the answer must come from a refined heart to be honest and forthright, and possibly effective on the audience and judges. Most of the questions the judges pose to the contestants are opinions about a current event and how she would handle the situation. Tactful, politically correct, and sincere-looking answers win over any other honesty that cuts against the mainstream media and liberal minds who are more critical in nature to a nice, sincere response.

It is not how much you say but how you say it. The more concise your statement, sometimes the more powerful it is.

It is very important to note that the more *proper* and *formal* you want to be, the less you can just voice an opinion, particularly if it is based only on hearsay or on someone else's opinion. Know the facts. If you have not had time to research the facts, and you are asked your opinion, you can always say that you have not had time to study the matter and would like to pass on giving an opinion that would not be based on truth. I once asked a friend of mine who she was going to vote for in the presidential election. She told me and I asked her what made her decide on that candidate. She said because he said he was pro-women. If that was all she had developed in her mind on that man's platform, she did not research very deeply. I believe all the candidates that year mentioned being supportive of women's issues, but she happened to hear him say that and it made her decision.

It is not how much you say but how you say it. The more concise your statement, sometimes the more powerful it is. It is quotable. It is a sound bite. It can be tweeted. Your social grace is intact when you are in control of what you say and how you act, and you get the kind of result you really wish for.

One last word about giving your opinion. Do not go where you are not confident on the subject matter. It is better to look shy and quiet and listen intently rather than to begin to speak about things you are not well versed on. You must *temper* your conversation with a good attitude of listening. You know what you know but you do not necessarily know what they are going to say. It makes life more interesting to begin a conversation, so memorize some good conversation *starters* then step back and look very interested in what they are saying and they will continue to talk.

This is what shy people do all the time. They take the focus off themselves and put it on another person. They are good at it because it is too painful to have so much attention by so many. One on one is not as frightening to shy, timid, introverted people. We would rather listen to a good debate than try to interject something, even if it is the wisest thing said during the evening. It just does not pay to curb the interesting conversation with facts or information that will dampen the light-heartedness or enjoyment of the conversation going on.

It is wise as a guest to take part in the entire evening including the conversation, and it is always good to have someone talk about themselves to allow you to listen and take it all in.

USING YOUR CONVERSATIONAL SKILLS

Remember those old college study habits? They are actually essential and good preparation for becoming a great conversationalist. Oh, and forget your shrewd ability to debate! That is not acceptable in social conversation – conversation is more like the rallying of a tennis ball as being better than winning the point. The objective is to learn more about the opponent (the persons you converse with) rather than show off what you know.

This somewhat restrained attitude might seem strange to some type "A" personalities who think conversation needs to be about them – what they know, who they know, and how they got where they are. Well, it may be all right if you insist on tooting your own horn, but it is far more sophisticated and tasteful to allow others to speak of themselves and casually get to know you, particularly if you are someone notable in society. The more notable the person, the quieter *you* become, knowing that the person showing interest in conversing with you will enjoy it as both of you exchange witty and intelligent thoughts as interests and hobbies slowly surface to the conversation.

Do your research on topics, recent news, important people in our generation, and other aspects of good conversation: art, politics, science, geography and travel. The topics to discuss are endless when everyone is innately intelligent (and the intelligent do keep up with current affairs) or else has done some research prior to a social event. And even if you do not get to discuss the information you researched, you have gained that knowledge for yourself and future discussion. The chances are very high that the major topics of the day will be discussed and that opinionated personalities will keep the conversation lively with their own opinions on the subject. And with the conversation being lively, intelligent and stimulating, it may entice you to develop a new hobby or discover a new talent or interest of your own. Always anticipate where the conversation may go and the questions you may be asked, but balance that with active listening skills.

Speech

Your speech and voice are just one element of becoming a good conversationalist. Keeping a good pitch in your voice – retaining a well-modulated or controlled tempo and sound – is always good manners. Refrain from being too loud (choose to whisper at times) and articulate your words; these two habits are good form for speakers as well as those that would like to carry on a good conversation.

Using too many "buzz words," colloquialisms or slang can make your conversation seem very "country" or crude and unrefined rather than proper and interesting.

A monotone voice or a sing-song voice can bore or irritate the listeners and cause them to lose interest in your conversation. When you speak in a monotone, others hear only a few words you say because the pitch and tone seem to wane in their ears. When you end every sentence on a high note, you sound like you never completed your thought but ended it in the middle of the sentence; this is called "uptalking," and it is frowned on in every situation, including job interviews. Try speaking out loud or reading sentences from a book to hear how you really sound when you speak. It is worth the effort to maintain a good voice that has an easy pitch and tone, while varying your words to retain interest.

Homework – List three conversation starters you are comfortable using with someone. Practice your tone, attitude, and demeanor in front of a mirror until it becomes natural to you. Video yourself and watch it for body language, tone, ease of speech and a slower pronunciation, perhaps – practice this and it will become second nature to you in meeting others.

Vocabulary

The importance of a strong, growing vocabulary is a significant factor in becoming elegant and refined. Our choice of words, or lack of, exhibits who we are to the world.

A good purpose for learning new words and expanding your vocabulary is that you will be able to choose words with greater precision. You will be able to communicate with more ease and less misunderstanding of your meaning. Your vocabulary is your communication toolbox. The more tools, the better you will communicate by choosing the stronger, more descriptive and precise word to suit the occasion. By learning more words and increasing your vocabulary, you not only increase the words you know, but understand the words you already know much better, because you can integrate the new ones to fully explain the ones you already knew, and that will lead to a better way to communicate thoughts, ideas and information.

Using synonyms and a thesaurus will help you to communicate better overall, however, you cannot always research a synonym or open a thesaurus while you are conversing at the dinner table. You must understand the roots of the words you know and then you can better explain something if there is an inquisitive stare back at you from someone at the table.

Vocabulary "Don'ts"

1. Anything vulgar – not just curse words, but crass words
2. "And," "uh," "you know," and other slurs of speech
3. Coined phrases such as "awesome," "random," and any words that come to mind in that category
4. "I hate," "I never" "I refuse," and words that express strong negative feelings or finality – it is only on a rare occasion a refined person will show extreme emotion when speaking, and because negativity changes one's demeanor, it should not be used excessively
5. Belittling words – words that express talking down to someone – like: "Oh, I already knew that …" or "yes, everyone knows... "
6. Colloquialisms that are common phrases and express the feeling that you cannot think for yourself, such as "you could have fooled me…" or "as we speak…"
7. Slang words: "zillion" and "fantabulous" or words that are a gross creation of several words together.
8. Public terms of endearment – this is a tricky one because there is no rule against being endearing to someone or that person being endearing to you, and you *can* express it tastefully, however, there are times and places it is not acceptable by refined people, such as when it excludes the other parties in

the group and makes them feel uncomfortable. Remember, a classy lady desires everyone to be comfortable and at ease.

9. He said, she said – this is information you cannot take back and usually regret saying . . . (gossip – need I say more?)
10. Off-color jokes/stories, including disrespectful jokes about those in authority

INTRODUCTION FORMALITIES

Getting started in a conversation can be the most difficult part of the evening unless your host or another guest knows the art of introductions. Introductions are basic and simple but there is a protocol to formal introductions. We all know the "rule" – introduce the lower person to the higher person, or the younger to the older, the less influential and decorated to the most. The more prestigious name is mentioned first and the younger, less important is introduced back to that person: Doctor Preston, may I introduce Miss Lily Wesley, who just graduated from Duke University last spring in economics. Ms. Wesley, Dr. Preston, Director of Engineering at Tulane. This is the way it is done – to formulate an introduction that not only gives the name and title ("Miss" and "Doctor") but tells something about each other to assist in starting up a meaningful conversation.

The beginning of a party is the most awkward time. Once people have gathered together and are excited about the venue and evening ahead, there usually is sufficient small talk to keep it lively.

Now that you can introduce those you know to others at the dinner party, what else is absolutely critical to being a perfect guest? Arrivals and departures are very important to the host. She is counting on everyone to attend and have a wonderful time and although there may be a good reason for pre-punctual arrivers and fumbling latecomers, the guest who knows what time to arrive and leave is assisting to dictate the flow of the evening with the host.

Much can be said on how a pre-dinner cocktail hour should function. It is intended to allow everyone to meet each other and become cordially relaxed before being seated and resigned to several hours with only two choices of partners in conversation (this is where all your research may benefit you). The objective of a great evening includes desiring to stir up both sides of conversation with current events and interesting historical information, the kind of information that may be relevant to the party, the host, the city you happen to be in and other appropriate topics – practically anything that will bring good-natured banter between you and your right-side and left-side conversationalists.

When preparing for the party, remember that the host may or may not have any formal pre-dinner entertainment or requirements planned. Some hosts feel they have to have entertainment during this time (more than a modest threesome or piano) and this is unnecessary, since the idea of the hour before dinner is to mingle. Distractions or planned activities steal that social time away from the guests to learn a bit more about each other; afterward they will be seated at a table where it is polite to only join in the conversations directly to their right and left, and perhaps overhear some of the conversation across the table. This dinnertime limits the ability to get to know more than perhaps four individuals. If your neighbor is an incessant gossip, you will learn more than you want to know about many persons. That information is never reliable and always frowned upon at a dinner party; partaking in gossip shows a lack of taste and lack of appropriate social behavior.

The final word of caution at a dinner party: Be prepared to start a conversation. If you are not prepared with some news from today's paper or other means of interesting up-to-the-minute news developments, do not expect the other guests to have much to start a conversation with either. The beginning of a party is the most awkward time. Once people have gathered together and are excited about the venue and evening ahead, there usually is sufficient small talk to keep it lively.

A guest should always be ready to discuss a recent best-seller as well as important but not scandalous news, and always try to find the balance in personal and general information to ensure the other parties are not bored or embarrassed at becoming too intimate in conversation. Alcohol during the time before dinner can sometimes create a noisy and friendly situation, however, it can also get out of hand if the persons consuming are also the persons who cannot have intelligent conversation under the influence of alcohol. Although you have been invited to have a good time and enjoy yourself, this is definitely not the place to consume more than is necessary to enjoy yourself or to relieve the stress of the day by getting intoxicated or obnoxious. Remember that your duty as a guest of your friend requires a delicate balance in having an enjoyable evening and supporting your host as an involved participant who is cordial, aware of her surroundings, and makes attempts to include even the shyest of people into conversation and into the fun of the social hour.

Boring or Interesting

Now, you have just been introduced and asked the simple question: "How are you?" The interesting answer is to be brief but open-ended. Start with perhaps the last place you traveled, what you have read lately, or how you enjoyed some current event. Then close by telling that person you are doing well, and how is she/he? That is sufficient information to refrain from being boring, and allowing this person an opportunity to reciprocate information; you are hoping to strike up a great conversation.

It is easy to refrain from being a bore: discover what interests you in conversation and try to emulate that. Listen to what others are discussing and find the most interesting speaker and follow that person around for a while and learn from him/her. This will help you in the future. Once you have observed others in conversation, you will find it is easier than you thought and you will be more at ease over the course of the evening. Do not give up and leave when you feel you are not hitting a home run on your conversation skills. It takes time to develop them, and you will only get better by sweating it out and practice. As self-conscious as you may feel at first, no one even notices that because they are enjoying the event and would willingly include you as you walk up to talking groups.

The best conversationalist is prepared, kind, considerate, patient, a good listener, does not interrupt, is pleasant to the argumentative guest out of respect for her host, and has a sense of humor that will open others up to conversing.

Interesting people are automatically good conversationalists. They have already figured out that knowing something and conveying it are two different matters. Did you know that the average woman spends at least 75 percent of the time in a group conversation listening?

Conversation peppered with *"sort of"* and *"you know"* have meanings that relate to downplaying our own knowledge of something.

Be an enlightened listener. When you are speaking, try to include everyone – this takes work and effort and concentration on all the persons around you. Divert attention from your own ideas to learn others' ideas. Look for the alert person whose eyes sparkle at the topic being discussed. They probably know a lot more than they are actually telling; a little coaxing may bring out much more.

Even in small talk there is a great compliment to both the hearer and speaker: they both pay respect to each other that they are worth speaking with. Conversation peppered with "sort of" and "you know" have meanings that relate to downplaying our own knowledge of something.

Gifts

There is a definite art to giving. The general rule is to give a "thoughtful gift" no matter what your budget. Although I rarely think that a gift card or cash is an endearing and thoughtful gift, a friend of mine while building a house was so busy and involved in the details of the home that she ended up buying a coffee shop gift card. Along with the card she included an endearing note stating that although she did not have time right now, as soon as she could get free she wanted to catch up over coffee. The gift card was her way of letting me know she was thinking of me, and planned to get together at some point in the not-too distant future. Her time was the most precious gift she could give, so she gave it in the future – when she had more of it to give. And it goes without saying that no one realizes how much it costs to build a house because of the little surprises that occur along the way. Her gift was thoughtful and within budget. Perfect!

A gift should never in any way be interpreted as expecting something in return. It should be quiet graciousness toward the recipient.

Terms of Gifting
1. Make sure the gift is appropriate in the most formal sense; an off-color or extravagant gift – even a gift to a male person of interest –may turn against you and become worse than no gift at all. If in doubt of the recipient, keep it formal. I once gave a gift to a client and had it monogrammed. His new wife thought the gift was too personal. I had kept it very formal, yet it was misconstrued even so.
2. Make sure you can easily afford the gift you are giving. We all realize that each person has limits to funds. It is also inappropriate to be extravagant to someone who cannot return the same type of gift at a special occasion in your honor.
3. No strings. A gift should never in any way be interpreted as expecting something in return, whether it is a favor, gift, honor

or special treatment. This is most dishonorable in the business world.

4. Think: *Thoughtful rather than expensive* – remember that a gift is something to be cherished by the recipient, not something that is so out of their reach they are intimidated by receiving it. And remember that the best surprise is always *beautifully wrapped,* so they will enjoy opening it up as much as the gift itself.

5. Timely giving. Make sure the gift is given in a timely fashion. The idea of the thrill of gifts at a party or wedding (or prior to the wedding, if it is a formal affair) is part of the fun and excitement for the recipient!

Receiving and opening gifts at an occasion can be daunting. It is important to think of the giver and her/his intentions as being genuinely loving when you are opening the gift in front of them, in order that you will be truly gracious with your heartfelt *thank you.*

Gifts opened away from the giver always deserve a handwritten thank-you note within three days of the opening of the gift with few exceptions.

If a recipient opens the gift and comments to you on it, they are not indebted to send a thank-you card. They have thanked you in person, and that is precisely proper. I asked a mutual friend about surprising our friend on his birthday. Her response was that he would be "mortified." It is the thought that counts, *but so many people do not like surprises* or being made a fuss over. <u>Consider the recipient</u>. Your lovely thoughts should be simple, tasteful and quiet, and the receiver will remember that much more than a lot of fanfare, particularly if they are private people.

One is not obligated to anything but a warm and genuine thank you when gifts are opened in front of the giver. If it is a particularly memorable gift of some expense, a handwritten thank you is nice, but should not be expected by the giver. Gifts opened away from the giver always deserve a handwritten thank-you note within three days of the opening of the gift. Exceptions would be large parties where many gifts, condolences, flowers or donations are received (such as open houses, weddings and funerals). Everyone understands these rules and makes allowances depending upon the circumstances; no one would expect more than what proper etiquette requires.

Thank You Notes

First of all, you should commit to actually writing thank you notes. And if you are going to spend the time doing this, here is a brief "lesson" on making the most of it.

In writing personal thank you notes, you may consider this outline:

1. Make reference to the gift.
2. Mention how you will use or enjoy the gift.
3. Communicate how appealing the gift is.
4. Express a sincere expression of gratitude.
5. Create a special closing sentence relaying the giver's thoughtfulness or kindness.

Other ideas: a photograph with the gift in use, reference to others admiring the gift, your secret desire for that gift, how perfect the gift was at the time it was sent. Once your mind is on this track you will think of several ways to be very personal in your words that will warm the heart of the giver and cause them to read your special note more than once.

There is no better way to exemplify your elegance and graciousness than through entertaining, particularly, hosting a dinner.

THE ELEGANT TABLE

Just as we would want our gifts to reflect our fine discrimination, we also desire our dining and hosting to reflect that simple good taste as well.

It is just as important to have a finely set table as it is to make sure the food is elegant, tasteful and plentiful. The table setting assists the host in setting the mood of the evening. It tells her guests that they are special to her and that she has planned an evening of delightful fellowship and conversation centered on good food, drink and laughter.

Setting the Table

The most gracious tables I have been invited to have contained the finest place settings and most beautiful flower arrangements and centerpieces. The entire experience was delightfully elegant from the aroma of the soup placed in front of me to the subtle rose scent of the centerpiece, to the charming people seated across from me, to the soft conversations all around the table.

An elegant table will have the china, silver and crystal all in concert with the rest of the table, making one want to stay as long as possible to enjoy these fineries.

The idea of having attractive tableware at your disposal is to make your time with these special people more delightful and to show forth how much you consider their presence at your home. The best reason to obtain fine tableware is for entertaining – whether it be with your favorite date, longtime husband, your daughter and friends visiting from college, or your next-door neighbors.

For those who are just dabbling in entertaining, there are ways to set a fine table with very little expense. The idea of having white dinnerware from a discount department store can stir you to be creative with the food you serve, in the colors, textures, taste and aromas. Using a white palette can be the most elegant table setting you could have. Plain glasses call for more creativity and flair when filling them with drinks and additions such as orange or lime slices. Color is always a way to cheer your guests, so do not be afraid of using color on a simple background. There are many books on entertaining, but the simple rule in setting a table is to place the silverware that will be used from the outside in.

Remember that drinks are on the right and bread on the left. D-R-I-N-K and R-I-G-H-T, F-O-O-D and L-E-F-T. Five letters in drink and right, four letters in food and left. The other way to remember which side is which is by forming a "B" in your left-hand index finger and thumb, and a "D" with your right-hand index finger and thumb.

Choosing China, Silver and Crystal

There are so many choices today in table settings that a rookie can become confused as to how to elegantly coordinate a table. There are colors that you can mix and match with various patterns, and there is the French design versus the British and Oriental designs. Here are a few ideas to keep your table interesting but coordinated. While British patterns can be a bit stronger, and French tend to be ornate and more feminine, as you place these patterns together, you will notice if it works or it does not. Generally, you can use the British silver across the board since it is usually strong and simple. The idea of an ornate dinner plate does not seem as elegant as a nice bone china dinner plate with elegant color and décor around the rim. The best choices of this are the Woodrow Wilson and George W. Bush patterns as shown in the China Collection of the White House "regular" tour.

China	Crystal	Silver
French	British	French
British	French	French
British	French	Oriental
Oriental	British	British
French	French	Oriental

With these simple "rules" you can create the perfect "go-together" fresh look every time. Things to remember: Never use more than one touch of Oriental in a table setting, unless you are attempting to host a "theme" party. British should be used sparingly with French. They can sometimes clash and other times they actually work together nicely since too much French on the table can weary your guests!

THE INVITATION

Sitting at someone else's table can be such a delightful experience. Imagine going to someone's home and not really knowing what to expect. It keeps you on your toes in anticipation of what is in store for the evening and what persons you will be meeting, conversing with, and dining with over the course of the evening. Before we look into being the perfect guest, let's discuss the acceptance of an invitation.

1. The RSVP is not an option.
2. RSVP no later than one week after receiving invitation, unless the event is less than three weeks away. Then you should respond within two to three days.
3. Regrets after accepting an invitation should be as soon as possible, accompanied by a card, flowers or small gift. If regretting by phone in order to give an explanation, follow up with card or small gift, or flowers on the day of the event, letting your host know how much you will miss being a part of the festivities.
4. Think about how you would want to be treated and act accordingly.

Being invited to an event, whether dinner party or picnic, requires a decision either to accept or decline. A commitment is required. If there is a reason you cannot attend an event, the sooner you notify your host, the more courteous you are being, as she can fill your seat with another dear friend or acquaintance. The RSVP is not an option. Depending upon how well you know the host, you should be considerate enough to reply within a week of receiving the invitation, unless the event is in less than two weeks. The idea of being invited is first of all an honor and a compliment to you. The host feels you will (1) fit into the event and (2) will enjoy the company she invites. If there is a conflict you are trying to work out in order to attend, and you and the host are very good friends, call her and explain your situation and let her know that you understand if she would prefer to invite someone else. She can then tell you if she will leave a seat open for you or if she needs a specific head count; and if she is civil, she will soften the disappointment by telling you she will definitely include you in her next event. This is the gracious way to handle not being able to commit within one week – you have considered her situation and made it easy for her to tell you one way or another.

We were invited to a charity event and had been invited to join friends at their table. We were not sure if we could attend because we had a potential conflict out of town on or near that date. The event was less than two weeks away and it was critical for them to know if we could attend the day we were invited. We decided that the potential trip was a priority and we could not determine the exact date, so we gratefully declined, letting our hosts know that if they ended up with two extra seats at the last minute and our trip was definitely on another date, we would be happy to attend. This left our hosts very happy to be able to fill the seats, but also helped them understand how much we wanted to be with them at the event, but could not commit at that time.

 Think about how you would want someone to handle an RSVP to you, then be at least that gracious in your responses to invitations YOU receive. The RSVP is a response to the generosity of the host including you. Considering you are responding to her generosity, the thought might cause you to take more consideration in submitting a reply.

This is common courtesy and should be attended to with vigor and seriousness. Please remember: the RSVP is *not* an option – even if the invitation does not specifically request an RSVP, you should send one anyway to commit to the event. If you have committed to attend the event, why not let the host know of your eager and joyful anticipation of attendance? The RSVP is a gracious gesture to show the host that you are delighted in being included and would either love to attend or you regret that you have a conflict. It is that simple and easy to reply. No long explanations of why you cannot attend, unless of course you had accepted the invitation and you are now replying that you cannot attend after all. This calls for as much of a dear explanation as you can muster, because the host has been planning for your attendance and will be very disappointed that you can no longer attend. The host will or will not be able to fill your vacancy, depending upon the date of your regret and imminence of the event. Sometimes it is impossible to predict situations that cause you to decline after you have accepted an invitation (funeral, family emergency, sickness, business situation, or other dire emergency). This is when you count on the graciousness of the host to understand your need to cancel your commitment.

Flowers, a small gift, or a card as a gesture of regret is always appropriate, since you cannot fully explain how much her invitation meant to you, how terrible you feel for disappointing her at the last minute, and how sincerely you looked forward to attending her event. It is *never elegant* to give too much attention to this endeavor, nor to spend a large amount of money on the gift or flowers. It is elegant to send a small, sincere, kind gesture; it is vulgar to spend a lot of money on the gift or flowers, as that takes away from the intimacy of your message. This thoughtfulness ensures good will with your host and possibly consideration of an invitation to the next event.

Changing your mind about attending an event is a concern for the hosts, because they have put considerable time and resources in the event and are counting on your attendance, along with the other guests. If all of the guests, or a good portion, decide they have something more important to do on that day, the event will be irreparably spoiled by their absence. Remember, it is a gracious gesture to host anything – it takes an effort – and great hosts are rare. Your consideration of this should inspire you to RSVP and to do it as early as possible so that the host can plan accordingly. It should also inspire you to be the perfect guest.

A Refined Host – Gracious Generosity

As every good refined host understands, the purpose of hosting any event is for the enjoyment of her guests. Every need is catered to, ensuring a delightful evening, breakfast, luncheon, tea party, or whatever the event might be.

There is more to being the perfect host than just time and money– you have to have a certain air that says: I want to bring all my talents together to have a venue for friends to flourish, meet new people, and be introduced to new ideas.

The host is fully aware that she has the burden of making sure all of the pre-planning is geared to that effect, and the follow-through to the day of the event is scheduled out to the finest detail for staff, caterers, chefs, florists, and many other entities involved. The planning of such an event requires manpower and resources the host is willing to expend in order to have a genuinely wonderful experience for her guests.

There is more to being the perfect host than just throwing time and money at a party – you have to have a certain air about yourself that says: *I want to entertain and enjoy my friends and guests! I want to bring all my talents together to have a venue for them to flourish and meet new people with new ideas. I want to be a catalyst for enjoying company and good food.* With this idea in mind, the dinner party was born. It was (and still is) also a way to introduce eligible bachelors to women and make it easier for them to get to know each other. Sir Paul McCartney was invited to many dinner parties given by Barbara Walters in attempts to introduce her cousin, Nancy Shevell, to him. The introduction and ensuing dinner parties allowed the couple to get to know each other, only to find out they both owned homes in the Hamptons where they also spent time together, and married in 2011. Do not make that your sole objective of a dinner party, for the obvious is always bad-mannered. According to articles written on the subject, Ms. Walters invited the most interesting people in the world as incentive for McCartney to attend her parties but sat Ms. Shevell next to McCartney at the table.

Designing a Dinner Party

If you have never hosted a party before, it is nice to have a mentor, or a seasoned entertaining person who is a co-host, to guide you through it. Here are a few tips to get you thinking about how to begin:

1. Keep it simple. From table, to décor, to menu, to guests – keep it simple.
2. Keep a notebook. Put all the details of the event in one place – either in an electronic file or handwritten notebook. You will refer to these notes time after time for contact information of providers, and notes on your experience – the things that went well and not so well.
3. Get professional help. Go online to find good catering tips, or get a good local caterer to do part of the work – you will learn so much from this experience that it will pay off in the future, particularly if you find you love hosting events.
4. Budget the event. If you decide you cannot afford a dinner party, try hosting a two-hour evening wine and cheese or afternoon tea – get your feet wet and see if this is your thing. If you just love having people over and hosting, then you will find the finances to fund your passion. I do not recommend having a *pot luck* as one of your first events. There are many tricky variants to organizing women to bring dishes to complement the menu you want or even coordinate with the theme of the event.

5. Experiment with baking. This is where a lot of the cost goes to caterers: handmade and decorated desserts. If you try out some simple things, such as lemon bars, turtle cheesecake or madeleine cakes, and they turn out well, you may want to try hosting a tea where you can showcase these items from your very own kitchen. You can also package a few tea cakes and hand them out to your guests as they leave. But to host a sincerely memorable event, the food is critical. Only the finest will do and the perfect host understands where to find the finest of each delectable fancy she chooses for her menu, whether it be catered, baked in her own kitchen, flown in from a faraway place, or otherwise. Make sure your ingredients and foods are of the very best quality, taste, color and texture for a beautiful and memorable presentation.

6. The host always remembers the event is *all about the guests,* and not all about the planning and work she expends. Keeping it simple will help her guests feel comfortable, particularly if it is their first time at her home or the venue of choice.

7. Fresh flowers are the epitome of finery. The finest dining is not complete without flowers and color and elegant displays of silver, china, and crystal on the table. It is to be an extravagant affair and the way you coordinate it all will clearly set you apart. Nothing says welcome with elegant splendor and graciousness than beautiful flowers and table settings. The flowers must be fresh and perfectly arranged, as well as the table settings. Create a beautiful place for your favorite people. Everything must be fitting for the occasion and placement.

8. Plan to have everything ready thirty minutes before the guests are to arrive. Some may arrive a bit early since they have to plan on traffic or other reasons. If your dearest friends arrive early *to help*, be sure to have a few ideas to keep them busy, such as laying out napkins, straightening silverware, taking plastic off food plates, or placing ice in glasses. Make sure to give them something to drink and then slip out to freshen your makeup while you breathe deeply.

9. You, the host, are the one to put everyone else at ease by being the conversation starter. Prepare by catching up on the latest news, international and local, as well as knowing something about each of the guests that will enhance the introduction of your guests to each other.

10. Do not underestimate ambience. The music, flowers, lighting and candles all add a flair and elegance to entertaining. Look through entertaining books and find various ways to elevate the experience of a delightful evening with friends.

Top Ten for Dinner Party Guests

1. RSVP as soon as possible. An RSVP should be sent at least two weeks prior to the event, or within two days of receipt of invitation if it is less than two weeks from the event.

2. Be punctual. For a formal dinner party, 10-15 minutes after the time on the invitation, for informal, 15-20 minutes after the time that is set. This allows for the hosts to have additional time, if necessary, to attend to any last-minute unplanned situation.

3. Know when to leave. Watch the crowd, or follow suit if you are not sure. If you have another engagement that evening, be sure to let your hosts know ahead of time about your early departure to avoid any display of disappointment or wonder at your early exit.

4. Attend prepared. Glance at the newspaper or online news sites in the event there was an incident that happened during the day that everyone will be discussing. It is also a good idea to prepare for the dialog with a few ideas for starting conversations.

5. Be an interested listener and conversationalist. Pay attention to the person you are speaking with. It is of the rudest behavior to be looking around the room to see who is in attendance while someone is trying to have a conversation with you. It is appropriate to glance once or twice during the conversation, particularly if it is a long, dull monologue from your speaker,

however, it is not polite to show you are constantly wishing you were somewhere else. The best way to retreat from this situation is to find a final or closure statement such as: "*Well, we both know* . . . that will never happen, or it will never change, or the situation is terrible . . . It has been a pleasure talking with you. Enjoy your evening." That will let both of you disengage on good terms.

6.   A great dinner party is a give and take, all in the hopes of the hosts honoring you and the others with an evening of fine dining, wine, or other specialties, and spending time with interesting people.

7.   Do not bring gift items to the party that will cause your host to stop and do something with the gift (for example, flowers that are not already arranged and in a vase, or a food item that must be put away).

8.   Be attentive to the person you are facing, and always indicate they are important. This sends the message that you honor your host by conversing with any and all guests she has at the party.

9.   Send a sincere thank you (note, flowers, candy) within three days of the event.

10.   Reciprocate, if possible, or run the risk of being removed from their guest list.

Hosting the Party

There is nothing more elegant than a great dinner party. The French are known for their home entertaining, and it is no wonder. If you have been to any restaurant in Paris of prominence (particularly the Michelin restaurants), you realize that hosting their guests is a career for these superb servers and *sommeliers*. They put everything into making your evening pleasurable and memorable. The same goes for home entertainment. Entertaining at home is performed like a symphony; it flows from greetings with champagne or wine aperitifs to being seated, to course after course to the grand finale of desserts, cheeses, espressos and liqueurs.

Suggestions:

1. Have a purpose, such as someone's birthday, pre-opera or ballet, new home, introduce a political campaign, annual bash, or other good reason. This focus will help you with limiting the invitation list and how formal to make the occasion.
2. Plan ahead.
3. Get the right kind of help/assistance.
4. Don't overdo it. Make sure the party reflects who you are, or it will look like you are trying to impress.
5. Mix it up with interesting people. A great party is 50 percent people and 50 percent accoutrements. If both are unforgettable, your party will be unforgettable. Purchase quality items, but always what is fitting for your lifestyle or venue. If you can only afford a great dinner party for six, don't invite 10 and dilute the effect of what you like to serve.
6. Relax, enjoy the party and be gracious to all.

Homework: Commit to hosting a party this year. Purchase a special notebook, put recipes and photos of table settings, favorite themes, flower arrangements – everything you find interesting and elegant –go back to it often, to inspire you to host an event: dinner party, tea, barbeque, or brunch.

Hosting Weekend Guests

Hosting weekend guests at your home is such a delightful experience but it is becoming a rare occasion unless you have a home at the beach or lake or mountains. Here is the opportunity to enjoy someone's company in an informal way and really get to know them. Sometimes the invitation might be to introduce them to your area, other friends, or just a way to catch up.

1. If possible, stay overnight in the suite you plan to have your guests stay. This will accomplish two important things: assessing the functionality and appropriate amenities.
2. Create a thorough checklist for guest house/room, such as:

- Air properly flowing and not blowing directly on the head of the bed.
- Drawers emptied and cleaned out for use of the guests.
- Comfortable pillows, blankets, sheets, pillow cases.
- Pen, paper and note cards, stamps, postcards if you are located in a vacation paradise.
- Fresh flowers, if possible.
- Place a basket of fruit, water, baked goods, and candies in the room for late-night snacking.
- Instructions on use of television, telephone, intercom, or other electronic devices (coffee machine ready to go?).
- Towels, soaps, lotions, shampoo, Kleenex – stock the bathroom the way you like it – dryer, comb, brush, new toothbrush, toothpaste, makeup mirror.
- Slippers/robe or other amenities.
- Good lighting and bedside reading lamps.
- Paper, pen, notepad.
- Fresh flowers or fragrant candle/oil.
- Orientation sheet to go over with guest – how to turn the hot/cold water, special shower instructions, air conditioning/heat, lights, windows, shades, emergency exits.
- List of planned events/meals, times, locations.

The Perfect Guest

Well-mannered ladies will be remembered long after the party is over by their tasteful response, but even more, by their grace, poise and participation – even when it might not have been enjoyable to do so! Some events are intended to honor a favored guest, which means you will be expected to make that guest feel extraordinary and catered to. You may be expected by the host to entertain or talk with someone who is not as interesting to you as an old friend you have not seen in a while. By participating as your host expects, you will gain far more respect and appreciation than just being there for your own selfish reasons; she might begin to accept you as one of the rare well-mannered women of elegance, and you will indeed stand out in a crowd.

You have just accepted a formal dinner invitation – what do you do now? What should you wear? Who will be there? Why did I commit to this? How do I act? What do I talk about?

If you have found yourself in this situation more than once, it is time to get prepared. Now is your chance to understand elegance and etiquette at its finest moment – among friends and new acquaintances in a formal dinner setting, where refinement is the way of life.

A host can find any excuse for a party she chooses but, actually, the excuse is simply because the host loves people – all kinds of interesting people.

This is your opportunity to understand and be a part of the best civility on the planet. How, you say? Preparation. Research. Diligence. And *then* you can flow through the party, doing a glide on autopilot and truly enjoying the moment and the occasion – you will be ready and prepared and actually looking forward to the evening more than ever before – with a few of the following guidelines and suggestions.

Guideline 1 – Know your host. By this we mean, know the "understood, but not spoken" expectations of your host. If this is your first formal dinner party, become a good observer and watch everyone – how they interact, what they talk about, how they dress and act: make mental notes of this event so that you can better prepare for the next event – or even when you host one yourself. Really become a good listener and find out what makes some parties 'tick" and why some parties are dull as doornails.

Guideline 2 – Know your audience. If you know your host well enough to be invited to the occasion, you should understand a little about what is expected. Is your host crazy, witty and charming? That host will assuredly be the life of the party and you just follow suit. She/he will make sure everyone is comfortable and entertained. There is very little demand on you to do anything except show up with a good attitude and a few interesting conversation starters.

So what type of friends will be invited? Again, this depends on the way the host prefers to entertain. If he loves to circle a few great friends around a big table in his wine cellar and just family-style it with great bottles of wine, then you can expect a more relaxed atmosphere, no matter the fare served. If your host seems formal and gracious, he/she will have expectations of his/her guests to chime in and *make* the party – it will not be about the food or great wine, but the personalities sitting around the table. The interaction between guests is what charms the host in this instance. That type of host may invoke a more emotional evening by inviting personalities who would not normally be seated together to charm the guests – a very memorable affair, one that may be talked about for weeks after.

A host can find any excuse for a party he/she chooses but, actually, the excuse is simply because the host loves people – all kinds of interesting people. If your host did not consider you delightful and interesting, you may not have been included, so gear up and realize you have an opportunity to be the perfect guest.

Once you have accepted the invitation, think about the gathering that you are going to spend an evening with: find out what the intent of the event is. If it is a fundraiser for a medical cause, perhaps the mood is more somber than if it were someone's twentieth wedding anniversary. Know the mood of the event.

Guideline 3 – Know your manner, know your limits. Some things are perfectly acceptable at informal gatherings that would not be acceptable at formal events. For example, your arrival and departure can be at your own choosing for an informal gathering, however, at a formal event, timing is everything. You never want to be the first to arrive or the first to leave. It is an art to arrive at the moment you should and tasteful to leave when appropriate. The time between those two situations should be filled with the duties of the perfect guest (see below).

Simply put, manners consist of doing the right thing at the right time and appropriate behavior always. Knowing appropriate behavior is more of a learned talent than a science, as progressive people always try to push the envelope, particularly in proper etiquette and manners.

Manners stem from a person's "manner" or behavior. If a man is a gentleman, he knows his place – always. He knows his duty and what is expected of him. He rarely deviates from the appropriate ways of the well-bred, and then only perhaps to make the rest of the company feel at home and relaxed. After all, good manners make everyone else feel important and special and acknowledged.

If a woman is a lady, she is gentle, kind and civil in all her ways. She is not uncouth, and she understands what being courteous is (not just in speech, but dress, talk, behavior, and treatment of others). A refined woman knows her worth, and is not afraid to regard others as equal, but never does she place herself beneath someone – that would not be the place of a refined woman but a servant, which she knows she is not. Nor does she take any liberties in putting others in their place; rather, by taking her own place, those in opposition or antagonistic to her will end up in their own place with no effort on her part. Cream always rises to the occasion (the top).

Normal Behavior versus Etiquette for the Occasion: You would be surprised what the normal person does at a dinner party. It's all about drinking and eating, right? Wrong. The event hosted by a friend who included you is much more than a planned meal and cocktail hour. It is an event where the host wants to introduce her friends to other people in a warm, inviting setting. The purpose of a dinner party is to share friendships with others and include those who might benefit from the introductions to others not already known to them.

The best etiquette will not get you far if it is something you are acting out because you read about it. It then becomes rules you must adhere to, and there is no elegance in that. There *is* an elegance in confidence and genuine hospitality. Etiquette and manners include preparing sufficiently for an event so that you and everyone around you get the most out of the time spent together. Think of the planning that goes into the event by the host. Getting dressed for the event is not the only requirement of a perfect guest but is one integral part of preparing for a fine dining experience: Think of it: you will be seated between two gentlemen or two ladies where, for most of the evening, they see only the crown of your head to possibly your waist. Flawless nails, hair, jewelry and makeup are essential. It is the refined look and charm of a woman of great poise and grace who can sit at a table for hours and look elegant and at ease in an open-front dress, using her gentle nonverbal expressions to charm the dining partners to her left and right. Her hairstyle is designed in such a way as to enhance her facial features and overall appearance.

Evening makeup is always more dramatic and elaborate than daywear. The refined woman takes this opportunity to highlight her greatest facial features. When putting on final accessories before going to a dinner party, think quiet, not noisy. Bangle bracelets are not tasteful, whereas a nice simple gold-braided filigree or diamond bracelet will bring the sparkle of the champagne and conversation to your wrist.

Getting started in conversation: If you have done your research a few hours before preparing for the event, you will have sufficient conversation starters. Now that introductions are a simple matter for you, let's discuss arrival and departure.

Only a very close friend would think of arriving before the stated time on the invitation.

As mentioned in Guideline 1 – arrivals and departures are very important to the host. Your host is counting on everyone to attend and have a wonderful time and although there may be a good reason for early arrivers and disheveled latecomers, the guest who knows what time to arrive and leave is making points with the host and takes her place as the perfect guest, who seems to know when to arrive and when to leave.

Arriving is a very subjective matter. The better you know your host, the more you will know when to arrive if the invitation is to the host's home. Only a very close friend would think of arriving before the stated time on the invitation, and the expected time for guests' arrival is twelve to fifteen minutes after the time stated on the invitation. Most dinner parties include "cocktails" or aperitif time (usually no more than forty-five minutes – no one wants to drink more than one or two cocktails before eating a meal with an impressive wine selection intended to impress the guests. If the guest has had too much alcohol before the dinner, how can she appreciate the exquisite wines that were carefully selected to be served with each course?

So, this aperitif or cocktail "hour" prior to being seated at the dinner table has much the purpose of a relaxing interlude between scenes in an opera – it is a time to take a deep breath, say hello to some acquaintances, and greet your host. This prelude allows time for everyone to make their way to the address through unforeseen traffic, to "decompress" from the events of the day, and greet those you know before being seated between two people who will share conversation with you for the remainder of the evening, or until everyone leaves the table.

Much can be said for how a cocktail hour should function – it allows everyone to visit before being seated, and allows your host to informally greet everyone and make the rounds before dinner. This is where your research comes into play – and if you are able to glean more interesting information during cocktails, you are "loaded for bear." You will not be the totally silent guest but able to stir up both conversation partners on current events, interesting historical information (relevant to the party, the host, the city you happen to be in – anything that will bring good-natured banter between you and your right- and left-hand seated), and other fashionable conversation of the moment. Social media can be a topic of interest to old and young – the young understand it, use it and abuse it and will tell you how they do. Older guests will be enamored that you actually navigate through a world that they are not quite able to grasp so easily. And off you go . . .

The host may or may not have any formal pre-dinner entertainment or requirements planned. Some hosts feel they have to have entertainment during this time (more than a modest threesome or piano) but is not necessary, since the idea of the hour before dinner is to mingle. Distractions or planned activities steal that social time away from the guest to learn a bit more about the other guests since they will ultimately be seated at a table where it is polite only to join in the conversations directly to their right and left, and perhaps overhear some of the conversation across the table. This dinner time limits the ability to get to know more than perhaps four individuals (unless your neighbor is an incessant gossip, then you will learn more than you want to know about a good many people, but *hearer beware,* since that information is never reliable and always frowned down upon at a dinner party, therefore partaking in it at all is vulgar and shows no taste in manners or etiquette or social behavior at all).

The final reminder for preparing for the dinner party: if you are not prepared with some news from today's paper or internet or radio or television news hour, don't expect the other guests to have much to start a conversation with either. A guest is always ready to discuss a good recent best-seller, important but not scandalous or litigious news, and always tries to find the balance in personal and basic information to ensure the other parties) are not bored or embarrassed at being asked for overly personal information at a first meeting. Alcohol during the time before dinner can sometimes create a noisy and friendly situation, however, it can also get out of hand if the persons consuming cannot have intelligent conversation under the influence of alcohol.

Although you have been invited to have a good time and enjoy yourself, this is definitely not the place to "let it all hang out" or relieve the stress of the day by getting intoxicated or obnoxious. It is a good thing to remember that you will be partaking of a lovely and well-planned dining experience, with refreshments throughout the evening, so there is no need to run the risk of not seeing the occasion through with a graceful demeanor by overindulging in alcohol prior to the main event. Remember that your duty as a proper guest requires a delicate balance in having an enjoyable evening and supporting your host as an involved guest who is cordial, aware of her surroundings, and makes attempts to include even the shyest of people into conversation and into the fun of the social hour.

Always remember that the formal dinner is more than a meal together. It is the place where friends, family gather around a table to enjoy social contact and share experiences, opinions, and each other's company. Food is to be taken in a quiet, leisurely manner, as if it is secondary to the event of conversation. Enjoyment of the company comes first.

General table manners can be found in almost every etiquette guide today, but here are a few rules that might be beneficial to review prior to an evening engagement.

General Table Manners for the Guest

1. Napkins are placed on the lap either once you seated or else when the host is seated.
2. Glasses are set in an order – they are normally from the outside in, depending on each course and the wine selection for that course.
3. Flatware is set to work your way from the outside in; for dessert courses, the flatware at the top of the plate is usually what you use, unless servers replace the silverware after courses.
4. When cutting meat, cut one piece at a time and eat it, then cut another.

5.   Place all silverware on your plate after use – do not place silverware on the table once it has been used.

6.   Knives should be placed with the sharp side facing the middle of the plate.

7.   When you have completed a course, place your silverware together at an angle across the plate. When a knife and fork are companions of a course, place them both across the dish even if you have not used the knife (parallel in 11/4 o'clock position) prior to the server taking up the course.

8.   Elbows are never placed on the table. Sit straight up in the chair, never leaning against the back of the chair.

9.   Food should be taken on the fork in small portions and chewed sufficiently.

10.   One forkful of food is taken on the fork. Too much food is vulgar. Never take half the food off the fork into your mouth. The fork should be directed straight toward the mouth and not sideways as if to shovel the food into your mouth.

11.   *Always* keep your mouth closed when chewing.

12.   Talking with food in your mouth or taking a sip with food in your mouth is uncouth.

13.   If you have something in your mouth that should not be swallowed, such as a fish bone or olive pit, place your two fingers at your mouth, take the item between those fingers and place it on the edge of your plate. It is more important to get the item out of your mouth than to look absolutely elegant. Some people use their napkin, but that is even more obvious and blatant than to quietly just remove it from your mouth and resume your meal.

14.   Soup spoons are to be pushed from the front of the bowl toward the back, then headed directly into your mouth in such a way that no one hears it go into your mouth – if you have to suck the food from the spoon, you have taken too much on the spoon to go quietly into your mouth. This takes practice, so do not expect to get this correct immediately unless you have seen it done. You should be attempting to do this at home whenever possible.

15.   Forks are for most foods other than soups.

16.   Passing bread or other foods: When something is on the table and directly in front of you, it is appropriate to offer the plate or items to the person on your left, then take your own portion, then pass the dish to the right, counterclockwise always. This allows the next person to take the dish with their left hand and serve themselves with their right, then hand the dish to the person on their right and so on.

17.   Upon rising from the meal, you carelessly drop your napkin on the left side of your place, never folding it or smoothing it out.

18.   Finger bowls are a rarity but are brought to the table after the fruit course to remove all acids from the fingers. Dip fingertips lightly, one hand at a time, and then dry on the napkin.

Homework: list five things you want to improve in your table manners. Write them down on a card and keep in your purse. Review them before you sit down to dine, or before meeting a friend at a restaurant.

Did you know?

- Latecomers begin with the course being served at the time, not the first course.
- Breads are broken one piece at a time and buttered separately; Place butter from the dish onto your own bread plate for use.
- Asparagus is not a finger food but is meant to be taken in small portions by your fork or, even better, individual asparagus tongs.

A WEEKEND GET-AWAY

There is much ado about what to pack for a vacation: remember the objective: it is a vacation! That is where you get to regroup, relax, enjoy and maybe learn something new, but never forgetting who you are and your genteel manner.

Packing for the weekend:

1. Personal care products in small amounts: toothbrush, paste, floss, mouthwash, perfume, skin care, makeup, hair products/items (brush, comb, dryer), nail kit, and personal hygiene items.

2. Appropriate clothing: one basic pants set, three tops, one or two dresses (one day, one night), evening attire (if called for), walking shoes, and heels. Bring running shoes and workout outfits if you plan a run or walk or class over the weekend.

3. A great read. Don't expect someone else to be in charge of all of your free time (catch up on those magazines).
4. A thoughtful gift /beautiful card – something special for your host.
5. A good attitude – no matter who or where, be "wonderful you".
6. Items communiqué (iPhone, Pad, PC, Apple watch, other).

Homework: Prepare for your next vacation get-away by having a pack-your-luggage "fire drill." Pack everything, then unpack and list the items. Then pack again, and try the following: place heavy things toward the bottom, and toward the "feet" of the suitcase. Fold blouses and pants in tissue and place the least likely to wrinkle first, with the most delicate blouses on top. Place jackets on top of everything – Put socks into shoes and then in shoe covers; save space by rolling pajamas and intimates and placing them at the bottom of the suitcase; the suitcase pockets should be kept for small items such as gloves, belts, scarf, makeup bag. Always double-bag liquids in zip plastic bags when flying.

CHAPTER 10 – A REFINED LEGACY

"I would like to be remembered as a decent human being, and a caring one." Grace Kelly

Your Personal Image to the World

Your personal image is something that will constantly change and you can continue to make it wonderful and fresh. Your image will specifically portray who you really are *when it begins on the inside.* Once your internal image is secure and settles there, you must maintain your *outside* to show the real you.

Someone I know once looked at her own photograph and exclaimed in humor: "I am much more beautiful in my own mind." This was simply the truth to this woman. She was exclaiming to us that she pictured herself differently from the woman she saw in the photograph (and really, who photographs well in *selfies?!)*

How wonderful and refreshing to think as that woman. She had confidence inside. She quietly expressed her desire by that comment. She wanted to portray that woman she believed she was on the inside. She wanted us to see her as she truly is. In reality, she was extraordinarily beautiful on the outside and humble on the inside.

If you want to become someone extraordinary, it begins inside. This is the first step in developing your personal image. Then you groom the outside to suit the inside nature that you already possess, and you become refined.

Refinement NOW and FUTURE

There is no *everyday* manners and *formal* manners – they should always be the same. There is a refined way to do things, which should be done always. That is the way of the refined woman.

It is not improper to be informal on occasion. *It is improper to be vulgar at any time in any manner.* The whole idea of manners is to have a rule of thumb to gauge your everyday actions, to determine if you are behaving properly in a given situation, so that eventually it becomes natural for you to behave civilly and well-bred. It takes time and effort (and possibly making some mistakes along the way) to finally settle into your own form of refined manner that is not in great contrast to those around you, but is truly who you are.

Remember to be genuine, fair and equitable to all. Putting others at ease is the first rule of refinement. Take into consideration those less fortunate, and associate fairly with them. Our lives are only completed at the end, and therefore being kind and civil to all will reap many benefits over your lifetime.

Aspire to Your Goals

A refined woman aspires to attain her goals in all areas of her life. Once you have established some goals, try to incorporate your wealth and wellbeing targets, as well.

Wealth management and wellbeing go hand in hand, and by establishing goals in those areas, you will always be on track for your future and the plans you hope to attain. You can improve your standards in these areas throughout your life with some effort and energy.

You are your own LLC (Limited Liability Company). Becoming a refined woman includes the ability to make good choices for your own life and welfare; this includes your own goals for your wealth portfolio. It is never too early or too late to begin working on building wealth, and that is certainly one of the most interesting and challenging things you can do with your time.

Financial savvy is more like chess rather than checkers. It has many facets that need to line up correctly to win.

In order to develop this wealth, you must decide to live *below* your means. This is something that, while it might be difficult to grasp, holds the keys to being content and happy with who you are. *Wealthy* and *rich* are two different concepts: wealth has to do with your overall attitude and gross assets; rich has to do with outward material show. Once you understand the concept of *wealth*, you can be wealthy if you are doing exactly what you are passionate about, and also reap financial rewards while doing it.

The concept of *working for a living* is a lower aspiration than the way you should be thinking. Working for a living is a way to get by in life, as opposed to wealth building, which mean aggressively and passionately pursuing a career that you believe in and are becoming an expert in. Wealth includes the value of the persons you meet along the way. Sometimes these individuals will be partners or can assist you in building your career and wealth portfolio. Some of them will become a support to you, and even perhaps a mentor.

Some people live very meagerly in terms of outward material wealth, but are truly wealthy individuals. They have developed the *living well* concept of never *working* a day of their life because they are pursuing their passion and are reaping money *in exchange for spending time on that passion.*

Another concept of wealth building is the exchange of time for assets (or money). You must value your time and you must decide what your time is worth. If you have a small child and realize that she will grow up very quickly, perhaps your taking a lower-paying, less fulfilling role in the workplace is the best value for you in order to spend more time with your small child. Everyone has to balance their life with time versus value. Once you are smart about this concept, you will have more control over how you make money, save money, and spend money.

REFINED ENTERPRISE – WEALTH GOALS

Maintaining a budget is not just allotting how much you will spend or save each month. It is more than that. It is a strategy that learns the right time to buy and the right time to sell. The savvy woman understands the stock market sufficiently to know there is ebb and flow (*bull* and *bear* markets); surprisingly, so many people do not take the time to understand finances in their own lives.

Just like the stock market, a woman's budget is devised on needs, wants and desires. She has priorities, demands and wishes, which might be very emotional drivers. She is learning a very important concept about refinement. She is selective in her choices and she is better for making tough choices for her and others' futures. Should she wish for something for years and never attain it, she still holds fast to the wish, the desire for that lovely thing, perhaps never owning it, but recalling all the reasons she put it off. There may be good reasons such as children, travel, education, husband's goals, charities, or an improved way of life.

She understands what it means to sacrifice immediate gratification for the more important goals and demands of life. She is learning that delayed satisfaction is a discipline to attain the longer-term goals she has set. She is pleased in knowing how much her planning has accomplished and how much her energy, placed where it is needed most, is the greatest asset in her budget. Many women have a shallow idea of finances.

Financial savvy is more like chess rather than checkers. It has many facets that need to line up correctly to win. Financial savvy is:

- Asset building at its finest.
- Planning at its most strategic.
- Your ideas about money, not just the money itself.
- Taking an opportunity to change something for the better in exchange for the money (and the energy spent on gaining that wealth).
- Sleeping well at night because bills and taxes are met timely and sufficiently.
- A stress-free life of knowing where you are and what you want.
- Waiting until you have the necessary finances before purchasing a luxury item that is not essential to your life.
  - The fountain of youth – because however small your budget is, you have control. When you have control, you are more relaxed at the thought of refraining from that purchase, or just letting your money work hard for you by researching investments and prospects for growth of your wealth.

Financial savvy is *not:*

- Risking more money on investments than you can afford to earn back in sufficient time.
- A chance month-to-month allotment of money.
- How much money you gain each month.
- Going into debt for anything that would cause damage to your overall goals and dreams.

At one point in my career I had only a small amount of money to invest, so I researched and purchased penny stocks. I made a little money and also lost a little money, but I learned a lot, and I never risked more than I could afford to lose. The education I gained was worth the risk, and in the end I did end up with a small sum of money above my initial investment.

The woman who is on a budget understands more and more about investing, and always humbly admits she could know more. She understands that a purchase really costs more than just the price tag – it also costs her energy and time to research and choose the purchase, the taxes involved in that purchase, the income taxes paid on that money prior to any purchase, the inherent value of that purchase, and the life value of that purchase.

Most women who maintain this kind of sophisticated budget knowledge do not purchase anything to feel better about themselves. They rarely purchase without research or thinking about the purchase overnight, and very rarely purchase on a whim, particularly if it is on a sale rack or in the sale area, including mattresses, clothing, cars or furniture. A thoughtful woman looks for the best she can afford and waits to find it at her convenience, not someone else's. She does not rely on a credit card, unless she has managed to figure in the cost of the interest and has a budget that incorporates credit card spending as part of her annual spending routine (or she buys on a credit card for frequent flyer miles and pays it off at the end of the month!).

There is a scene in *Family Man* where the characters are shopping in a Mall. The actor Nicolas Cage finds a $2,500 suit that he decides to buy to feel better about his miserable life. His wife, played by Tea Leoni, suggests he put the suit back and instead they'll go to the Food Court and purchase a funnel cake! He sarcastically says that a funnel cake will be the highlight of his week. It is only a scene in a movie but relatable here, since we can all empathize with the down times in everyone's lives when we do need something to cheer us up a bit. Better a funnel cake than a $2,500 suit.

Rather than sell the farm, just sell some milk and get a little something *extravagant*. A $6.00 coffee at a designer coffee shop can represent for many of us that funnel cake we need to feel better about our life at that moment. The decidedly refined sophisticated woman will understand others' need to do this and may indulge herself from time to time, because it *does* make you feel in charge and a little extravagant. However, we all regroup, gain our composure, lift our heads, and realize sometimes the wait is part of the pain, but it also makes attainment so much sweeter. To wait for gratification once we find what it is we are adding to our life is a good discipline in an undisciplined world, a world where we are surrounded by advertising that tells us to *get it now and pay later.*

This is not the refined woman's point of view on life. She is not living at the whim of advertising or *impulse-buying* gimmicks. She is very aware of how things work in the retail world and is savvy about how she accumulates her possessions. After all, possessions are hers to take, give, sell or buy. They do not possess her. The loss or gain of them is temporal and, as beautiful or useful as these tangible items might be to her, she is not dependent on them to fulfill her life.

Leaving a legacy is more than philanthropy and charity – it is much more personal and larger than that.

You, as a refined woman, will always want to become part of something bigger than yourself. We learn about being philanthropic, about volunteerism in high school, with opportunities at the local hospital, nursing home, community center or library. If this was instilled in you during your youth, you understand and already carry this in your thinking. You also know the pleasure and good feeling you get when giving.

The rest of us may not have participated in giving back to society as much as we hope to now. Volunteering starts out small, and as you develop your time, efficiency and organization skills, you can increase your volunteer time. I was always taught to give a little bit of what I had to the poor. Giving is the basic concept, whether it be tangible or intangible.

Leaving a legacy is more than philanthropy and charity – it is much more personal and larger than that. It is the desire to leave the world a better place, to make a difference in some way while on this earth, making a positive difference in lives while you are here. Your integrity and values are the things that will inspire and motivate others once you are gone. The intent is to leave a legacy behind that is honored, respected and valued by others. The meaning of legacy is "a gift by will of money or personal property." Legacy is inheritance. It is the gifts we leave behind. It is your acts of gratitude.

A friend of mine is leaving a beautiful family tree with photographs, news clippings, and interesting facts about more than 2,300 ancestors he has researched on his family. This endeavor took countless hours of effort and dedication to ensure his children have the best information about their ancestors; this family tree he created will not only be something left for them, but for other family members who will benefit from his work. What a legacy!

Legacy is more than material acquisitions. As stated before, it is the influence and impression you leave with others, including integrity, guidance, mentorship and ideas, a cause served or a charity started. It is passing on the torch of the good values inherited from those before you. You are essentially willing them or passing them on to the next generation. It is the love, integrity, wealth, possessions, and investments you have made that will leave others better and enrich their lives. Legacy is passing on what has been instilled in you and in the way your life was lived in front of others.

This is where refinement comes in. You are tremendously important to the overall scheme of things once you become refined. More is developed in you and now more is required of you. Think of royalty. They have responsibilities to everyone in their sphere. Throughout history they were the ones to make sure the laws were fair and decent, ensuring better living for those who could not fight for their own rights. Your responsibilities as you become refined only get larger and more real. The way you live your personal life now becomes important. Others are watching.

People live their lives, work with their heart and soul, and leave behind the results after their lives have been completed, or even set things in motion as they live out their lives. They cannot change their past. It becomes the legacy to those left behind, no matter how that testimony reads. This is the time to become refined and choose to plan a legacy in your name. It is the responsibility of those with much to invest in others. Your life is lived in such a way that you leave a legacy to be proud of.

The way you live your personal life is important. Leaving a legacy by personal actions might include leading an exemplary life of good values and virtues. Your legacy might depend on the development of good habits whereby others emulate your actions, observe your productivity, efficiency and usefulness; they see it and desire to prolong it.

The way you live your public life is also important because it affects society. Your positive contribution to the community and society paves the way for the development and enhancement of many lives. One person can make a difference to society and the world. Live it the way you want to be remembered, and the way you believe it is to be true to yourself. Your social life can become the role model of many others and inspire them to live a better life.

REFINED STYLE – SOCIAL RESPONSIBILITY
Benevolence

The refined woman has a sense of herself and what she can accomplish. She has goals, and she finishes what she starts. She also has a sense of what she can offer alongside others. She is accomplished in her own right and flows in others' worlds as well. Finally, she has a sense of benevolence toward others and is very definite in her way of accomplishing things that matter. She does not spread herself too thin, thus accomplishing nothing of value to her fellow citizens, but she develops a passion for a few important issues that matter to her and the world around her.

The refined woman is selective and restrained in her volunteerism, knowing that her name on something reflects her integrity. She researches all projects for which she will endeavor and will not rubberstamp issues that are not fluently valid. When Kate Middleton married Prince William she was approached by many charities. Princess Diana chose certain charities that she was passionate about, and Catherine, her royal highness Duchess of Cambridge, had to do the same, realizing that there are many worthy causes, but in order to make a difference, she had to limit her time to those philanthropies she was actually passionate about. Rightfully, Kate researched the endeavors she thought she could undertake and made her selections thoughtfully. We must do the same if we expect to see any lasting imprint of our work in the lives of others.

Reasons you would desire to take on more responsibility:

- There is no one else more fitting or accomplished in your talents and abilities to do it.
- You are time-conscious and realize that your family is an integral part of the team and you desire to mentor them in good things of value by undertaking outside charities and social events.
- You have a good sense of opportunity and enrichment of others and want to provide this for a few who are worthy.

- You desire to be an example to younger women to make their mark on people in a world larger than their own household.
- When the timing is right, you delve into the project after studying it, and allotting the needed resources, manpower and time.
- You are organized and kind, and those attributes add to any endeavor of value.

REFINED OBLIGATION - PHILANTHROPY

 Our time is our own and what we do with it dictates our lifestyle and goals more than any other one thing. We can devote all of our time to family, or work, or ourselves, and in the end, our life will have a mark based on the sum of what we did – it will be meaningful and fulfilled, or there will be regret.

Victoria Beckham in a walk-through interview was asked to answer 73 questions. One was: "What should everyone be required to do?" Her response was immediate and pointedly simple: "*to participate in a philanthropy.*" The idea of everyone understanding and participating in philanthropy is an ideal for the woman who wants to excel in life. She is usually introduced to this concept of responsibility to society at an early age. Volunteering in high school? I was asked to coach a local fifth grade girls' basketball team and it never occurred to me that I should not do it. I understood the obligation of the older girls to the younger girls and of course I obliged. (I had to learn more about basketball, since I didn't really play the game). I realized then that even fifth graders were watching older girls as role models, which was humbling.

The idea of being philanthropic just comes naturally to some women. To others, the idea might be daunting or intimidating, or too demanding. Every woman who has undertaken a philanthropic activity or project will attest that the rewards of what you put into it are greater than the time, resources, and energy you expend.

Homework: Plan a lunch with a like-minded friend and map out a way to start a philanthropic idea: It could be as simple as gathering clothing from five of your friends to take to a Women's Shelter each season when you both go through your closets.

HOW TO BEGIN PARTICIPATING

If you are sincerely interested in being a philanthropic individual, you will have more than sufficient opportunity to give.

Your biggest threat is to spread yourself too thin and be of no value to any charity or organiztion. Once you determine the role you wish to play and the organization you wish to invest your time in, it is a matter of contacting the organization, joining or being introduced to the group, and learning more about that organization or philanthropy. You will quickly learn what it stands for and decide if you agree with the mission statement and path it is moving on. No matter the cause, you will find ample opportunity to give of your time and talents to a need.

I researched the opportunities of the mid-sized town I was living in, and found that the symphony, Red Cross, and arts were well invested in by so many other women that I found myself offering my time to the obscure local zoo as a docent.

I learned over time how my volunteering influenced the families and small children who visited, as well as other volunteers. It also broadened my awareness of how important it is to participate and be an example and a leader to those around me, continuing to learn about and give back to my community.

Volunteers are necessary and important to every nonprofit organization functioning for the good of the community. Political activists are also an avenue of becoming involved in the community and becoming watchdogs for the way it is evolving from the government standpoint.

You will find opportunities and make great friendships through philanthropy; this giving will help you in developing a refined way of life because a leader is always looked to, admired and emulated. You will work with people of varied backgrounds and taste, and advance as a social leader and trendsetter; this will challenge your refinement and set you apart, as the idiom says, *the cream rises to the top*.

You will develop your character through giving of yourself. Your wisdom and graceful way of doing things will grow as you gain insight into human nature and exercise your awareness of how to behave in all circumstances and situations.

My desire to become a refined individual is a continuing goal, and I do not feel I will ever reach the apex of grace and poise. It is a lifelong ambition for me and an exciting and invigorating one. I desire to continue to refine my taste and way of life to suit my best interests and happiness. Every refined woman must choose how she desires to live and then get on that path and enjoy the trip.

I seem to learn something new every day about etiquette and manners that I did not know. A friend recently asked me where to put the lemon wedge from the iced tea rather than slip it into the tea glass. Well, I wonder if anyone bothers disposing of it on a plate or the saucer under the tea glass. These situations run across my mind daily. The idea that we can even know all rules pertaining to proper dining is preposterous! It is impossible. But in refining your manner and your elegance, you will do the right thing at the time, without thinking of any rule – and that's refinement.

MENTORING AS A LEGACY

"No legacy is so rich as honesty." William Shakespeare

Your legacy puts your stamp on the future. We hope that by living our lives in such a manner we have influenced others for the better and that they will desire what we had in our lives. By mentoring and being available to others and influencing them, you leave a legacy behind in what you have invested and instilled in others. If you sincerely desire to leave a legacy, there are core principles to live by to ensure you are leaving the best behind that you can possibly leave.

Mentoring others will give your work meaning and purpose and motivate you to do your best.

You must carve out your own set of principles if you are going to stand for anything, but here are a few of mine.

1. Maintain integrity at all costs. Be a person of principle.
2. Life is best lived in service to others while obtaining the best for yourself.
3. Consider other's interests as important.
4. Love people. Loving people has to do with your actions. Liking them has to do with emotions.
5. You reap what you sow.
6. Hard work is never a waste.
7. Do not give up when you fail. Try again.

Mentoring others will give your work meaning and purpose and really get you motivated to do your best. When you have such a life of investing, it can instill a pride and joy that keeps you focused. Now is the best time to begin to mentor those who are worthy. I have this on my 100 list and already have a charity and mentorship program started during my first year of designing my list.

FINANCIAL SAVVY

In order to leave a legacy and have a great life, it is important to understand the financial world. I probably started late in grasping the things I should have learned about finances. I recall hearing about Heather Locklear who, in her early career, worked very hard, had two full-time shows on television at one time, and yet found time to go to the local college to take a few courses in bookkeeping and accounting. She was determined to make sure she understood her finances as she began making large sums of money in the entertainment business. We should all take heed: knowing something about accounting is very important to any woman in the world, and it is never too late (*think: Melanie Griffith in the movie <u>Born Yesterday</u>*). If you have not read Rich Dad, Poor Dad (original version, of course), get it. It will keep you motivated to be creative in your financial advancement. Watch a show a month on financial advice (Suzie Orman might still be on YouTube).

 Homework: Seriously, look at the ten things listed below, and if one or two stand out to you as being important but you are not knowledgeable in those matters, do some research and learn more about them.

Ten Things You Should Know About

1. Stocks, bonds, and how Wall Street works. It is important to understand the overall history of the market so you can see the big picture and understand risk versus reward and how it all works. (Some people believe only a bull market works, and some believe it must be a bear market for it to work).
2. Real estate –how to purchase a home, rental property, commercial real estate, and investment property.
3. Understand your credit score.
4. Financial goals for your lifestyle, age, income bracket, risk factor.
5. Designing a personal portfolio and updating it.
6. How to maintain a budget (prioritize paying off high-interest debt first).
7. IRS, tax credits, tax exemptions, and changes each year (consult a CPA).
8. Credit card debt and borrowing money.
9. Fraud and how to protect yourself.
10. Regular saving and investing.

Guidelines for Living

Limitations are those things that you place upon yourself without ever defining the parameters.

- Do not settle for anything that does not suit you. You should be joyous over it, and not complacent.
- Desire and pleasure are not the same thing: your desires will lead you to better yourself, pleasure alone will make you bored.
- Keep alive those things that are challenging and difficult to endeavor; they strengthen your character.
- Know yourself.
- Limitations are those things that you place upon yourself without ever defining the parameters.
- Anticipate the future, learn from the past, and live in the now. This will keep you focused and clear-headed.
- Be an inspiration to someone.
- Become interesting by having diverse interests. Narrow-mindedness is unbecoming.
- Listen before you speak.
- Treat others as well as you treat yourself.
- _____
- _____
- _____

BRIEF HISTORY OF ETIQUETTE

The history of an idea or principle gives root meaning to the concept that you have been introduced to. In this case, even a brief history about refinement and etiquette might be beneficial to your overall approach to the subject. This is the beginning of the manner of the well-bred and refined individual.

The origin of courtesy is thought to come from the Middle English "corteisie," from Anglo-French "curteisie," from "curteis." Its first known usage was in the thirteenth century. As the very word indicates, courtesy is the blossoming of the courtly ideals of the Middle Ages, and the word was originally used in connection with the court. Later came the word gallantry or gentility, in connection with the gallants – the men of the world.

Courtesy is defined as a behavior marked by polished manner or respect for others – a courteous behavior. Courteous behavior is also understood as an indulgence, for courtesy was giving allowance to individuals despite the facts – it was the kind consideration, cooperation and generosity in providing something (such as a gift or privilege). By the time of the Middle Ages, restraint of the impulses and regard for the rights of others formed the foundation of social law.

When the British colonists began to move to America, they brought with them the style they were accustomed to: they were frugal and straight-laced. Their furniture was made to be comfortable, but practical and efficient. With a huge new country ahead of them, they began to blossom and relax their standards of civility, realizing that it was more important to get along and work together than to have a structured pompous social framework inherited from generations of nobility and social hierarchy. A regard for others was what made life pleasant and agreeable.

The forefathers of the United States of America believed in civility toward all and used it as the foundation of their social standards in the Colonies. They believed there must be a cultural standard of behavior that set them apart from native, or island behavior, and it was considered uncivilized to ignore social protocol in the presence of civilized persons. It was also understood that such boorish behavior would not be tolerated. These ingrained attitudes of etiquette and protocol were a part of who these people were, right down to the core. It is said that Marie Antoinette, in walking up to the guillotine where she was beheaded, stepped on an executioner's toe while climbing the scaffold; her last words were, "Pardon me sir, I did not mean to do it."

Over the centuries, etiquette and manners have been a fascination of some people and a required by protocol of those "of court" as well as statesmen, ladies, and the "well bred," no matter which century they were born in.

Now, etiquette and manner in the last hundred years has stabilized in general American society, after several hundred years of noble standards being refused by the common man. We can now attest to the need and desire of our country for the strong sense of civility and proper manner of British and French courtiers of old, with a sensible attitude as an American. But we are not forgetting the refinements of living that grew out of the Renaissance. Our American etiquette is clearly wholesome, creating a sense of ease and comfort in social interaction rather than a feeling of stiff formality and restraint. The woman who would go beyond this standard in developing a keen sense of *refinement and manner* may stand out as simply tasteful and elegant, and she will surely enjoy that benevolent behavior of a refined and more fulfilling lifestyle, no matter where she may find herself.

References and Thank You

Although I have listed a few recent books and writings that I have studied below, I owe my research and knowledge to many sources over many years. In Refinement *I have attempted to compile all of the wonderful things I have learned while applying them to my own life. There is no way I can fully acknowledge all the sources of wisdom I have discovered and had the privilege of knowing firsthand. All these women have made my life more elegant, rich and refined, in one way or another.*

Remember, it is a lifelong journey of refinement, and as some of the information in this book comes to mind, think of those who went before us to write ideas and knowledge for more enriched lives as elegant women. I salute all of those gracious women as well as many not mentioned and say thank you.

A few references

The Book of Etiquette, First Edition, Lillian Eichler
Vogue's Book of Etiquette, Millicent Fenwick
Emily Post's Etiquette
Letitia Baldrige's New Manners for New Times
Amy Vanderbilt's Complete Book of Etiquette
The Art of Conversation, Catherine Blyth
50 things every young lady should know, Kay West
Manners Made Easy for the Family, June Himes Moore
The New Rules of Etiquette, Curtrise Garner
The Art and Power of Being a Lady, Noelle Cleary
Becoming a Woman of the Finest Class, Eunice Leong-Tan

Melanie Jarrell resides in Lafayette, Louisiana and continues to write and learn about a refined lifestyle. Her summers are spent in Paris and elsewhere discovering the way of life of women who have become icons of taste. She has designed an elite line of Platinum stud earrings (www.Galtlineplatinum.com) and continues to consult as an environmental expert (www.environmentalstratreg.com) to entities across the United States. This book is available to purchase online at www.refinementofmanner.com and on Amazon Kindle Store.